STUDIES IN AMERICAN LITERATURE

Volume XVIII

☆☆☆☆☆☆☆☆☆☆☆☆☆☆☆☆☆☆☆☆☆☆☆☆☆☆☆☆☆☆☆☆☆☆☆

CONRAD RICHTER'S OHIO TRILOGY

ITS IDEAS, THEMES, AND RELATIONSHIP TO LITERARY TRADITION

by

CLIFFORD D. EDWARDS

Wisconsin State University

Platteville

1970

MOUTON

THE HAGUE · PARIS

LIBRARY OF CONGRESS CATALOG CARD NUMBER: 79-85902

Printed in The Netherlands by Mouton & Co., Printers, The Hague.

To Neva, Mark, Marilyn and Cecily

ACKNOWLEDGEMENTS

It gives me pleasure to acknowledge the inspiration of Austin Warren, whose theories of literature have helped shape my conception of literary criticism. I am especially indebted to Joe Lee Davis for the seminal and perceptive suggestions he gave me in the initial stages of this study. I also wish to express my gratitude to the late Conrad Richter for his patience and willingness to answer long and tedious questions in our correspondence over a period of two years.

A grant from the Institutional Research Committee of Fort Hays Kansas State College provided for the typing of the manuscript. I would like to thank Professor Verna Parish for her kindness and encouragement.

PREFACE

In 1936, Conrad Richter, a native Pennsylvanian exiled by fate to New Mexico, published a collection of his Western short stories in a single volume entitled *Early Americana and Other Stories*. Although Richter was already forty-six years old, this publication marked for him the real beginning of a lengthy and distinguished career as a writer of stories and novels about American backgrounds. In addition to *Early Americana*, he has written three novels also set in the Southwest: *The Sea of Grass* (1937), *Tacey Cromwell* (1942), and *The Lady* (1957). Richter's other novels of the wilderness frontier, set in the pioneer times of the Northwest Territory, include the Ohio trilogy – *The Trees* (1940), *The Fields* (1946), and *The Town* (1950) – and three less successful novels, *The Free Man* (1943), *The Light in the Forest* (1953), and *A Country of Strangers* (1966).

But Richter was never limited to fiction of the frontier, although all of his narratives are concerned with the relationship of the past to the present. Like Henry James, he delighted in "a palpable *visitable* past" of nearer distances and clearer mysteries, and five of his later novels explore that era contemporaneous with his youth and young manhood: *Always Young and Fair* (1941), *The Waters of Kronos* (1960), *A Simple Honorable Man* (1962), *The Grandfathers* (1964), and *The Aristocrat* (1968). In the best novel of this group, *The Waters of Kronos*, he suggests only as much of both the past and present as can be made to sustain the illusion of reality in the framework of fantasy; in *The*

Aristocrat, published just before his death in 1968, Richter becomes unduly repetitive, but he still manages that elusive equilibrium between a sense of the past as strange and a sense of the past as familiar.

In addition to various medals for literary achievement and an honorary *Litterarum Doctorate*, Richter has won the Pulitzer Prize for *The Town* and the National Book Award for *The Waters of Kronos;* his literary reputation is secure. His masterpiece, however, is the Ohio trilogy, recently issued in a single volume edition entitled *The Awakening Land*. Since the trilogy represents Richter's finest achievement, this present study fulfills a need to make a detailed critical analysis of the triology's ideas, themes, and relationship to literary tradition.

The strength of the American writer lies in his ability to keep in touch with the living muscle and tissue of actual experience, to keep the destiny of the common man central in his vision. Few American novelists have been gifted with Richter's powers of observation and insight into the pulse of life which throbs even in the meanest of incidents, the most trivial of experiences; fewer still have shown such understanding of the quality of manhood developed by the great experience of pioneering, settlement, and growth that is the story of America.

Richter's sense of the continuity of past and present has enabled him to weave into a meaningful whole the epic strands of the American experience: the nomadic penetration into a primeval wilderness, the cultivation of the fields, the growth of community from the soil, and the emergence of an industrial civilization and mode of life which threaten to destroy something vital and noble in the human spirit. The trilogy is significant not only because of its artistic transmutation of historical materials and its suggestive mysticism, but because Richter's dramatization of cosmic necessity in the historical process, of the inevitability of suffering, and of the emasculating effect of time is a tragic commentary on the universal human condition.

The detailed analysis of Richter's philosophical and psychological theories in this study illuminates his artistic interpretation of the enigmatic pattern of existence; moreover, it enables us to relate his ideas to the philosophical tradition of evolutionary naturalism, and to explore the relationship of his discursively expressed theories to the intuitions of art in the structure, texture, and meaning of the Ohio trilogy. Since the initial conception and primary research for the trilogy coincided with Richter's composition of *Early Americana* and *The Sea of Grass*, however, considerable attention is given to these two works in an effort to trace the growing significance of his theories of man and the cosmos for the technique and substance of his fictional recovery of the past.

Richter's knowledge of the American past provided him with a well-defined historical image of a change in the human condition attended by a cultural loss. The Ohio trilogy as an historical novel of the soil offers an interpretation and judgment of this change and loss by means of a thematic structure of affirmation and protest: an affirmation of enduring primitivist and transcendentalist values, especially the stoic conception of *amor fati* and the need for roots, and a protest against those forces of an industrial and urban civilization which uproot man and alienate him from the rhythmical order of nature.

If Richter's trilogy did no more than to translate us by the considerable power of his imagination into the American past to observe and to share that unique pioneer experience of building and growth, it would have done enough; happily, it does much more. It fulfills the criterion of good fiction by helping us to touch on life at many points, by enlarging our consciousness and awareness not only of others but of ourselves as well. Elton Trueblood, the Quaker philosopher, has recently observed that modern society suffers from the disease of contemporaneity – the self-obsessive notion that all our problems and dilemmas are peculiarly contemporary and that consequently, the past has nothing to say to us. Although specific problems such as the horrifying threat of nuclear over-kill, the population explosion, and the spectre of famine are undeniably contemporary, the human condition as such remains unaltered. In our everyday existence we are still faced with the same problem of living and dying that preceding generations faced. Furthermore, whatever we are as individuals and as a nation, we are bound up inextricably with our past, and the Socratic maxim, "Know thyself", has always implied the need to know something about our roots.

The need for this historical sense of continuity between generations is crucial in an age which has discarded the past as if it were a plucked flower. As a "cut-flower" generation, to borrow another forceful term from Trueblood's glossary, we need to discover the value of knowing our antecedents, and it is Richter's unique ability to provide this knowledge in a believable and compelling narrative of the American experience that recommends him to a growing body of readers.

The special value of literature is that it gives form and shape to life so that it may be analyzed and understood. The artist imposes order on a fragment of human experience; in doing so, that fragment is rescued from the stream of time to become timeless. As structured form, it is no longer a fragment, but a whole, and it becomes our experience to explore and to share. It is my hope that this critical study of the Ohio trilogy will aid both in discovering the principle of order that gives wholeness to Richter's vision and in evaluating the significance of that vision for contemporary man.

TABLE OF CONTENTS

I

CONRAD RICHTER: NOVELIST AND PHILOSOPHER

1. RICHTER'S LITERARY REPUTATION

For the past three decades, Conrad Richter has quietly and stubbornly forged for himself a respectable place in American literature, and his thirteen major works of prose fiction represent solid achievement, particularly in the genre of the historical narrative. Richter's reception has not only been favorable, but reviewers and critics have been generally perceptive of his chief skills and talents as a novelist. His favorable reception began with *Early Americana*. The reviewers agreed that here was an "admirably trained intellect with fine perception of character reproducing impressions of life", an artist at transforming historical materials, who showed promise with his "finely drawn studies of character" against a background of "skillful atmospheric restraint".[1]

As his fiction grew, critics came to realize his talents were not restricted to Western stories. Richter is "limited neither by one region nor by one fictional type", writes John T. Flanagan.[2] The

[1] See Charles J. Finger, "The Old Southwest", *Saturday Review of Literature*, August 8, 1936, p. 7 and E. L. Walton, "Pioneer Tales from the West", *New York Herald Tribune Books*, August 2, 1936, p. 6.
[2] "Conrad Richter: Romancer of the Southwest", *Southwest Review*, XLIII (Summer 1958), p. 190. N.B. Flanagan finds Richter's novel of the Southwest to be "romance in the Hawthornian sense: while not encouraging a false picture of the human heart, nevertheless allowing the writer to mellow, deepen, enrich the atmosphere in any way which would contribute to the desired goal" (p. 190).

publication of the Ohio trilogy, of course, insured Richter's literary status. These are "rich and satisfyingly earthy books", says Edward Wagenknecht. "They pulse from beginning to end with the passion of the land, the flesh, and the spirit." [3] The general approval these novels evoked is expressed by Dorothy Greenwald's review of *The Trees*: "No detail is out of place, no word jars, no episode seems forced or ill-considered. Language, incident, character, mood – the writer's imagination has fused them all. The result is whole and complete, a serene, beautiful and moving book." [4]

Fellow novelists, too, have seen much to admire in Richter's fiction. The late Louis Bromfield wrote:

I doubt that any one writing today in this country is closer in understanding and treatment of its pioneer life than Conrad Richter ... He has that gift the first and most important in a novelist – of creating for the reader a world as real as the one in which he lives, a world which the reader enters on reading the first page and in which he remains until the last. [5]

Not one of [his] characters is dull, for the author has that power of good novelists which finds interest in everything, so that he is able to make even the bore an illuminating study of boredom. [6]

Walter D. Edmonds, speaking of *The Trees*, says, "Nothing very grand happens in it, but when you finish it you will have lived in its time ... I would have given an arm to have written it myself." [7]

Richter's most recent fiction has continued to be warmly received. *The Waters of Kronos*, although criticized by some for being too portentous and privately mystical, has been generally enthusiastically welcomed. Coleman Rosenberger writes, "Conrad

---

[3] *Cavalcade of the American Novel* (New York, 1952), p. 437.
[4] "Forest of Ohio", *Boston Evening Transcript*, March 2, 1940, p. 1.
[5] "A Fine Novel of Pioneers in Ohio", *New York Herald Tribune Weekly Book Review*, March 31, 1946, p. 3.
[6] "Another Volume in Mr. Richter's Fine Frontier Saga", *New York Herald Tribune Book Review*, April 23, 1950, p. 5.
[7] "A Novelist Takes Stock", *Atlantic Monthly*, CLXXII (July 1941), p. 77.

Richter remains too little recognized for what he of a certainty is – one of the finest creative talents in American fiction . . . I know of nothing comparable to *The Waters of Kronos* among American novels." [8] And *A Simple Honorable Man*, in the words of Richter's publishers, "has had magnificent reviews".[9] David Dempsey writes of it, "A paean to goodness, this is a tender and beautiful book." [10]

Critical attention to Richter's literary accomplishments, considering the remarkably consistent welcome and praise his novels have received over the years, has been slow to recognize the range and complexity of his talent. The few really scholarly essays on his works have been perceptive, and remarks such as Bruce Sutherland's that Richter is "one of the greatest of . . . modern humanists" to write historical fiction,[11] and such as Orville Prescott's that Richter is one of America's "most rewarding contemporary writers",[12] show that in some quarters he is highly esteemed. Recent studies suggest that Richter is finally receiving the attention he deserves. He has been the subject of two useful doctoral dissertations,[13] and Edwin Gaston, Jr.'s critical-analytical study of Richter for the Twayne's United States Authors Series has provided an excellent general overview of Richter's achievement.[14] Most of Richter's critics have been impressed by his simple and compelling realism, by the careful artistry of his tales, which are characterized by classical condensation and emotional restraint, and by his talent for writing pioneer and autobiographical novels packed with homely, realistic

---

[8] "Mr. Richter's Magic Touch", *New York Herald Tribune Book Review*, April 17, 1960, p. 1.
[9] Correspondence to me, May 16, 1962.
[10] "In the Footsteps of the Nazarene", *Saturday Review*, April 28, 1962, p. 19.
[11] "Conrad Richter's Americana", *New Mexico Quarterly Review*, XV (Winter 1945), p. 413.
[12] *In My Opinion* (New York, 1952), p. 145.
[13] Marvin LaHood, "A Study of the Major Themes in the Work of Conrad Richter and His Place in the Tradition of the American Frontier Novel" (unpublished Doctoral dissertation, University of Notre Dame, 1962); David Lee Young, "The Art of Conrad Richter" (unpublished Doctoral dissertation, The Ohio State University, 1964).
[14] Edwin W. Gaston, Jr., *Conrad Richter* (New Haven, 1965).

detail integrating character, action, setting, language, and style.

The fact that Richter's best works are historical novels partly accounts for the critical neglect and misunderstanding he has endured. For the historical novel itself as a literary genre has suffered considerable neglect, and unfortunately there persists a form of literary bigotry which disdainfully regards the historical novel as the unwanted miscegenetic bastard child of history and fiction.

In addition to being considered as nothing more than a historical novelist, a skilled craftsman in a limited field, Richter has suffered at the hands of those critics who have not understood his philosophical and spiritual motives. It is a mistake to consider him as merely a "traditional story teller" within a "recognizable and authentic folk tradition".[15] Such an appraisal does not really perceive the use Richter is making of the historical novel to present a distinctively philosophical way of looking at man and at history. His novels are not doctrinaire, but they do originate from a more complex way of looking at life and at human destiny than is apparent on the surface of his narratives.

2. RICHTER'S PHILOSOPHICAL ENDEAVORS

Although Richter's fiction is consistently welcomed and praised, few critics have been willing to admit the importance of his personal inquiry into the mystery of human nature and destiny. It is most significant to note that among Richter's first three published books, two – *Human Vibration* [16] and *Principles in Bio-Physics* [17] – were not fiction at all, but serious if amateurish treatises, which attempted to arrive at an understanding of first causes, and to explicate his peculiar theories of human vitality, of the relationship of mind and body, and of creative or purposeful evolution. Only two of Richter's earlier critics, Frederic I.

---

[15] Dayton Kohler, "Conrad Richter: Early Americana", *English Journal*, XXXV (September 1946), p. 368.
[16] (Harrisburg, Pennsylvania, 1925).
[17] (Harrisburg, Pennsylvania, 1927).

Carpenter [18] and Bruce Sutherland,[19] attempted to make meaningful connections between his early speculative works and his later
novels. Both rather summarily dismissed the former after only a
superficial consideration, finding them to be merely curious relics
out of Richter's past, having little relationship to his later writings.
More recent studies have continued to argue the irrelevance of
Richter's mystical and philosophical notions for an understanding
of his fiction.

It was, doubtless, a surprise to those who know of Richter's
early works – especially those who discounted them – when he
continued to expound his theories in yet another philosophical
work, *The Mountain on the Desert*, published in 1955. If Richter's first non-fiction works based upon his own observations and
studies of man had been merely an early flexing of the intellect as
some have thought, we may well have discarded them. With the
publication of this latest essay, however, Richter has made it clear
that he considers its content an important continuation of the
theories underlying all of his fiction, a more precise statement of
the principles that explain, at least to his satisfaction, the pattern
of life, the reality beneath the appearance.

The Mountain on the Desert, he points out, is not another
of his novels (despite the dramatic structure), but it is 'a continuation of the philosophy that underlies them, particularly the
trilogy, *The Trees*, *The Fields*, and *The Town*. Not that he has
written the book to explain or further develop his novels. Indeed,
it "is and was quite the other way around".[20] It should be stressed,

[18] "Conrad Richter's Pioneers: Reality and Myth", *College English*, XII
(November 1950), p. 78. Carpenter, after citing Richter's early works,
writes, "Of course, these failed and might well be forgotten, but they
make clear that his mind has always sought to analyze and to explain
human phenomena through conscious symbols and that he has always
rejected the simple philosophy of mechanistic naturalism."
[19] Sutherland, p. 416. After summing up briefly Richter's assumption
concerning the mechanical nature of the human organism and the importance of inheritance from countless ancestors in determining man's
actions and reactions to stimuli, Sutherland concludes, "This reasoning
may be neither scientific nor philosophical, but it helps to explain Mr.
Richter's deep interest in those people out of whose present the future
of America was being formed."
[20] *The Mountain on the Desert* (New York, 1955), p. ix.

however, that his novels were not necessarily intended to serve as "test cases" for his theories; the complicated processes of what Richter calls psycho-energics are too subtle and difficult to grasp to illustrate clearly in the kind of dramatic situation demanded by the art of realistic fiction. Nevertheless, his theories of human behavior and destiny inform his point of view and provide a basis for the mystical overtones and "hand of fate" apparent in the trilogy. It is clear, then, that Richter considers his mystical and psychological interpretation of life crucial to the meaning and significance of his fiction. "As mentioned in the foreword to *Mountain on the Desert*", he confides, "these theories have never let go of me. On the contrary they still hound and allure." [21] His philosophy of psycho-energics has become for him an *ideé fixe*, and his compulsion to make known his view of purposeful evolution has been no passing whim but a life-long moral obligation. His ideas have become a grievous burden on him, he writes, "a tiger by the tail demanding to be harnessed and demonstrated before a skeptical world". [22]

In view of the importance Richter attaches to his theories – and especially in light of his pointed reference to *The Mountain* as a continuation of the philosophy that underlies his novels, particularly the Ohio trilogy – we cannot avoid asking this salient question: to what extent has his unique philosophical and mystical point of view informed his fiction and contributed to, or impeded, his art? He has pulled back the curtains on life's stage to reveal a cosmic drama ostensibly working out man's fate for good; but what, exactly, is the *modus operandi* in this drama that permits nature to become the mystic arbiter of human destiny? To answer these questions, we must examine Richter's philosophical ideas as closely as we can in order to determine not only the pattern and texture of his thought but the relationship of his formally expressed ideas to philosophical traditions. The deficiencies of his philosophical system may soon be apparent, but Richter deserves as generous a treatment as we can afford him within the confines of this study.

[21] Correspondence to me, July 4, 1961.
[22] *Ibid.*

II

RICHTER'S THEORIES OF PSYCHO-ENERGICS:
A RESTATEMENT OF EVOLUTIONARY NATURALISM

1. THE QUEST FOR MEANING

When Richter began around 1912 to record his observations about
the nature of man in an effort to provide what he thought to be a
reasonable and factual explanation of the eternal enigmas, he
hoped to keep his feet well planted on the substantial earth. As a
very young boy he was unable to accept Christian explanations
of the human condition because of the supernatural dogmas of
the faith, a state of affairs which resulted in heated arguments
with his Lutheran clergyman father. His aversion to certain of the
Biblical doctrines and rites of his father's church grew so strong
that he was actually repelled by them, and the thought of attending church and Sunday school often made him physically ill. [1]
Only respect for, and fear of wounding, his father and mother
prevented him from anything like constant and open rebellion.

The implications of Richter's rejection of his father's faith are
far reaching and crucial to an understanding of the motives and
directions behind both his philosophical and his fictional works.
This spiritual crisis in his personal history has impinged itself in
one way or another on all he has done and is reflected in a pervading sense of tragedy as well as in themes of guilt and alienation in his fiction. [2] Not only did it precipitate a rupture from

---

[1]   Correspondence to me, September 22, 1961.
[2]   I follow Edwin W. Gaston, Jr., *Conrad Richter*, p. 24, whose discussion
of the theme of "quest for the father" is extremely helpful.

tradition and a subsequent search for a more empirical explanation of human destiny, but it explains his sense of urgency, and
partly accounts for the stubborn tenacity with which he has clung
to his beliefs for over half a century. His philosophical theories
derive partly from his need to justify his rejection of Christianity
and to vindicate his course of action; consequently, he has an
intense emotional investment in them.

The way in which this aspect of his spiritual biography relates
to his fiction will be made more explicit later in this study; at this
point it is only important to know that he found Christianity too
restrictive in concept, and that he inaugurated a quest for a more
latitudinarian belief. He recalls reading as a child an account of
the feats and miracles performed by a holy man of India. "It
struck me that he had as strong, devout and proven a faith in his
religion as my grandfather did in his, yet each called the other's
deity and beliefs false." [3] As his mind developed, Richter continued to wonder if there could be an explanation for divergent
spiritual phenomena, such as faith and belief, no matter what the
particular creed or doctrine. In short, he reasoned, faith and belief
must be a means, not an end – but a means to what? Richter's
repudiation of Christian orthodoxy set him on a life-long quest
for meaning.

Richter was reluctant to explain life's mysteries or the purpose
of being in terms strictly of supernatural doctrines or traditional
metaphysics, and so by the age of thirteen or fourteen when he
declined a scholarship that would have taken him through pre-
paratory school, college, and seminary on the condition that he
become a Lutheran clergyman, he had already resolved to follow
his quest to whatever conclusion it might lead him; however, it
would certainly not lead him to the church. In looking back over
his youthful decision, he does not see his choice as involving a
conscious conflict between religion and science. He had accepted
the assumptions of science with as much faith as his grandfather
and father had accepted the assumptions of Christianity. [4] Thus
Richter saw himself more in the role of the seeker than of the

---

[3]   Correspondence to me, September 22, 1961.
[4]   *Ibid.*

lost when he turned to the inviting theories of science to help him explain the mysteries of life.

Richter's desire to answer the big questions of ultimate concern within the framework of scientific facts led to his interest in and subsequent familiarity with widely discussed notions concerning the construction and make-up of the living cell, the evolution of living organisms, the atomic structure of matter, and the principles of electricity and related aspects of physical and biological science.[5]

The intellectual milieu was conducive to Richter's efforts; it was an era of freewheeling scientism and scientific idealism. Intriguing notions sprang up from all directions. From France drifted Emile Coué's principle of self-mastery by autosuggestion ("every day in every way I am getting better and better") and Henri Bergson's doctrine of *élan vital*, the notion that ultimate reality is a process of creative evolution capable of being grasped intuitively if not scientifically. The English and American penchant for the popularization of science prompted Scottish biologist Sir John Arthur Thomson to publish such works as *The Outline of Science, Concerning Evolution, Darwinism and Human Life,* and *Everyday Biology*,[6] while the English physicist and writer, Sir Oliver Lodge, filled in the gaps with *Life and Matter, Electrons, Making of Man,* and *Beyond Physics*.[7] All of these

---

[5] This interest coincided with – and perhaps was stimulated by – an attempt among scientists to explore the electrical basis of life. The following articles selected from scientific and popular periodicals of the time reflect this interest: G. Hucky, "Human Body as an Electrical System", *Scientific American*, LXXXII (July 1, 1916), pp. 2-3; L. H. Hyman, "Suggestions Regarding the Causes of Bioelectric Phenomena", *Science*, XLVII (Nov. 22, 1918), pp. 518-24; "Electrical Theory of Memory", *Scientific American*, CXXVI (April 1922), p. 249 f.; E. P. Cathcart, "Energy of Expenditure", *Scientific Monthly*, XXI (November 1925), pp. 508-510; D. C. Seitz, "Life Maintained by Electricity Within the Body", *Outlook*, CXLIII (August 18, 1926), pp. 540-542; and "Birth of the Mind", *Literary Digest*, XCIV (July 9, 1927), p. 24.

[6] (New York, 1924); (New Haven, 1925); (New York, 1917); (New York, 1924).

[7] (New York, 1907); (New York, 1907); (New York, 1924); (New York, 1931). The sub-title of the last work clearly indicates the metaphysical drift of these works: "An Idealization of Mechanism in a Philosophical and Psychological Direction."

books were published in this country, and both men apparently reached wide reading audiences. At home popularizers of science were turning out such titles as *Mechanics, Life and Personality, Mechanism and Meaning of Life*, and *Outwitting Our Nerves*.[8] Furthermore, the misty notions of Christian Science and New Thought contributed to the intellectual smog.

It was in this heady and confusing atmosphere that laymen such as Richter and his contemporary fellow novelist and correspondent, Stewart Edward White, took up the cudgels for science and deity. The "answer" – like Hoover's prosperity – seemed to lie just around the corner, and there was an apparent need to reshuffle thoughts and beliefs. A brief glimpse at White's analysis of the need of the hour and his attempt to meet it, paralleling as it does Richter's efforts, will suggest the tenor of independent thought springing up in various corners.

White insisted that the crucial need was for "orientation among the bewildering new conditions of the century", a need for speculative works "to admit fresh ventilation to modern thought", and to provide a "stretching exercise" for modern man's imagination.[9] White's response to the need was his speculative book, *Credo*, in which he outlined four expansions in modern scientific knowledge which required a new synthesis: (1) evolution and the process of mutation and growth; (2) better knowledge of the electron by which matter was discovered to be reduced to nothing but energy and force; (3) the expanding knowledge of chemical-psychology, which had opened up a world of parallelism, behaviorism, and mechanistic response; and (4) psychical research, which had "de-occultized" the sacred and abolished the exclusive reliance on mysticism to explain the imponderables.[10] White was confident

---

[8] J. S. Haldane (New York, 1928); G. Gates (New York, 1928); J. A. Jackson and H. M. Salisbury (New York, 1928).

[9] *Credo* (New York, 1925), preface.

[10] *Ibid.*, pp. 6-7. N.B. In view of White's appraisal of the intellectual milieu and of his friendship with Richter, it is interesting to note further the distinctives of his thesis put forth in *Credo* the same year Richter published his first work. White first postulated the existence of an all-pervasive cosmic consciousness and a trinity of omnipresent attributes in all "things": (1) substance, the material of embodiment; (2) life, the force or dynamism;

that man had progressed far enough to cooperate with the processes of "spiritual" as well as physical evolution.

2. THE MECHANISM OF MAN AND DEITY

It was in this intellectual atmosphere, then, that Richter's interest in a "factual" basis for human behavior and destiny developed. He unquestioningly shared the general emphasis among scientists and some philosophers upon a reductive view of phenomena. Scientists were trying to reduce physical and biological phenomena to their basic qualities of matter, motion, and energy, and naturalistic philosophers were attempting to reduce mental phenomena to the same basic categories. Thus, for Richter, the search for warranted belief on the one hand led him in his first book, *Human Vibration*, to a reductive interpretation of human phenomena:

After thirteen years of reluctant concession to nature, I have become convinced that the only fact or truth we know is mechanical. All that exists in life and matter is but the effect of mechanical, that is to say, natural laws.[11]

All phenomena of life, including the intricate and vastly complex phenomena of man's mental and spiritual behavior, operate on principles of law and order. "The primary elements of man are material – not philosophical. They can be tested ... more easily than electrons, atoms and other super-sensible objects admitted by science." [12] This is the basic assumption that underlined his effort to "invent backward" the mechanism of the human body and mind.

On the other hand, Richter could not rest contented in a purely reductive view of human nature or the universe. He had con-

---

and (3) consciousness, the guardian of the Idea. By mutual interaction, these omnipresent attributes, said White, assist each other up the spiral of evolution, and progress – including the emergence of man's spiritual nature – is made toward the perfection of each quality of consciousness.
[11] *Vibration*, p. 15.
[12] *Ibid.*, p. 22.

vinced himself that a mechanistic interpretation of human nature does not negate man's higher attributes, or deny the reality of a Supreme Power:

That truth or fact is mechanical does not imply there is no Supreme Intelligence, no immortality, no higher beings than we. It simply means that there is no mystery, only mechanical laws which we have not as yet grasped.[13]

Richter insisted on the mystical dimensions of the cosmos, and the speculative system he began to fabricate was, and is, based on mystical and teleological assumptions. We should understand, therefore, that Richter's conception of natural law is heavily tinged with the notion of numenic forces. Phenomena can be explained in terms of mechanism, but behind the mechanism there is a final cause, whose natural laws are superintended by "higher beings".

The "designer of the Universe" has thus provided natural (or is it supernatural?) laws that control and account for every petty detail of our lives. Indeed, Richter continues, the Creator has provided mechanistic processes to insure the growth of our highest human attributes – benevolence, sympathy, and understanding. The earth we tread on is "a huge intelligible machine, turning out individuals of various sorts and refining them eventually to the point of caring mechanically for the well being of each other". We are, he avers, human automatics; and it is a mechanical fact that

Some of these human automatics in moving about their orbits are made to catch the unhappiness, suffering or trouble of other human automatics and to pause and try to relieve it. This to me is the greatest mechanical marvel on earth . . .[14]

In view of Richter's lack of formal training in either philosophy or psychology, his early and sustained attempt to define the "scientific" basis of what he took to be the pattern of life is nothing short of astounding. He had a firm grip on his central thesis which he has refused to relinquish for forty years: through com-

[13]   *Ibid.*, p. 24.
[14]   *Ibid.*, p. 26.

plex mechanical laws, the human organism (body and mind) obtains and builds up energy for "creative" or evolutionary growth only in the presence of "inharmony" – i.e. discomfort, adversity, hardship, suffering, or pain, both physical and mental.

The reception of *Human Vibration* was enough to delight any fledgling writer. Not that it attained a wide reading public, but certain prominent scientists and authors, whose opinions commanded respect, were quite enthusiastic in their acclaim of Richter's attempt. Dr. Joseph Collins, who reached a large reading public with his popular "The Doctor Speaks" series, wrote, "*Human Vibration* is a gold mine." [15] Stewart Edward White, already a well-known novelist and nature enthusiast, whose *Credo* has been cited above, said, "I am immensely interested and stimulated." Thomas L. Masson, for years the editor of the humorous magazine, *Life*, commented warmly, "It expresses the whole human process clearly, and is so much more a work of literary art than Kant's *Critique*." In a personal communication with Richter, Masson wrote, "For many years my life has been ordered on the principles laid down in your little book." [16]

The famed naturalist, Luther Burbank, was extremely encouraging: "I am convinced you have discovered some of the fundamental principles of life which have never before been understood." Although Professor William Lyon Phelps of Harvard generally encouraged fledgling writers, it is still significant that he had high praise for Richter's thought-provoking work: "*Human Vibration* is full of challenging ideas. I have read every page with interest and profit. I never had it explained so well as here." And the reviewer for *The Bookman* wrote, "Mr. Richter's book is one of the most suggestive and instructive since Alexander's *Space, Time and Unity* [sic] . . . [17] One gets more from the second reading than the first."

Encouraged by this reception, Richter immediately set to work

[15] The following comments on *Human Vibration* appeared in various sources including personal correspondence to Richter. Unless stated otherwise, they all appeared on the back cover of his privately circulated book, *Principles in Bio-Physics*.

[16] Correspondence to me, July 4, 1961.

[17] This should be *Space, Time and Deity*.

on a second book with the awesome title, *Principles in Bio-Physics: the Underlying Processes Controlling Life Phenomena and Inner Evolution*, which he circulated privately two years later. This ill-advised work is smaller, an attempt to condense and refine the conclusions arrived at in *Human Vibration*, and to present them in a symbolic language to facilitate discussion of the vague principles.[18]

Despite the fact that his symbolic language actually impedes the expression of his ideas, this book also evoked encouraging responses from men whose opinions were well worth having, and served thus as an encouragement for Richter to continue in his line of thinking.[19] To give a single instance, Lee Wilson Dodd, then a well-known popular novelist, wrote Richter that he had observed in himself some of the processes set down in *Principles in Bio-Physics*.[20]

The conception of man's mechanical nature in intimate relationship with a purposeful universe continued to guide Richter's thinking in his most recent essay, *The Mountain on the Desert*. This is by far the most interesting of Richter's philosophical essays because of the dramatic structure. Michael, a rug-weaving

---

[18]   For example, A = the cell's energy voltage, B = resistance in cell and circuit, A/B = energy flow (current), C = expenditure rate (vibration pitch), Cn = rate of a cell group, $Cn+$ = lean energy flow, etc. By using alphabetical symbols, Richter established formulas for such mental activities as pain, memory, and desire. To give a single illustration, $Cn+$, CA/B designates "desire".

[19]   Richter now considers the book badly named and a "crude record" of his past thinking, an effort to set down empirically some of the explanations that came to him at the time. Correspondence to me, September 22, 1961.

[20]   Correspondence to me, July 4, 1961. N.B. It might be well at this point to clear up an issue concerning the existence of a third book supposedly written by Richter in this early period. Some critics have mentioned a book entitled *Life Energy*, which apparently they believe was published after *Human Vibration* (e.g. Carpenter, p. 78; Sutherland, p. 416; Young, p. 10). Indeed, the book is listed in *United States Catalog, Books in Print, 1928*, under Richter's name. Richter, however, disclaims having written such a book. "So far as I can recall there is no book of mine called *Life Energy*. Several correspondents have mentioned it ... but it remains a mystery to me" (correspondence to me, September 22, 1961). It is apparent that Richter's early works have not been carefully assessed by those scholars who have supposedly consulted them.

mystic-shepherd figure, takes four college students on a philosophical journey across the New Mexican desert and attempts to relate to them his intuitions of the primal relations of man and his environment, of the mysterious life force within the human organism that explains man's compulsions and drives.

In refining his theories and articulating them through the dialogues and oracular utterances of Michael, Richter abandons for the most part his early penchant for symbolic formulae, and he now designates the corpus of his beliefs as the philosophy of psycho-energics. He has come to regard the mechanism of mind and body as infinitely more complex than he had earlier thought. The organism of mind and body is not something

limited, crude or mechanical but of infinite and sensitive capabilities ... If I ever use the term 'mechanism' it doesn't follow that it's purely mechanical. By mechanism I mean that it uses energy, its physical parts, its so-called mental parts, and any possible finer instrument connected with it whose substance and purpose are unknown.[21]

Despite Richter's assertion that the human mechanism is more complex and intricate than his earlier conjectures, this latest expression of his beliefs remains in essence indistinguishable from his initial efforts. Therefore, in the following attempt to abstract the basic outline of his "system", it will be the practice to refer chiefly to *The Mountain on the Desert*. Reference will be made to his earlier essays only when it appears that advantage can be gained by doing so.

3. ENERGY: THE BASIS OF LIFE AND ITS PHENOMENA

Michael, the rug-weaving philosopher of *The Mountain*, had jotted in his notebooks two basic postulates: (1) the distinguishing feature of life is limited energy, and (2) the basic primal motive is energy hunger.[22] These two postulates go to the heart of Richter's theories. But before they can be understood, it is necessary briefly to examine his conception of the nature of energy,

---

[21] *The Mountain*, p. 13.
[22] *Ibid.*, p. 7.

and of how energy operates in the living cells of the human organism's nervous system.

Modern science had shown that matter, which was once thought to be stationary, is actually made up of supersensible units of motion. The differences in forms of matter could be accounted for by the differences in vibration rates of the elements composing the matter, i.e., figuratively speaking, the rotation of satellite electrons around a nucleus in the miniature solar system of each element of matter. The more complex the matter, the swifter or more intense the vibration rates; animate matter – the cell of living tissue – is characterized by vibration rates in its molecular make-up which greatly exceed in speed and intensity those of inanimate matter. Furthermore, the vibration rates of very complex animate cells – e.g., the cells of the human brain – are higher than those of simple life forms such as the amoeba.

The conclusion Richter drew is that energy must be considered the basis of all life phenomena if all matter, whether that of a chunk of uranium or of the brain of man, is characterized by an ascending scale of motion or vibration rates. By analogy, Richter theorized that the primary life element of the countless millions of microscopic cells in the human organism can be considered a bio-electric life energy which accounts for all complex activity in the nervous system. Furthermore, such complex phenomena as we observe in human behavior must have their corresponding vibration rates of physical energy in the nervous system: the more complex the behavioral phenomena (such as man's higher passions), the greater the energy vibration associated with those phenomena.

His conception of this minute life unit is analogous to the energy unit of electric current. The nervous system (the psycho-energic instrument), therefore, is conceived to be a sort of electrical apparatus permitting the instantaneous flow of energy throughout the organism. For these theories, he found some support in the infant fields of electrophysiology and bio-physics, in contrast to classical physiology with its more conventional explanation of vital processes in terms of chemistry and glands.

For our purposes here, it is only necessary to understand that

Richter came to consider the human organism (mind and body) to be somewhat like a bio-electrical dynamo. It depends on the energy it can produce and refine in the psycho-energic instrument, whose chief function seems to be the further development of inherited and acquired energy patterns by building up higher energy rates and flows.

Through the endless mortal network of nerves, the recording matrix of which is the brain, the energy rates of one cell group (which stands for inherited and acquired experiences) can be picked up by that of another group having similar rates, much as the plucking of one violin string will make another of the same pitch vibrate:

Now when we see an object there are set off in us cells associated with aspects of that object which strike our eye at about the same time. Each cell thus animated by the object through our eye set off its own series of associated cells we call a cell group.[23]

Thus, in human experience, every association is characterized by expenditure rates in the nerve cells which stand for that association in the brain. Pleasant associations are those in which energy flow is available to meet the demands (harmony), whereas unpleasant associations are those in which the demands exceed the supply (inharmony). By means of a psychological mechanism analogous to the physical law of sympathetic vibration, the combined energy flow of a number of cell groups representing pleasant associations can be tapped to relieve the high energy needs of a single unpleasant association. Once this combination has been formed, the general level of energy flow in the organism remains at the higher rate demanded by the inharmonious sensation.

The sum total of the numerous energy rates and flows representing the memory of infinite blends of sensations, both inherited and acquired, makes up the psycho-energic instrument or "realman". The realman represents the essential being of each person and controls him "as effectively and accurately as the tuning in of a radio receiver selects the wave length that may

[23]   *Vibration*, p. 127.

come through it".[24] It not only represents his personality, his temperament, his drives and compulsions, but it represents his contact with destiny, for it is the one aspect of man that partakes of immortality or survival.[25]

The most curious thing about this psycho-energic dynamo is that it cannot produce enough energy to supply the need. It is always in want, consciously or unconsciously hungering for energy night and day. The human organism, therefore, must learn to obtain energy for the continual energy needs that are a part of its natural state. To do this, man has evolved and invented "release processes", which bring relief to the high vibration or "expenditure rate" of one dominating cell group (which stands for consciousness) by tapping or robbing energy from another cell group or group combination, whose vibrations are similar and whose needs are not so desperate.

In reality, thought and physical action are sequences of such release processes built up by instinct and experience, one needy cell group setting off another for the benefit of its energy flow ... Energy release processes are being touched off all the time and their power charges appropriated and spent. Often two, or three or more of our cell groups are active simultaneously.[26]

The release process never ends simply because the plan of life insures a continual energy deficiency for purposes of evolution. Furthermore, the release process helps define for Richter the basic mechanism of the life impulse:

"... consider this psycho-energic definition of life impulse – the basic hunger of primary cell groups for more energy and their consequent incitement of secondary groups to spend energy so the primary groups can get hold of some of it".[27]

---

[24] *Principles*, p. 23.
[25] Richter's notions of survival reveal his peculiar kind of scientific transcendentalism. If survival is real, it is not to be considered immortality in the Christian sense, but a continuity into future realms of being, where further refinement takes place in the "realman" until at last it reaches those ultra-high vibration rates and energy flows which represent the Original Source. Richter makes it clear that he is only speculating about this; he is more convinced of survival than of what exactly happens in the "future crisis of existence". Correspondence to me, September 22, 1961.
[26] *The Mountain*, pp. 24-25.
[27] *Ibid.*, p. 30.

Release processes, whether conscious or unconscious, govern our lives. Whenever we bite our lips, grind our teeth, brace our shoulders, utter a prayer, cling to a belief, or relieve the suffering of our fellow man, we are, in the physiological realm, setting off energy flows to be appropriated by the currently inharmonious group.

4.   CREATIVE GROWTH: THE PURPOSE OF BEING

It has been the aim of Richter's philosophical writings to show the purpose of life in raising man up the evolutionary chain of being, away from the animalistic and toward the spiritual level. The laws of inner evolution have a message about the purpose of life, he asseverates, and that purpose is the "raising of expenditure rates and flows" and the "multiplication of them in groups", the physiological prelude to the growth in our sympathetic understanding of our fellow man. The basic physiological process Richter imagines as involved in the inner evolution of the psycho-energic instrument is unnecessarily complex. For our purposes here, it will only be necessary briefly to outline the fundamental psycho-energic principle, which Richter terms "Expansion and Contraction of Energy Expenditure" (E C E), in order to show the role of pain, conflict, or inharmony for evolutionary growth.

The expansion of energy rates is always accompanied by pain or sensations of inharmony, and the contraction of energy expenditure is accompanied by pleasure or sensations of harmony. One of the basic postulates of psycho-energics is that energy flows aroused by release processes to meet the expansion of energy subside more slowly than the demand, resulting in sensations of harmony. Life is a continual sequence of inharmony and harmony. Nature, of course, is a vast storehouse of experiences that elicit this process in man: storm and clearing, night and day, confinement and liberation, sickness followed by health, fatigue followed by rest, loneliness followed by reunion, and on and on.

A look at the psycho-energic basis of music and beauty may help illustrate the working of the E C E process. Music is one of man's release processes, which releases energy "according to the flows established by our inheritance and experience with music and life". Music symbolizes life:

I mean we can't hear anything without energy rates and flows being set off in us. Life is a continuous sequence of such rates and flows and their effect upon our conscious and unconscious well-being. Now music is a setting off of these same rate-flows of life. They may be unrecognized in us but are there. These symbols of the energy rate-flows of life give music its infinite resources and explain how from only a relatively few notes there can be all the vast literature of music.[28]

Violence in music, when followed by movements of peace and beauty, elicits the E C E process. The violence in the musical score suggests or awakens expenditure rates of inharmony; as soon as the sounds of violence subside, there are released energy flows (which subside more slowly than the expenditure rate) bathing the "softer more melodic parts of music with the harmony of surplus energy". The subtle reflection of life's processes – such as suggestions of hunger followed by food, being tired followed by rest, the gloom of a dark hallway followed by the brightness of airy sunshine – is what gives music its meaning and beauty. Thus, in one sense, beauty always has pain in it. The beauty the common man sees in a pleasant still life or landscape painting may be the result of the obstruction he has encountered during the day – high expenditure, for example, from hard work, financial problems, or boredom with the hustle and bustle of life.

The important thing to note here is the physiological necessity for pain in the psycho-energic scheme. Pain, Richter believes, is the "mother of psycho-energic growth":

Simple nonexistence of pain isn't sweet in itself. It's only when some E C E process has released energy to the cell groups in question that the lack of pain becomes delectable. So the harmony of today is the direct product of the inharmony of yesterday. The Creator's purpose appears to be the raising of our expenditure rates and energy flows for our increased power and our appreciation of good and beauty, the multiplication of our groups to give us wider experience and under-

28   *Ibid.*, pp. 95-96.

standing, and the establishment of more transfer points to enable us to resolve our own deficit problems.[29]

The method of creative growth, then, is the process of increasing expansion of energy expenditure. When expansion occurs, that is, when circumstances of inharmony (hardship, suffering, privation) evoke higher energy rates, these new rates are permanently established in the nervous system with greater volume and longer duration than the previous highest rates were capable of. These rates, once established, can be set off again to release energy for new, greater expenditure demands.

The higher the rates and flows, the closer man approaches to the Original Source, and the more his energy streams are connected with the spiritual side of life.

Now our concept of the Creator is of a being of infinite power not only in energy resources but in the scale and sensitivity of His energy spending. Therefore a process that establishes a higher rate of power in us we might loosely call a process of creative growth, for it tends to make us more like our Creator.[30]

Richter is careful to point out that the mechanism of man does not instinctively want evolutionary development. The blind urge within the organism is to provide energy flow for energy deficits. One way to supply this flow is to avoid circumstances of inharmony which increase expenditure, and to seek only circumstances which evoke harmony. In his first book, Richter calls this blind urge "desire", an unintelligent force that wants energy, not evolution.[31]

Desire itself has undergone its own peculiar evolutionary growth, however, and one of the most significant developments in evolution has been the emergence of desire "not only for the reduction of one's own inharmony but for the reduction of the inharmony of another". If this has been worked out by an Intelligence, Richter remarks, "it appears as though that Intelligence knew us well enough to take no chances on us and so wisely tied

29 *Ibid.*, p. 214.
30 *Ibid.*, pp. 193-194.
31 *Vibration*, pp. 83 f.; *Principles*, pp. 37 f.

up our happiness with the happiness of others".[32] The real mark
of evolutionary growth is this sympathy and understanding of the
suffering of others.[33]

The scale of existing mankind represents a vast range. At the
bottom of the scale there is the primitive, brutal, totally self-
centered man, calloused and indifferent to the feelings of others
(i.e., the man whose total rates and flows are extremely low).
Above him, in what for convenience may be called the "intermediate class", one finds the compassionate and sensitive man,
whose painful awareness of the suffering of others may cause him
in unreasoning sympathy to try to relieve his fellow man of those
burdens which seem cruel, but which in actuality are raising the
victim's rates and flows. Paradoxically, until experience teaches
him differently, the man in the intermediate class works against
the creative plan when he permits himself to be overcome by his
own sympathy.

Above those who "feel overwhelming another's distress and
rush emotionally to remove his burden, even the beneficial
burden", are the most highly advanced. At first glance, the most
highly advanced may seem cold and removed; in actuality, they
have come to the painful realization that suffering and pain are
instrumental in evolutionary growth: "the higher man goes, the
farther he can see, the grander his view of the over-all picture,
the greater his interest not in helping his fellow beings stagnate in
too much relief and pleasure but in freeing them from the wheel
of fate".[34]

The more highly advanced men will be manifestly more spiritual; their greater "energy flows appear connected not so much to
pleasures of the animal world as to things of what we roughly
call the spirit".[35] These persons of sensitive spirit who have
evolved the greatest "understanding" depend on those higher
release processes such as love, imagination, and especially, the

---

[32] *Vibration*, p. 93.
[33] Cf. ". . . the sharing of one's substance for the welfare of others is a
characteristic of what is called spirit, increasing in intensity and intelligence
as the spiritual scale rises" (*The Mountain*, p. 218).
[34] Correspondence to me, March 8, 1962.
[35] *The Mountain*, p. 229.

denial of the reality of pain and evil. To one who understands the function of pain in evolutionary development (or spiritual growth), Richter points out, evil is recognized to be nothing more than an illusion. Once we obtain "surplus energy to the cell groups representing the problem, there's actually no evil, only pleasure and stimulation".[36]

Three of the most advanced release processes for the spiritual sensitives are (1) belief in a higher power and respect for providence ("What a man believes in depends on his mental and spiritual evolution. But at every stage of that evolution, the energy stream of a powerful belief can support him and clear his deficit groups for his well-being"); [37] (2) prayer (supplication for energy from the highest creative power the mind can conceive); and (3) personally identifying oneself with the creative power in the universe (arousing powerful energy in the psycho-energic God-concept by saying and believing, for example, that "I and the Father are One").

Richter would have us realize, however, that real understanding, the mark of the most highly disciplined, obtains in those spiritual sensitives who, like Christ and Gandhi, have consciously cultivated the higher release processes, and repudiated the lower release processes.[38] Furthermore, at this stage of man's "spiritual" evolution, there are very few who reach the status of a man like Christ. Most persons will be a mixture of traits and drives, a blend of a few high release processes and groups of low release processes.

We see that in Richter's philosophical scheme, the spiritual aspect of life is based on a mystical conception of the evolved and developed physiological make-up of man. On the one hand, the spiritual life is a *naturalistic* relationship with the powers-that-be behind the universe. On the other hand, this relationship is unmistakably mystical and metaphysical. In his effort to reconcile the mystical and spiritual cravings of his mind with science, Richter has erected a philosophical system which attempts to

[36] *Vibration*, p. 159.
[37] *The Mountain*, p. 182.
[38] Correspondence to me, March 8, 1962.

yoke the mechanical and the spiritual. Psycho-energics, he insists, is the basis for all human mental and spiritual phenomena: "It has no water-tight compartments. Religious, philosophical and psychological fields are human aspects of the same psycho-energic principles." [39]

5. COOPERATING WITH DESTINY

Since the business of the universe is the creative growth of man, and since this growth is accomplished by expanding rates and flows in the psycho-energic instrument, Richter would have us understand the function of those circumstances which evoke the E C E process in order that we might participate in the creative process. Problems, burdens, hardships, obstruction – i.e., any inharmony which is brought on by natural events, fate or destiny – trigger creative growth.

But man may participate directly in his own creative growth and "remove himself from the statagems of destiny established in his own evolutionary behalf".[40] By practicing self-discipline, Richter theorized, man might by-pass the harsher blows slated by fate or the inevitable consequences of a weaker course.[41] When one attempts to encourage his own creative growth by practicing self-discipline, he is only cooperating with natural law by providing situations which help build up the expansion of energy flows. "To the Universe", such a practice "has the advantage of graduating a student to a higher and more intelligent method of growth".[42]

The ability of man to participate directly in his own evolution presupposes a freedom of the will, an ability to choose and direct one's own destiny. Although man is an automatic mechanism physiologically responding to natural law, he enjoys a "higher freedom to direct and order certain parts of his whole".[43] This

---

[39]   *The Mountain*, p. 183.
[40]   *Ibid.*, p. 204.
[41]   Correspondence to me, January 1, 1962.
[42]   *The Mountain*, p. 204.
[43]   Correspondence to me, September 22, 1961.

higher freedom of volition thus permits an individual to bargain with fate, and to participate in the destiny laid out for him by choosing to practice self-discipline. If this freedom of will is not exercised, fate will administer natural adversity to insure creative growth.

6. RICHTER'S RELATIONSHIP TO PHILOSOPHICAL NATURALISM

It is not to be supposed that Richter's formal philosophical essays have had even the remotest influence on American philosophy. Our purpose in analyzing them has been chiefly to illuminate his fiction. By reducing his system to its essential postulates, we are better able to define his conception of the cosmos and of human behavior, both collective and individual. At the same time, the analysis we have made of his thought does help to relate Richter's theories to their antecedents. Most critics of Richter doubt that his system can be related to any tradition because of the heterogeneous mixture of concepts that characterizes it. Several have recognized that one of the chief weaknesses of his philosophical essays is his failure to indicate the intellectual authority of his basic assumptions. There are few internal clues in his earlier works.[44]

David Young doubts that Richter has *any* authority whatsoever for his system, and concludes that, divested of the scientific jargon, his concepts are commonplaces acquired apparently at home.[45] To some extent Young is correct, for, as we shall see, many of the broader generalizations of Richter's theories (e.g. hardship and adversity effect physical hardihood) belong to that

---

[44]   Gaston notes Richter's appeal to the notions of Michael Farraday and George Washington Crile, p. 44. N.B. Richter made use of Crile's *A Bipolar Theory of Living Processes*, edited by Amy F. Rowland (New York, 1926). When I asked Richter if he relied heavily on Crile, he replied that Crile's theories "appeared to be based on a purely mechanical philosophy and my thought in mentioning them was to convey to the reader that the electric basis of energy wasn't something dreamed up by me". Correspondence to me, January 1, 1962.

[45]   Young, pp. 22-23.

body of commonplace truths which are no less true for being self-evident. And as the discussion earlier in this chapter suggests, the intellectual milieu of Richter's first endeavors provided him with stimulating if confusing directions. However, it is possible and profitable to relate Richter's theories to a well-defined tradition – that of philosophical naturalism.

Naturalism is not so much "common agreement on specific ideas as in general attitudes", writes Y. H. Krikorian. It does not represent a body of doctrine or a specific set of beliefs, but rather, a set of somewhat broad tenets that provide a common ground. Most importantly, man is treated as an integral part of nature. His career and his destiny as well as his mental and spiritual attributes are explicable in terms of natural phenomena. His mind is a manifestation of the "existential and causal primacy of organized matter in the executive order of nature".[46]

As a movement, naturalism has experienced several important changes since assuming shape late in the nineteenth century. The complete story of this history has been told elsewhere.[47] For our purposes here, it is necessary to trace only in broad outline the three phases which define this historical change in order properly to relate Richter to a specific variety of naturalism: (1) "evolutionary naturalism", whose influence and greatest expression came with the works of Herbert Spencer and John Fisk, but whose influence continued for three decades into the new century; (2) "reductive naturalism", whose beginning can be traced to the positivism of Auguste Comte, but which coincides with, and extends beyond, evolutionary naturalism; and (3) "constructive naturalism", which is a reaction against reductive theories, and which represents the most recent expression of philosophical naturalism.

Harold Larrabee has shown that the evolutionary naturalists played a leading role in the history of American naturalism. The

---

[46] *Naturalism and the Human Spirit*, ed. Y. H. Krikorian (New York, 1944), p. vii. N.B. Several essays used in the following discussion are contained in this work which will hereafter be referred to as *Naturalism*.
[47] See esp. Harold A. Larrabee, "Naturalism in America", *Naturalism*, pp. 319-353.

writings of Edward L. Youmans, John W. Draper, John W. Powell, J. A. Thomson, and John Fiske have done much to shape the movement in its beginning.[48] A keynote in the writings of the evolutionary naturalists is their attempt to mediate between science, theology, and philosophy by showing that "evolution 'properly understood' only confirmed creation and design 'properly interpreted' ".[49] Although man's behavior and spiritual growth could be understood in terms of natural law and mechanistic or physical principles, there was, believed the evolutionary naturalists, a final cause beyond mere mechanism which gave purpose and direction to man's evolution. Their evolutionary systems thus took on the undertones of the deep ethical purpose they discerned in the universe.

Reductive naturalism rejected this mystical and teleological emphasis in evolutionary naturalism as unscientific. John H. Randall defines reductive naturalism as

... a body of beliefs founded on a reductive analysis of all processes to the motion of masses, on the materialistic dogmas of nineteenth-century physics, and on the materialistic metaphysics which regarded the scientific enterprise as the simple discovery of the physical and biological laws 'governing' events.[50]

The "old", or reductive, naturalism, later naturalists charged, was too simplistic and mechanistic – in short, too willing to reduce all aspects of human experience, including man's religious, artistic and spiritual achievements, to "nothing but" chemico-physical relationships of matter, motion and energy. Such a reductive naturalism, John Dewey points out, tends to cultivate a pessimistic attitude toward man's career and destiny, reducing all "distinctly human values, moral, aesthetic, logical, to blind mechani-

[48] Since Richter was acquainted with the writings of Thomson and Fiske, it might be helpful to mention their principal works: J. A. Thomson, *The Outline of Science, Concerning Evolution*, and *Darwinism and Human Life* (all cited above in footnote 6); John Fiske, "Cosmic Philosophy", *The Miscellaneous Writings of John Fiske*, I-IV (New York, 1902).
[49] Larrabee, *Naturalism*, p. 348.
[50] "Epilogue: The Nature of Naturalism", *Naturalism*, p. 360.

cal conjunctions of material entities – a reduction which is in effect their complete destruction".[51]

Naturalists, claims William Dennes, have been transforming their naturalism from the "old" to the "new" by abandoning as basic categories "matter", "motion", and "energy", and adopting such basic categorical terms as "events", "qualities", and "relations".[52] By escaping from the blind alleys up which the reductive naturalists were leading naturalism – reducing man's higher phenomena to nothing-but-physics in a blind chance universe – the constructive naturalists hoped to build philosophies which would not minimize all of human experience. "The world as a whole", writes Randall, "the sum of all natural processes, is to be understood as making living and knowing possible, as furnishing the materials for the organization of the Good Life".[53]

Although Richter shares with reductive naturalists the belief that the vastly complex experiences of physical and mental phenomena can be reduced to a few basic bio-physical laws that govern events, and with constructive naturalists the profound respect for the higher human vision that sees the value of love, religion, and art for man's biological and mental well being, his ultimate affiliation is with neither. For both reductive and constructive naturalists agree on "one reductionist or liquidationist thesis: There is no 'supernatural'. God and immortality are myths." [54]

Richter, of course, is in fundamental opposition to such a thesis:

I want to make sure that nothing I have said might be taken to misconstrue my fundamental belief in the infinite capacities of God and to a lesser extent of those unknown beings that must be nearer him. One can't face the facts of the magnificent universe with its countless stars and worlds without becoming convinced of a tremendous unseen organization of superior beings, some looking after the vast mechanical problems, some after the staggering numbers of inferior beings struggling along the complex paths. Where the mechanical influence

[51]   "Antinaturalism in Extremis", *Naturalism*, p. 2.
[52]   "The Categories of Naturalism", *Naturalism*, p. 271.
[53]   Randall, *Naturalism*, p. 361.
[54]   "The Naturalism of Frederick Woodbridge", *Naturalism*, p. 295.

of the Creator's network of laws and processes ends and where the personal influence of superior beings begins, none of us can accurately say.[55]

Richter's mysticism and his conviction that what exists in the universe is not a product of a final mechanism, but rather something beyond, which goes toward explaining that mechanism, then, clearly relate him to the earlier tradition of evolutionary naturalism. It is significant to note that in *Human Vibration,* he cites two of the leading evolutionary naturalists, J. A. Thomson and John Fiske, to support his notion of "purposeful" evolutionary development and the ethical dimensions of the cosmos.[56]

A very brief analysis of John Fiske's mind-body theories will be sufficient to suggest how much Richter is indebted to the assumptions of this late nineteenth century movement. It will also suggest that much of what Richter has to say in his psycho-energic theories is anachronistic and out of touch with recent developments in philosophy and psychology.

John Fiske's four volume *Outline of Cosmic Philosophy* published at the turn of the century is a prime example of evolutionary naturalism.[57] Fiske viewed the system of evolution as purposeful growth toward a higher and more spiritual perfection. The nature of man could be understood by scientific analysis and an inductive search for the laws of nature behind human consciousness. Fiske assumed that man, as a product of the universe, is subject to the laws of matter, motion, and force that control the action and substance of all phenomena.

It is in Fiske's theory of the nervous system that we observe the most marked antecedents to Richter's basic assumptions. Fiske defined the nervous system as composed of cells of matter subject to the law of rhythm or oscillation. The basic cell is made up of elementary substances characterized by oscillatory movements which have combined and recombined into countless

---

[55]   Correspondence to me, January 1, 1962.
[56]   Richter reports that he has not blindly followed their theories, but rather that he has reinforced his own conclusions with their opinions. Correspondence to me, January 1, 1962.
[57]   (New York, 1903).

patterns. Nervous energy itself, liberated by the basic cell, rhythmically flows along definite channels from one nerve center to another. This recording of nervous energy passageways takes place in the cerebrum and cerebellum, where ideation is continually going on. Fiske inferred "that the transfer of an undulation from one cell to another is the objective accompaniment of each subjective unit of feeling of which thoughts and emotions are made up".[58] A cognizable state of consciousness is "attended by the transmission of little waves from one nerve cell to another, so that the ultimate psychical element of each conscious state must correspond to the passage of these little waves". From this parallelism, Fiske postulated the ultimate unit of the mind to be composed of a "simple psychical shock, answering to that simple physical pulsation which is the ultimate unit of nervous action".[59]

Of more interest than Fiske's theory of consciousness is the ethical inferences he makes about human behavior; for Fiske anticipates Richter's notion of "creative growth", the development of altruism as passion, and the role of pain or "evil" in human evolution. Fiske assumed that man was evolving from a primeval state of savage isolation to a relative perfection of life in a state of civilized interdependence. A latter manifestation of evolutionary progress is the *generic* evolution of sympathy – the pain occasioned by the sight of another's suffering. This is what Richter eulogized as "the greatest mechanical marvel on earth".

Fiske also remarkably anticipates Richter in interpreting the problem of evil. Both assume that as man ascends the ladder of evolution, he is more disposed to revere the Intelligence behind the universe and to realize ultimately that suffering need not indicate malevolence. Fiske's statement of this notion reflects his ethical interpretation of the Darwinian doctrine of "survival of the fittest":

To be delivered from evil, we must avoid the maladjustments of which evil is the consequence and the symptom. Hence, while to the aboriginal man malevolence was the only conceivable source of suffering, the reverent follower of science perceives the truth of the

[58]   Fiske, III, pp. 206-207.
[59]   *Ibid.*, p. 190.

paradox that the infliction of pain is subservient to a beneficent end. "Pervading all nature, he sees at work a stern discipline, which is a little cruel that it may be very kind. . . ." Thus with Michelet, we come to regard pain as in some sort the artist of the world which fashions us with the fine edge of a pitiless chisel, cutting away the ill-adjusted and leaving the nobler type to inherit the earth.[60]

In an essay entitled "The Mystery of Evil" Fiske goes on to elaborate on the principle that since "the element of antagonism" is necessary for consciousness as well as for evolutionary growth, evil is therefore an indispensable part of the dramatic whole; thus Deity is the originator of evil – not diabolically and malignantly, but benevolently.[61]

In light of the mysticism which surrounds Fiske's theories, it is understandable why the stricter naturalists looked with distrust on his theory of "emergent evolution".[62] Such theories were dismissed as "panevolutionism" and "metaphysical genetics", having neither biological nor any other scientific authentification.[63] The tradition of evolutionary naturalism, to which Richter is so strongly related, could not survive the harsh and sustained criticism of later naturalists, and its philosophical efforts were relegated to the realm of pseudo-science and demi-science.

7. PSEUDO-SCIENCE VS. "ARTISTIC TRUTH"

Pseudo-science is a close or deceptive resemblance to science which results from a too-credulous acceptance of unverifiable "scientific fact". Demi-science, on the other hand, denotes a "scientific theory" based on the assumption that natural law in the universe is attended by numenic forces or demi-urges (supernatural beings imagined as creating or fashioning the world in subordination to the Supreme Being). Richter's philosophy of psycho-energics is both a pseudo-science and a demi-science.

---

[60]   Fiske, IV, p. 305.
[61]   "The Mystery of Evil", IX, p. 251.
[62]   Randall, *Naturalism*, p. 378.
[63]   Thelma Lavin, "Naturalism and the Sociological Analysis of Knowledge", *Naturalism*, p. 189.

Sir Charles Eddington, in his evaluation of Poe's pseudo-scientific theory expressed in *Eureka*, reminds us that the theories of those who depart from conventional scientific views in their effort to reconcile the scientific and the philosophical or mystical – no matter how ingeniously conceived and expressed – run the danger of putting forth "crank theories":

Any one of independent mind – a rebel against conventionally accepted views – is likely to hit the mark some times. That is particularly the case when it is a case of philosophical and spiritual intuition versus scientific progress.

I should say then that regarded as an attempt to put forth a new physical theory, *Eureka* would rightly be regarded as a crank theory by scientists of the times. (The trouble with cranks is usually not that they are not far-seeing, but that they have no appreciation of the immediate obstacles in the road.)[64]

It is doubtless an understatement to say that Richter, too, has "no appreciation of the immediate obstacles in the road"; the conclusion is forced upon us that his specific theories of psycho-energics are crank theories, ingenious but derivative from the superannuated tradition of evolutionary naturalism. It is no wonder that the critical reception of *The Mountain on the Desert* was so reserved and condemnatory. We cannot deny Richter a certain amount of philosophical and mystical insight; he has the emotional power of the poet to go beyond appearance to a deeper reality. Furthermore, if one overlooks the confusion of his basic assumptions, there is considerable tissue and muscle to his observations, and he demonstrates a remarkable ability to order and control his ideas. But we cannot escape the conviction that crucial aspects of his system defy both demonstration and rational analysis. Indeed, Richter himself has admitted the difficulty of expressing his ideas and his disappointment at seeing them misunderstood:

Perhaps I should mention my disappointment that although some intelligent men and women have read and commented warmly on these theories, few of those I talked to in person appeared to understand them. I must admit them difficult, tangled, and disguised in

[64]   Quoted in A. H. Quinn, *Edgar Allen Poe* (New York, 1941), p. 547.

life, thought and being. Only in certain states of mind can I perceive and follow them clearly myself. Often I have tended to doubt their existence and to suspect my own extravagant imaginings and fantasies until some situation in good light reveals them operating nearly exactly as noted before, and I am convinced once more that one day when rightly presented and perhaps corroborated by delicate measuring instruments of energy flow, they may be more widely understood, discussed and accepted.[65]

Basically, scientific inquiry is inductive and requires the scientist to observe, to record, and to control his data in order to arrive at valid conclusions, to discover the "meaning" and "pattern" of experience. Students of logic are familiar with the fallacy of the inductive leap: the incautious and hasty generalization based on insufficient data without proper consideration of exceptions. Richter not only is guilty of inductive leaps, but there is strong evidence that he has made leaps backward from pattern to data. This does not necessarily mean that he has been wrong in discerning the pattern per se; but it does mean that his arrangement and interpretation of specific data are open to serious criticism.

Several critics have noted discrepancies or contradictions in Richter's system. His failure to be conversant with continuing developments in philosophy, physiology, psychology and theology is a serious indictment. Young in particular calls attention to the anti-intellectual bias in Richter's conviction that education is fruitless because "being taught something isn't experiencing it", a conviction that undercuts Richter's entire purpose, which is to instruct and to play a tutorial role.[66] Perhaps the most serious deficiencies of his system have to do with his implicit reductivism regarding human behavior in general, and to the whole complex and intricate relationship between man and God in particular. To reduce belief and prayer to "energy release processes" may satisfy the deistic latitudinarianism craved by the youthful Richter; but it will not speak to the condition of those who have had an experiential relationship with God, such as that of the apostle Paul, St. John of the Cross, or Jonathan Edwards.

[65] Correspondence to me, July 4, 1961.
[66] Young, pp. 18-19.

Richter's reductivism forces serious obstacles in the way of understanding human moral and spiritual responsibility. The task of reconciling freedom of will on the one hand and mechanistically determined "choices" on the other is not really possible on a rational level. Man as a free moral agent is responsible for his choices; but if his choices are dictated by unconscious psycho-energic release processes, then freedom to will and to choose is reduced to a mere dynamic fiction. Richter has stumbled into the same pit he accused Freud of inhabiting when the latter related all of human conduct to the "blind sack of the genital gland".[67] Richter's concession to a "higher Freedom to direct and to control the whole" is an attempt to resolve the dilemma, but it does not succeed in doing so.

Before concluding this chapter, it is only fair to reflect briefly on the size of the task Richter attempted. In spite of the censure his detailed theories invite, we must keep in mind that science has not carried us very far in understanding the nature of mind. In an important symposium held at the University of California San Francisco Medical Center in 1961, some of the experts gathered to consider the control of the mind were forced to admit that very little is known about mind, either as a concept or as mechanism. Wilder Penfield, in concluding his discussion of the physiological basis of the mind, reminded the audience of this sobering thought:

... after all this progress, when we try to see the actual link between the patterning of electrical impulses in the brain and a change in the mind of man, we are still in the dark – as much in the dark as Aristotle when he asked so long ago, "How is the mind attached to the body?"

In conclusion, it must be said that there is as yet no scientific proof that the brain can control the mind or fully explain the mind. The assumptions of materialism have never been substantiated. Science throws no light on the nature of the spirit of man or God.[68]

The fact that as yet little is known in this area thus dulls some

---

[67] *The Mountain*, p. 119.
[68] Wilder Penfield, "The Physiological Basis of the Mind", *Man and Civilization: Control of the Mind*, a symposium edited by Seymour M. Farber and Roger H. L. Wilson (New York, 1961), p. 16.

of the harsher criticism that has been leveled against Richter. He has attempted to light a candle in preference to cursing the darkness; however, this does not obviate the fact that the flame has only been bright enough to bring the shadows into sharp relief. Perhaps greater familiarity with the conclusions of more capable and highly trained students of the physiology of mind might have chastened Richter's attempt, might have caused him to be more cautious, less dogmatic about his conjectures. The accuracy of his observations or the psychological validity of his interpretation of human behavior is one thing, but the psychological explanation of this behavior is something else and had better be left in the hands of those who know whereof they speak.

When we consider the enormous amount of effort Richter has put into the formulation of a system in a language so unlike his often lyrically moving prose fiction, we are struck by the force of Joseph Wood's appraisal of *The Mountain*:

There are truths which poetry has approached more closely than science and which are better adumbrated by analogy than stated as propositions. But I doubt that the poet is wise when he borrows a specific terminology from science and then uses it in a sense which science does not recognize when he attempts to identify analogy with proposition.[69]

Richter himself has admitted the failure of his philosophical essays and has realized that fiction is a more ideal vehicle for his perceptions. In the final book of his unfinished trilogy, he hoped "not to make the mistake of *The Mountain* in expounding and explaining, but to present as suggestions and symbols in life".[70] The trilogy was not finished before his death, but those novels written after *The Mountain* show the wisdom of his decision to rely on the symbolic possibilities of literature. To capture the felt patterns and rhythms of life in fiction is the proper task of a reflective novelist. It is a happy strategy whereby the real significance of Richter's vision can be determined in terms of his powers of observation.

[69] "In the World of a Hermit", *New York Times Book Review*, June 5, 1955, p. 18.
[70] Correspondence to me, July 4, 1961.

As we have seen, the water and oil of philosophical conjecture and mystical assumptions make at best an unstable mixture, and Richter learned painfully and slowly the valuable lesson that the insights of an artistic consciousness provide a way of knowing that need not be buttressed by the terminology and methods of the scientific laboratory. In an essay entitled "Science and Mysticism", Sir Charles Eddington once wrote, "It is reasonable to inquire whether in the mystical illusions of man there is not a reflection of an underlying reality." [71]

It has been only recently that much attention has been given to the kind of thought Eddington reluctantly implied in his concession to the "mystical illusions" of man. One approach taken by recent philosophers has to do with the problems of semantics and the limitations of language and of "scientific" logic. Perhaps the most seminal development to emerge from this new concern is the distinction being made between "discursive" and "presentational" forms of knowledge. Philosophical problems have traditionally been pursued only in terms of concepts which are clear enough to be handled systematically in conventional semantic forms; but Suzanne K. Langer has attacked the attitude of traditionalists for their tendency to regard any concept too elusive to be "projected" in discursive form as not really accessible to the human mind. Therefore, from the point of view of traditionalists, anyone who concerns himself with "the inexpressible realm of feeling, of formless desires and satisfactions", and of "immediate experience" is forever non-communicable; thus, conclude traditionalists, any thinker "who looks in that direction is, or should be, a mystic".[72]

This view, she feels, does not take into account man's unconscious and primitive (or essential) appreciation of *forms* as a source of knowledge. The traditional philosophical and scientific hostility toward that realm variously designated as "intuition", "deeper meaning", "artistic truth", "insight", and so forth has derived from an imperfect understanding of the primary role of

[71]   Cited in Quinn, p. 556.
[72]   Suzanne K. Langer, *Philosophy in a New Key* (Cambridge, 1942, 1951), p. 86.

symbolic thinking in our mental life. After all, in the process of conceptualization, pictures (the concrete) precede words (abstractions), and, as Langer argues rather cogently, symbolic perception furnished by our sensory apparatus is primary and immediate and often irreducible to discursive form.

The value of language is also its limitation in that words and semantic structures have more or less fixed equivalences, which makes it difficult to grasp what is non-discursive and untranslatable in human experience. On the other hand, the presentational form of knowledge, that is, wordless symbolism "does not allow of definition within its own system and cannot directly convey generalities". Thus symbolic meaning is meaning in terms of the whole, the inter-relationship of the total structure, and the kind of knowledge furnished by "artistic insight" or "poetic truth" is "involved in a simultaneous, integral presentation".[73]

In our analysis of Richter's fictional world, an analysis undertaken in light of his stated philosophical theories, it is important to keep constantly in mind that presentational symbolism – which can be extended to include the total inter-relationship of all the elements of Richter's delineation of reality – is a vehicle of meaning in itself. We can expect Richter at times to tend toward "discursive" narrative forms in his attempt to articulate his intuitions of man's relationship to the universe and to himself; we can expect "themes" to recur which relate to his psycho-energic theories; we can expect those psycho-energic theories to help form his conception of character, his choice of setting, and his determination of action. At the same time, we can expect to see the intuitive and insightful aspects of his vision, which originally gave rise to his discursive theories, to be apparent in his conception of the whole. The larger adumbrations of his interpretation of the cosmos, which do not necessarily rest on the details he has in the meantime worked out to explain them, no doubt inform his fiction with a point of view and a structural pattern – a mode of interpreting human experience which both complements and transcends the "system" of psycho-energics.

[73] *Ibid.*, p. 97.

III

COSMIC DESTINY: THE ROLE OF HARDSHIP AND DISCIPLINE AS A MEANS OF GRACE IN RICHTER'S FICTIONAL RECOVERY OF THE PAST

1. THE CONFIGURATION OF LIFE'S PATTERN

Much of his life John Donner had pondered that which secretly governed man and determined his destiny. Where did it come from and where in him did it reside? It could be found, he had observed, in the grossest of flesh and in the most sensitive and quivering. Seldom could he lay hands on it naked, revealed and labelled in the broad light of day. Sometimes he had caught a glimpse of it in a man's eyes, a snatch of it in his voice or its shape and pattern in what he did, and then in a burst of unwarranted confidence had called it life, spirit or soul, not knowing what he said, and finding out later that, however he named the unnameable, it remained elusive, formless and past his finding out.[1]

In this opening paragraph of Richter's second novel in his unfinished autobiographical trilogy, which attempts to explore further the psycho-energic make-up of man, we find a statement of the concerns that have occupied him as a writer of fiction since the publication of *Early Americana*. It reflects his attempt to show in his fiction that man is a complex entity secretly governed by some mysterious force, the nature of which is elusive, but the pattern of which is occasionally distinct. John Donner, Richter's alter-ego, confesses in this novel the difficulty he has had in grappling with the elusive, mysterious pattern. Perhaps the sense of caution and tentativeness expressed here reflect Richter's disillusionment in identifying – even to his own satisfaction – the

[1] Conrad Richter, *A Simple Honorable Man* (New York, 1962), p. 3.

hidden processes, the "shape and pattern" of that unnameable and formless force, which has compelled his imagination over the years.

Despite the elusiveness of the cosmic pattern, however, Richter's novels continue to be stamped indelibly with those tentative mystical and psychological conclusions he has drawn from his theories of psycho-energics. He realizes that his hypothesis of the formulation and operation of the "realman" must only be suggested in broad outline if he is not to subordinate realism to doctrine, art to thesis. But certain major themes central to the thesis of psycho-energic law emerge again and again as part of an overall life pattern; the meaning of Richter's fiction is related to his psycho-energic interpretation of this pattern.

The configuration of life's pattern, he believes, reveals the use by the universe of hardship and discipline to individual progress, bad means to a good end. Where self-discipline breaks down, there is a natural law insuring that the forced discipline of adversity takes over, both individually and nationally. By imposing this pattern on the details and circumstances of life contained in each episode of his novels, he is able to introduce form to his subject matter, to impose an intelligible order on the experiences of life. The implications he draws from this life pattern account for Richter's preoccupation with a few recurring themes that run like a refrain through his fiction: the themes of hardship and discipline as the means of grace, of the warning against the "cult of comfort", of the growth of higher intelligence wrought by experience, and above all, of the perception of a cosmic destiny ordering the affairs of men.

2. THE CULT OF COMFORT IN MILLENNIA

Richter's theories of emergent evolution threaten to run into serious difficulty concerning his notion of "spiritual" or moral growth. Discarding for the moment the whole problem raised by his assumption that the human organism is an evolving "mechanism", there is an apparent contradiction, or at best paradox, in

Richter's conception of the three stages (or classes or levels) of man in his supposed migration upward from primordial beginnings and toward the "original" source. As we noted in chapter two, Richter distinguishes the three classes of man to be (1) the brutal and self-centered; (2) the sensitive altruist, who unwisely seeks to destroy misery and hardship in the world; and (3) the highly advanced man of disinterested benevolence, whose intelligence and wisdom are equal to his passion, and who therefore refuses to interfere in the natural destiny of his fellow man.[2]

The problem of pain and suffering is thus at the heart of Richter's theories, and Michael's ambivalent feelings on the function and role of pain are actually those of Richter. Michael confides to the college students who seek his counsel that, although he recognizes pain to be the "mother of psycho-energic growth" effecting an ultimate good, he is often extremely troubled by the means. "I am the weak one who acknowledges the Creator's process of obstruction and suffering for our own benefit", he laments, "but who holds back painfully from using it on any living thing but himself." [3] Later Michael confesses that the sight of some poor souls suffering turns his convictions to water, and he is not satisfied with the knowledge that psycho-energically they are benefitting. "I can only think of their tragedy in human terms, and pray for their relief from the wheel of fate." [4] In correspondence to me, Richter admits that Michael's prayer for a "milder and gentler evolutionary system, for a good means to a good end", is his own.[5]

Richter's admission here of the anguish he experiences by accepting the conclusions forced upon him by his theories is an important clue to the tragic tone that pervades his work. The

[2] Richter writes, "the higher man is found on the scale, the more compassionate he is for other men's lives and the more passionate to share his substance, but this very substance may include the joys of higher advancement, and man must reach that advancement first, all of which means the sufficiently evolved and intelligent man would be unlikely to rush to remove those of man's burdens by which he himself attained his higher rates and energy flows". Correspondence to me, March 8, 1962.

[3] *The Mountain*, p. 111.

[4] *Ibid.*, p. 223.

[5] Correspondence to me, March 8, 1962.

glimpse into the machinery of fate brings a sad knowledge that heavily taxes Richter's emotions; and given the sensitivity of his own temperament, it is natural that sorrow and a sense of the tragic inevitability of pain and suffering will impinge upon his conception of human experience. Indeed, this same tragic vision will be evoked as Richter brings into stark relief the nearly total helplessness of man before such immutable processes.

For assuredly, this is a vision of man as helpless in a very real way; nor does Richter find any hope in the illusory panaceas of our contemporary urge to legislate out of existence any manifestation of what society calls misery. The problem is moreover intensified in our own age, Richter suggests, by the apparent fact that modern society collectively is just now entering the "intermediate" stage of spiritual evolution in which zeal for human welfare outdistances the wisdom of restraint. Richter concedes this to be one of the enigmas of existence, and he is convinced that it will force itself on mankind as an unalterable principle.

The temptation before any sensitive in the "intermediate class" will be to covet happiness for his fellow man; but, to repeat Richter's main contention, it becomes a mark of higher advancement when the sensitive man is given the wisdom and will to resist this temptation. Furthermore, says Richter, in what must be a remarkable understatement, the man who has reached this stature is rare and sure to be misunderstood. Understood or not, he will, from Richter's point of view, be the one to have attained genuine moral growth.

Moral growth is marked by an "impersonal" altruism. Unfortunately, the moral growth which attends the "spiritual" evolution Richter envisions cannot be taught: none of the higher virtues such as charity, tolerance, kindness, and generosity can be taught as principles. Morality is only a superficial acquisition if there has been no growth in the psycho-energic substance.[6] The obvious weakness in this notion has already been mentioned. It does emphasize a conception of human nature that will have a direct bearing on Richter's conception of character motivation in

[6] *The Mountain*, p. 202.

his fiction. Stripped of the psycho-energic jargon, it is a theory of determinism that rests on the tyranny of ancestral or "blood" consciousness. "Both the educated and the uneducated who respond to character education", writes Richter, "have the needed qualities already born in them or sharpened by their early lives, or both." [7] This then is the line of thought that translates Richter's essaical theories from speculation to social criticism. If any one catch phrase in Richter's writing best captures his attitude toward modern society, it is the notion that "moderns" [8] have succumbed to the "cult of comfort". Contemporary man, in his quest for comfort, has dedicated himself to the proposition that whatever promises the most security, welfare, and ease is the most progressive. In this view, hardships of any kind have latterly been shunned. Since the expansion of energy expenditure is accompanied by pain and suffering, Richter reminds us, it is unpopular and against the organism's will:

Today the Western world calls much of this process evil. Modern progress and science do their best to conquer it. They're confounded when it springs up more terrible than before in the very ashes where they thought they had destroyed it. What they don't realize is that it is apparently an integral process of the Creator and that the cards are stacked against those who try to destroy it.[9]

Since the mandates of the universe cannot be thwarted, he argues, a land flowing with milk and honey and reclining in ease and luxury will tragically find itself faced with adversity imposed by natural law. Some form of "obstruction" such as overpopulation, famine, sustained droughts, or the plague of war will in some fateful hour visit the people who, had they practiced self-discipline, might have been prepared to withstand the suffering.

Manifestations of the cult of comfort, Richter believes, are everywhere apparent, but they are most obvious in the general failure of restraint. The relaxing of restraints is perhaps the most

[7] Correspondence to me, March 21, 1962.
[8] "Moderns" is the noun Richter has used since 1936 to denote contemporaries who partake willingly of the "modern spirit", i.e., who have rejected certain historical values in the name of progress and enlightenment.
[9] *The Mountain*, p. 194.

serious symptom of modern degeneracy, for "moderns", Richter
charges, have fallen under the spell of "relieving" and thus see
no logic in disciplining their indulgence in desires, wants, sex,
pleasures, and most "so-called compulsions".[10] "It is", writes
Richter, "a process of lowering the evolutionary and manly
standard that our ancestors so laboriously built up." [11]

The most regretful and debasing product of the cult of comfort
is the attitude it engenders. "The modern American", Richter
complains, "is frightened, cowed, bewildered, beaten down by
life, and running with the sheep." He is dependent, bored, searching for happiness in material possessions, and lacking in energy
and vitality. "You can build understanding, culture, and progress
on manhood", he writes, "but you can never build manhood on
mere intelligence, culture and progress. Character strength and
manhood are from within." [12] It is the loss of manhood that
Richter charges modern society with: we have become emasculated, and he lays these evils to the cult of comfort and the
modern philosophy of benefaction.

Richter's only attempt to dramatize the values and attitudes
kindled by unrestricted social benefaction, and graphically to
portray the inevitable and ultimate disaster of the cult of comfort,
is a short and unsuccessful time fantasy entitled "Sinister Journey".[13] Written in the anti-utopian tradition of George Orwell's
1984 and Aldous Huxley's *Brave New World*, this is an eschato-
logical thesis story, a glimpse into an unattractive future. Although
deficient artistically, the story clearly illustrates Richter's vision
of what existence may be like in a society which has succeeded in
abolishing all want and deprivation.

Michael, the protagonist, is portentously translated into a future
dimension of time in which he encounters the long missing

[10] The chief culprit in the psychology of "relieving" is Freudian doctrine.
One of the main motives in Richter's writing *The Waters of Kronos* was
to give an alternative explanation of the Oedipus myth of son-father
hatred by exploring the implications of the Cronos myth.
[11] "That Early American Quality", *Atlantic Monthly*, CLXXXVI (September 1950), p. 30.
[12] *Ibid.*, p. 28.
[13] *Saturday Evening Post*, CCVI (Sept. 26, 1953), pp. 36-37.

Douglas Creel, an altruistic socialist in the former dimension of time, but now a captive resident of the totally planned state of Millennia. The meaning of life in such an apparently utopian environment is set forth in the subsequent dialogues between Creel and Michael.

In the state of Millennia, Richter depicts a world in which public claims destroy the possibilities of private life. The dwarfish, neutral Millennians have sacrificed their human personality to become a function of a process they are never allowed to understand or control. They have lost their imagination and capacity to apprehend reality, and in return they have accepted security. The cardinal principle of the State is freedom from want, and the officials will "tolerate no hunger, poverty, or housing shortage, no illiteracy or ignorance, certainly no medical or other lack that interferes with the peace, contentment and security of our people".[14] Privacy and independent opinions are scorned as subversive of the State maxim, and transgressors of the spirit of freedom from want are given "Benevolent Instruction" and training in "Benign Common Weal". Through such devices Richter shows his distrust of the questionable morality that predicates humanitarian projects imposed by the State for the common good at the expense of an individual's freedom to dissent from the "benefits" of these projects.

Creel, as it is to be expected, has radically changed his mind about his social ideals after having lived in Millennia. He has learned, above all, the effect of freedom from want on man's spiritual consciousness; for the biggest tragedy in this synthetic, imitation world is that where nobody wants for anything, there is no need for God; his Name and Idea are forgotten. Creel, who was an agnostic before sojourning in Millennia, now in a statement of faith presents the thesis of the story:

Oh, I have learned a lot of respect for God from his absence. Back home as a boy I was told everything good came from God. They didn't tell me that lack of good may be God too. I mean what makes you work and pray for something you don't have. Now I believe that's more of God than the other because it lifts you up and develops you

14 *Ibid.*, p. 99.

while monotonous goodness makes you stagnate like a frog in a swamp.[15]

Having initiated his protagonist into the prospects of the future, Richter manages to get him back to the present where, presumably, he will be a much more responsible person.

3. USES OF THE PAST: HARDSHIP AND THE DISCIPLINE OF PAIN

Happily, Richter never again attempted a time fantasy trip to the future, although his short story, "Doctor Hanray's Second Chance" [16] and his remarkable novel, *The Waters of Kronos*, which derives from it, are time fantasies which permit their protagonists to visit the past of their own consciousnesses. Richter's fiction has always been concerned in one way or another with the problem of time, or the lapse of time, but his real genius lies in realizing and evoking the past, not projecting his imagination into the future. His preoccupation with the lapse of time, of course, is related to his psycho-energic criticism of degenerative tendencies in modern civilization. The point to note is that this preoccupation provides him with a time perspective of contrast between past and present.

Indeed, one of the most effective devices Richter employs is to create a then-now tension by suggesting an implicit contrast in human experience between former and contemporary modes of existence. Thus his vision is dual in the sense that past and present are eternally juxtaposed one to another in his interpretation of human experience. This is made explicit in his essays and appears as an implicit protest in his fiction, a protest against the disintegration of modern man, who stifles creative growth by fostering a life of ease and comfort.

As a specific to this modern degeneracy, Richter turns to the past to rescue certain values needed to curb man's devolution. To the extent that this theme emerges in his fiction, Richter can be considered a social critic in the primitivistic tradition, a relation-

[15] *Ibid.*, p. 102.
[16] *Saturday Evening Post*, CCII (June 10, 1950), pp. 22-23.

ship which will be treated later in this study. But his criticism of modern attitudes and beliefs must be related to his theory of emergent evolution, for it is from this theory that he derives the intellectual authority for his protest; and it is this theory which distinguishes his criticism from merely nostalgic, conservative reaction against innovation and change.

Richter's highest achievements as a novelist are due to his familiarity and sympathy with the American pioneer. The great example for modern civilization by which it may regain its vitality and fortitude is the early American, and more specifically, that early American quality. This explains in part his lifelong devotion to historical fiction. According to Richter, the opposition of the wilderness developed the hardy and vigorous American pioneer, who is perhaps the best exemplification of the value of conflict for character growth:

The greater the difficulties of the pioneer, the more did his hardship, insecurity, danger and discomfort establish strong energy flows in him so that when resolved by hope and effort toward eventual victory over them, the released energy of these hardships gave pleasure, not pain. The idea of pain wasn't in the pioneer so much as in modern people with fainter energy flows who look back on the pioneer and invent tales of his suffering and despair to cut him down more to their own size.[17]

What Richter has tried to define in his researches into the early American character is the *source* of that quality which he believes was unique. The pioneers had in common, a "kind of hardihood and vigor beside which most Americans seem soft and squeamish today". There was, he insists, a dynamic vitality in their lives. In contrast to the emasculated modern character, the early American had about him a "manliness" – not physique, but a quality that made for an "independent crabbed hardihood that stood up for its rights and took you on at all odds", writes Richter. "It was a quality of mind and spirit rather than of body, still more of creed and belief." [18]

Richter's chief admiration for the early Americans, then, is for

---

[17]   *The Mountain*, p. 200.
[18]   "That Early American Quality", p. 27.

their common sense philosophy, which accepted the need for opposition and inharmony; they had "a greater value and respect
for the establishment of expanded expenditure, however painful".
The older generation accepted life's misfortunes and adversities
as "the wise dispensation or discipline of the gods".[19] They did
not rail at life or denigrate the mysterious fate that placed them
time and time again in cruel circumstances. Richter's conviction
that the early Americans had somehow divined life's pattern, and
had learned through experience the folly of rejecting Providence,
or cosmic destiny, goes far toward explaining why his pioneer
novels are his most vigorous and alive. "The sustained summoning
of effort and energies built up in some mysterious way the
spiritual and physical reservoirs of men and women [and] produced that breed whose record so dwarfs us spiritually and physically today." [20]

By turning his efforts toward the frontier era, Richter hoped to
contrast the positive qualities then so much in evidence against
what he feels to be the negative or emasculated qualities that
early began to vitiate the American spirit. The emergence of a
higher standard of living concomitant with the spread of industrialism in the mid-nineteenth century marked the beginning
of a cultural loss. "No one can long study the early days in
America" he writes, "without witnessing the strength of character
under hardship and its weakening under ease and high living
standards." [21] His purpose as a historical novelist is to present an
authentic account of pioneer vitality evoked by hardship and the
discipline of pain and to illuminate the meaning of certain changes
in the human condition brought about by cosmic destiny.

The Ohio trilogy represents the highest fulfillment of that purpose. However, in *Early Americana* and *The Sea of Grass*, the
two major works that precede the first book of the trilogy, Richter
struggled with the problem of articulating and dramatizing his
conception of life in historical fiction. An analysis of these two
works will be helpful in suggesting the increasing importance

[19] *The Mountain*, p. 199.
[20] "That Early American Quality", p. 30.
[21] Correspondence to me, July 4, 1961.

Richter attached to his theories of psycho-energics for his fictive interpretation of the past. Furthermore, an analysis will serve as a foundation for our understanding the relationship of his discursively expressed theories to his intuitive and perhaps unconscious revelation of the tragic overtones which characterize the Ohio trilogy.

4. EARLY AMERICANA AND THE SOUTHWESTERN FRONTIER

Richter's stories of the Southwest represent his first seriously artistic effort to translate the significance of the past into meaningful and revelatory dramatic episodes. His journey to New Mexico, necessitated by ill-health in the family and perhaps prompted partly by the need to redefine and clarify his own role as a writer, opened a rich vein of literary materials. In a characteristically mystical gesture, he attributes his relocation to the land of enchantment to a purposeful fate: "Blindly but surely events conspired . . . to make us sell our Eastern farm-home, burn our bridges behind us and cast our lot in New Mexican soil." [22] Richter was more than ever confirmed in his theories when he came to know New Mexican residents who had first hand knowledge of life in the territorial past or who had descended from pioneer parents.

The nine stories collected in *Early Americana* indicate clearly the thematic and technical direction Richter's frontier fiction was to take for the next two decades. Although the stories are not arranged in any conscious pattern of structural architectonics or united by the controlling consciousness of a central character, they are bound together into a complementary whole by the late southwestern frontier setting, the continuity of theme, the conception of character, the tone, and the technical devices which enable Richter to achieve atmospheric control and to suggest emotional restraint.

[22] "New Mexico Was Our Fate", *New Mexico Magazine*, XXXV (March 1957), p. 20.

In the foreword, Richter acknowledges his indebtedness to those men and women of the Southwest, whom he personally interviewed, for providing him with realistic "details and authenticities he wished to know, not of history, but of early life".[23] His aim was to set these stories "down on an underlying pattern of these endless, small authenticities, without which life would not be life either then or today, and in a style suggestive of those times . . .".[24] It is important to note, however, that Richter's conception of the "small authenticities" of life is not restricted to the homely and realistic details of frontier life; the emphasis rests on the "underlying pattern" of these authenticities. In short, the details are selected and invested with special significance in light of Richter's psycho-energic theories. The theories give point and direction to his use of the authentic details, for in Richter's view of life, no detail, however mean or trivial, is without its psycho-energic significance. We can expect, then, a rigid principle of selectivity and order in his presentation, not only of the larger episodes, but of the homely details with which he undergirds those episodes.

Each episode – and each story is chiefly built around one climactic episode which distills the meaning of life – involves a limited number of characters in a moment or period of crisis and traces their emotional and physical response to that crisis. Generally, one character provides the center of consciousness whose emotional growth or understanding is particularly revelatory.

The first tale, "Early Americana",[25] is the story of Laban Oldham's initiation into manhood under the most grotesque of circumstances. Laban, impatient to leave his parental home to join a group of professional buffalo hunters, arrives at Carnuel, a tiny remote settlement dominated by John Minor's buffalo post, where the residents are preparing for the wedding of Jack Shelby and Nellie Hedd. When the couple to be married fail to appear, Laban volunteers to ride the short distance to the Hedd homestead

---

[23] *Early Americana and Other Stories* (New York, 1951, first published in 1936), pp. v-vi.
[24] *Ibid.*, p. vi.
[25] *Ibid.*, pp. 3-37.

to determine what has hindered their coming. Discovering that Indians have murdered and mutilated the entire family, Laban returns to the settlement with his grim tale, and the four men and three women prepare themselves for Indian hostilities.

Knowing the cruelty and savagery of the Indians, John Minor persuades three of the men secretly to reserve one bullet each to use against the three women to prevent their falling into the hands of the savages should the Indians overwhelm the settlement. It is Laban's lot to kill John Minor's sixteen-year-old daughter, Catherine, should it prove necessary. Laban understandably is horrified at the prospect, and the ordeal is made worse by Catherine's presence, for she determines to give him companionship during the long night vigil. The Indian raid fails to materialize at dawn, and the safety of the settlers is assured by the belated arrival of the buffalo hunters. Laban's parents and brother, who had escaped the Indian attack, are with the hunters.

The most important development in the episode is Laban's new feeling for Catherine. Before the end of the week, the circuit rider, using the document originally intended for the murdered couple, marries Laban to Catherine Minor. The ordeal has matured Laban, whose early thoughts of a gay and carefree life of adventure with the hunters give way to a more compelling vision of homesteading with the resourceful and graceful Catherine. The story turns on Laban's ability to accept a man's responsibility that stern evening of vigil; but Catherine, too, demonstrates qualities of discipline and determination which are brought to the surface by the imminent crisis. In each instance, romantic fancies give way to sterner realities.

The story, despite the constant threat of violence, is characterized by intensely powerful emotions kept under strict control – particularly those of Laban, who, psychologically preparing himself for the responsibility thrust upon him, suffers through the night knowing that he might have to kill Catherine. The tension is intense, and Richter carefully selects details which relate to Laban's need to prepare himself for the dreaded possibility of a mercy killing. In terms of psycho-energics, Laban experiences a desperate need to release energy to meet the increased energy expenditure associated with the ordeal. He must tap deep reservoirs of strength to meet his dreaded obligation; this psycho-energic process is exemplified in the effect the enormous pile of curing buffalo hides has upon his resolution to carry through with the unprecedented task assigned him by fate:

The strong reek of the skins gave him something that he needed, like a powerful medicine brewed from the staked plains themselves. It reached where no whiskey could. Kiowas or Comanches were nothing. After what he had seen in the canyon this afternoon, he could mow the painted devils down all day and stay icy cold with hate and clear of regret. But a white person, a woman, and only a girl! For more than an hour he kept walking up and down between the dark piles, and all the while, in the tightened sinews of his arms and legs and in the growing flatness of his cheeks, he seemed to be curing, hardening, drying, almost like one of the buffalo hides itself.[26]

"Smoke Over the Prairie",[27] the second story in the volume, develops a much different conflict – that between the past and present, between a pastoral mode of life and the progress of civilization, symbolized by the coming of the railroad. Frank Gant, owner and ruler of a huge pastoral empire, exercises the authority of a benevolent despot over his family, his land, and his employees. Autocratic and absolute, he is a powerful man capable of both gentleness and violence. His conflict with the railroad is related to his personal hatred for Vance Rutherford, the young iron-willed railroad engineer, who marries Gant's daughter, Juliana, against her father's will. Not only does the railroad take his daughter, threaten his baroniel authority, jeopardize his freighting business, and bring him into conflict with his wife, who opposes her husband's resistance against the railroad, but it promises to bring "civilization and progress", which Gant knows means homesteading farmers, who will eventually violate the pastoral range in a vain effort to transform the desert grazing lands into farming country like the Kansas they migrate from. He is further embittered by Rutherford and his own wife's failure to realize that civilization has already existed for three centuries in the New Mexican territory, and that it has endured and triumphed

[26] *Ibid.*, p. 25.
[27] *Ibid.*, pp. 38-83.

because it has recognized the spirit of the land and has lived in harmony with it.

Within two years the steel tracks of the railroad which parallel the road into Capitan reach Gant's empire. Through political influence and deceit, the railroad manages to secure condemnation procedures on right-of-way land that transverses Gant's huge range. In a climactic episode, Gant – driving to Capitan to confront the officials who duped him – fatefully encounters the celebration train, carrying dignitaries to "open" the road officially. Grimly resolved to ignore the train, Gant soon finds himself racing against it in a symbolic show of strength. The railroad, of course, is destined to triumph over Gant's stubborn resistance, and just as it appears that the steel-nerved rancher has won the race, his buggy is struck at a crossing and Frank Gant is killed.

The story, in some respects, is a miniature tragedy. Gant, godlike in his defiance, is ennobled by his willful resistance against "progress", but, transcending his limitations in his fierce hubristic pride, he is eventually destroyed by his nemesis, a fatal force over which he has no ultimate control. The tragic tones are muted by the nostalgia and middle distance of the narrator, Gant's son, who tells the story in reminiscence. Thematically, the story represents an encounter between an idyllic past, in which men of heroic stature moved in slow and powerful rhythm with the earth, and a frenetic present in which "progress", represented by a shrieking, noisy, but powerful train locomotive, blindly destroys the rude baronial empire to bring the dubious advantages of Eastern civilization to the New Mexican desert. Gant's failure to accommodate to the new order is due partly to a tragic mistake in judgment, but Richter suggests very clearly that something grand and noble is irretrievably lost.

Despite its apparent advantages, civilization is somehow an enemy to the nobility and firm resolution of men like Frank Gant. Gant's son intuitively recognizes this: "I was only a boy, but I could tell, as I rode thoughtfully homeward, that in this thing my mother called civilization, there was no quarter, no compromise, no pity." [28] The technological luxury symbolized by the

[28] *Ibid.*, p. 67.

train suggests that the conditions which formed and shaped men like Frank Gant will disappear from the land. His ability to draw upon vast pools of strength from his own inner being to confront such a formidable enemy as the collective strength of the railroad has been due to the circumstances in his own development in a hard land. When individual strength is replaced by collective strength, something vital and very near the center has dropped out.

"New Home" [29] is the tale of a homesteading couple who encounter a number of hardships in establishing their home and claim to land on the New Mexican frontier. Seventeen-year-old Sabina Clark gives birth to their first child in a covered wagon parked on a choice site where Pleas has determined to settle. Handy with tools, the self-reliant young settler, who had built the wagon that brought them to the West, builds a tight log cabin; but trouble appears in the form of a grim warning from Fant, owner of the Cross Key ranch, whose cattle use the clear spring near the cedars and newly built cabin. In order to secure title to the land, Pleas must leave Sabina alone to protect their interests while he makes what would normally be a two-week trip to the nearest land office.

Three weeks elapse with no sign of the young settler. Sabina busies herself to occupy time, fighting hard to keep her anxieties under control; moreover, the ordeal is suddenly intensified by news of an Indian uprising. Although warned to take shelter at the nearby Cross Key ranch, Sabina cannot force herself to forsake their cabin and livestock to the savage Kiowa raiders. The climactic episode of the story is the night-long vigil. A glow in the night tells her the nearby Hurd homestead has been attacked. Later at night when an Indian stealthily attempts to steal her team, anger overcomes Sabina's fear, and she drives off the marauders, seriously wounding one with a shotgun blast. In the morning Pleas returns and explains his prolonged absence. Frustrated by Fant, who blocked his homestead claim application, Pleas had ridden one hundred miles farther on to purchase a railroad land scrip that entitles him to 460 acres of land anywhere in the territory. Fant, at last forced to acknowledge the Clarks' claim to the land, has agreed to live peacefully with the settler.

The drama of the tale is less in the external action and more in the inner tension and emotional experience of Sabina in her need to summon strength and resolution in the face of severe strain and emotional ordeal. Richter's psycho-energic theories are apparent in the conception of character; for instance, Pleas is described as having "blue, patient eyes which always told you that underneath his gentle manner lay inexhaustible wells of strength".[30] Part of the tale is devoted to demonstrations of his ability to draw upon this strength. Richter's theory of human behavior is perhaps more apparent in Sabina's emotional response to the three crises of childbirth, conflict with rival land seekers, and Indian raid. During the birth of her child she draws strength by calling to mind the familiar patterns of life back in her parental home. The description of the routine duties from which she draws energy during Pleas' absence serves the twofold purpose of making believable her behavior under stress and of giving justification for a detailed picture of frontier life. This is particularly apparent the night of the Indian raid. Sabina, to replenish her depleted energy stores at the sight of the burning homestead in the distance, attempts to convince herself aloud that it is only a brush fire to clear land, a practice she had often observed in Arkansas. The association of brush fires with Arkansas and her loneliness call to mind a host of memories which she encourages by reciting them aloud to her baby:

Your papa came out here to make our future. There wasn't much chance in Arkansas. But there were lots of people. We saw them at church every Sunday morning and evening and at Sunday school in the afternoon. On Saturday night we had specials. In the summertime we had church festivals. Neighbors always dropped in. In winter we went to school and studied the blue-backed speller and Ray's arithmetic and McGuffey's reader.[31]

Another singular instance of details invested with significance by

---

[30]   *Ibid.*, p. 87.
[31]   *Ibid.*, p. 113.

Richter's psycho-energic theories is Sabina's enigmatic attitude toward the pine trees near the cabin. Early in the story she is struck by something disturbing in their presence: "These pines always reminded her of something, but she never could decide what it was." [32] Later, during Pleas' absence, their presence becomes more clearly related to something in her subconscious: "But when the shadows of the cedars grew long and taciturn, she felt stirring under the stones of her mind all the unnameable memories of the race." [33] Finally, the evening of the day she receives the Indian warning, their significance epiphanizes for her:

She walked swiftly down to the spring and was conscious at last of what the two pines reminded her of. They were round no longer, but flat against the moon. Their triangular shape, their indentations from dark branch to branch and the long points at the top were tonight unmistakeably arrowheads against the sky.[34]

The fear elicited by this discovery strangely releases energy and enables Sabina to resolve her dilemma of whether to flee with her infant to safety or to stay. She receives the needed strength to meet the crisis head-on and immediately sets about securing the livestock against attack. Imbedded in her racial consciousness are "cell groups" of energy flows associated with the age-old conflict with hostile primitives, symbolized by the flint-points of arrows. Through the discipline of fear she receives courage and resolution.

The conflict in "Long Drought" [35] is not between human beings, whether civilized or savage, but between man and nature. The arid Southwest is itself the chief antagonist in this story of the great drought that extended from June 1889 to the summer of 1893. Lively, boyish, and attractive Joanna Davis, daughter of a prominent horse rancher in the Valle Grande, pledges her troth to Yancy McQuail, a quiet, resolute young cowman who is starting his own ranch. Joanna promises to wait a year until

[32] *Ibid.*, p. 94.
[33] *Ibid.*, p. 105.
[34] *Ibid.*, p. 110.
[35] *Ibid.*, pp. 119-147.

Yancy is financially more secure, but destiny intervenes and the lush range with its "rolling bonanza of grass" is turned into a wasteland of starving cattle. The grim ranchers watch helplessly, and the marriage is postponed for four years as Yancy takes the remnant of his herd to South Dakota to escape the drought.

When several of the remaining ranchers attempt to persuade Sylvester Davis to relocate with them in South Dakota, he refuses to go along. Shrewd and independent, he has faith in the wild spirit of the land and in the homely maxim, "When troubles come thick, they soon get their worst. Then they start to mend." [36] Davis moves his horses to the distant Sugareet Range, and in his absence the burden of responsibility falls upon Joanna, who is soon faced with a crisis more immediate than the drought. Her mother, ill and nearing childbirth, is in need of a doctor. Joanna's young brother, Elliot, is thrown from a horse and hurt in his attempt to ride for aid, and Joanna is forced to leave her mother and brother in the care of her youngest sister while she makes the torturous sixteen hour ride alone. Mrs. Davis survives the birth of her fourth child, but the family is grieved at the death of Sylvester Davis, killed by a horse on the Sugareet Range.

Just when the troubles have gotten "their worst", the land begins to heal. Yancy returns to manage the D-Bar ranch and to marry Joanna. Coincidental with his arrival, the rain returns to the parched earth and the long drought is over. Although the story's conclusion borders on contrivance and sentimentalism, Richter manages to suggest a realistic movement from tremendous deprivation to welcome release in a psycho-energic pattern of good out of evil. The land is imaged as hostile and malevolent in the period of drought, but there is the unmistakeable hint that the ordeal of drought has been instrumental in forming a more meaningful marriage union and in paving the way for an even more successful D-Bar ranch. This is the first story in the present volume clearly to demonstrate the autonomy of nature in the destiny of men, but it is a message written in hieroglyphics whose key is unearthed only in retrospect:

36   *Ibid.*, p. 136.

A year to come, and men were to say that all this summer the brand of fate had been burned in gigantic red strokes on the broad green page of the plain. But few men there were in the Valle Grande who read the warning without mistake until it was too late.[37]

Few of Richter's short stories have dramatized as forcefully the qualities of stoic endurance over a protracted period of hardship. In keeping with his psycho-energic theories, Richter conceives of his characters as strengthened by this ordeal. The external drought is not accompanied by internal drought, nor is the erosion of the land followed by erosion of the emotions or spiritual strength. Indeed, the obverse is true.

The journey from a war-ravaged Georgia to the wild and hostile plains of New Mexico is the structural vehicle of the tale, "Frontier Woman".[38] Richter could not have selected a better device for his presentation of frontier life, or for the fact that most Western emigrants became hardened frontiersmen on the trail West. The protagonist, Lalla Porterfield, is the psycho-energic center of consciousness; Lalla takes her mother on the great Western trail to reunite the family with her father, Major Porterfield, an ex-Confederate officer, who, in partnership with his brother, has preceded them to the New Mexican territory to mend his fortunes. Although accustomed to the genteel life of antebellum aristocracy, Lalla has been emotionally prepared for the ordeal by her experiences in the South during the Civil War. The underlying pattern of her strength, courage, and determination is directly attributable to this heritage of hardship. The war had required Lalla to turn from the delicate social training appropriate to her status in Southern aristocracy to the demanding responsibility of managing a doomed plantation and of attending wounded Confederates in the wake of Sherman's march through Georgia. It is this that enables her to summon the necessary courage to retrieve the body of her Negro servant, who is slaughtered by Indians on the trail.

The hazards of the trail are muted by the presence of Craig Whetherville, owner of the C-Bar ranch, who is returning to New

---

[37] *Ibid.*, p. 120.
[38] *Ibid.*, pp. 148-183.

Mexico after delivering cattle to Alabama. Their experience together on the trek across the Great American Desert forges a
bond between them that culminates in Craig's marriage proposal
at the end of the story. Although the successful romance suggests
Richter's relationship to popular magazine fiction, the underlying
significance of the story is the distinct connection between Lalla's
Civil War crisis and her transformation into a frontier woman.
Craig's proposal is accompanied by a warning that life will be
hard and lonely on the staked plains. His warning evokes a vision
of the hardship she will inevitably be subjected to on a remote
Western ranch; the vision itself releases flows of inner strength
which are clearly connected in her mind with the discipline of
pain in war-torn Georgia:

As if in answer to these pictures, a steady welling rose in her. She was
glad to feel it, to know that a week's bright gayety in Sante Fe had not
destroyed it – that it was still there to lean upon, a kind of flowing
armour in the blood, the strange sweet fruit of that bitter plant, defeat
in war.[39]

Unlike several other protagonists in *Early Americana*, Lalla is
more perceptive of the cause-effect relationship hardship has had
with her inner strength; she knows that pain is the chisel of
nobility which cuts away illusion and leaves the stern features of
reality.

Most of Richter's frontier stories involve in one way or another
the implications of marriage, but no courtship or marriage is as
strange as that in "As It Was in the Beginning".[40] Convinced by
a severe illness and the boisterous but good-intentioned advice of
several hunters and traders that a frontiersman needs a wife
– even if she is Indian or Mexican, Foard Hudspeth determines
to trade for Ursula Ross, a young white woman held captive by
Shaved Head, a Comanche chief. Confident of the success of his
endeavor, Foard prepares his trading post to receive his purchased
bride before leaving Taos for Bent's Fort and Comanche country.
Although young, Foard is a shrewd, hardened frontier trader,

[39]   *Ibid.*, pp. 182-183.
[40]   *Ibid.*, pp. 184-227.

whose ability to match wits with the crafty and cunning Comanche chief enables him successfully to bargain for the "squaw with yellow hair". Returning in quiet triumph to Bent's Fort, Foard is shocked and disgusted when Ursula, backed by the moral authority of a missionary, refuses to accept wifehood under these terms. Foard reluctantly frees her to return East and choose a husband in a civilized way. Unexpectedly encouraged by the missionary to ask Ursula to be his wife as one would propose to a white woman, however, Foard proposes marriage, and the story concludes with a frontier wedding at Bent's Fort.

On the level of technique, Richter's psycho-energic theories are apparent in the momentary flashbacks which occur when a word or situation unlocks in Foard's mind memories and associations which strangely provide the impetus for needed determination or action. Ursula, too, finds a special quality of strength in reciting lines from an old familiar hymn which relates to her former existence in white civilization. Furthermore, her experience with her captors, who have cruelly murdered her parents and brothers, fills her with a controlled but energetic hatred that enables her to bide her time for release and to resist total assimilation into the Indian's mode of life and psychology. On the thematic level, of course, the episode is a graphic demonstration of those early American qualities so necessary for survival on the frontier – qualities which are further nurtured by the exigencies of life in a primitive setting.

Although filled with the same adverse frontier circumstances and adversities that thwart and frustrate human plans, "Buckskin Vacation" [41] is not as successful in believably conveying Richter's vision of the West as the other tales in *Early Americana*. It is the story of a frontier marriage, once again accomplished after several unexpected obstacles have been overcome. Rosalie Porter, having made plans secretly to wed lieutenant Coates McDonald, is returning home for summer vacation after her first year in a female seminary in Missouri. Her return to the untamed prairies is marked by her increasing anxiety and fear that she will not reach

[41]   *Ibid.*, pp. 228-261.

home in time to meet McDonald at a Fourth of July dance, from which they plan to elope and marry. The train is stalled by the mass migration of buffalo, which causes Rosalie to miss her connections. Met by the coach her father sent to fetch her in, she determines to catch up with Gaius Bent's swift mule train. Indian violence threatens as they encounter the remains of a mutilated emigrant wagon; overtaking an ox train bound for the territory, Rosalie learns that Bent's pack train is too far ahead to catch up with, and she resigns herself uncomplainingly to a tedious forty day journey.

McDonald fails to see her during summer vacation, and Rosalie regretfully begins the return trip to school in Missouri. However, McDonald, fortuitously assigned to escort wagon trains over Indian territory, catches up with Rosalie's Eastbound group, and they are married out on the stark plains with good-natured emigrants providing the necessary witness.

The coincidences of this final meeting and the romantic intrigue of their wedding temper the realistic edge of this story, although once again the technique of flashback-reminiscence to summon the energy and strength needed for patient endurance is apparent. One particularly effective scene is the stern rebuke her inner-consciousness brings to bear on her carelessness:

Out from the recesses of her mind, a swarm of shadowy memories were emerging. She had been so many months in the sheltered East she had almost forgotten they existed. It was as if a button had been suddenly pressed, a curtain silently raised, and all about her on the prairie moved the shadowy figures of dim, ugly scenes that she wished might have been forgotten.[42]

Not only is she reapprised of the ugly reality of plains life, but she is thus enabled to respond more alertly to the incipient violence that threatens her safety and well-being.

"The Square Piano",[43] one of the weaker tales in the collection, is the story of a brooding conflict between two feuding ranches which erupts into violence the night of a community entertain-

[42]   *Ibid.*, p. 242.
[43]   *Ibid.*, pp. 262-294.

ment at which the territory's first square piano is unveiled. The principals in the conflict are the Piatts and the Lawlers, who trace their antagonisms to a rather trivial incident five years before – Jack Lawler's arrogant display of a cowhide having the Piatt's Rafter P brand. The elder Piatt and the oldest Piatt son were murdered early in the feud, and on the day of entertainment the atmosphere of mortality lies heavy on the town, particularly since the vendetta had been aggravated by a skirmish between the factions the night before.

The center of consciousness in the story is Cynthia Ann Piatt, a sensitive girl of ten or twelve when the events of the story take place. The focus of interest is the fate of seventeen-year-old Ewing Piatt, who takes Valeria Wingate to the social affair. The air is charged with tension, and not unexpectedly, the feud explodes into the open, although characteristically the violence takes place in the dark streets outside the entertainment hall. Cynthia is conscious only of shots, voices, and confusion. Ewing is seriously wounded, but the story concludes optimistically with a somewhat melodramatic exchange of betrothal vows between Valeria and Ewing. The feud is not reconciled, however, and Valeria's laconic pledge of troth is made in full awareness that her life with Ewing will inevitably be marked with recurrences of the old feud.

Once again it is Richter's feeling for an immutable destiny as well as his skill at creating an atmospheric medium that give vitality and force to an otherwise rather conventional story. His conception of a fixed order in the cosmos is reflected in Cynthia's sense that the vendetta was somehow "fated and inexorable as a scene out of the Old Testament". Details are deliberately selected for their psycho-energic adumbrations. For example, as Cynthia recalls the episode in reminiscence many decades later, she re-experiences the "strange alchemy" in her young blood she had felt at the sight of a dry Ute scalp nailed to the Lawler hide-and-wool warehouse. The effect of music upon her consciousness is described essentially in psycho-energic terms: as Valeria plays first the melodian and later the square piano, a kaleidoscope of pictures flash through Cynthia's mind, sublime notes calling up visions of the towering Jicarita Mountains, the gentle, rocking movement of the bass notes eliciting sensations of the vast grassy sea of the Rafter P range. In each instance, Cynthia – cognizant of the impending danger to Ewing, and prescient about Valeria's feelings for him – envelopes the young couple in a kind of ominous musical mist. Richter's theory of music's power to elicit certain "release processes" is definitely reflected in these details. Characterization too is related to Richter's intentions to affirm the psycho-energic frontier experience. The unflinching, resolute manner of frightened yet courageous people in a violent land is exemplified in Mrs. Piatt, Ewing, Valeria, and Cynthia. Firmness and self-reliance are not mere options; they are requirements for survival.

"Early Marriage",[44] the last story in the volume, is reminiscent of "Buckskin Vacation" in that the protagonist undergoes a trial of hardship to reach the one she plans to marry. Nancy Bellem, seventeen-year-old daughter of Asa Putman, operator of a frontier trading post on the Sante Fe trail, is preparing to travel to the distant Rio Grande country to marry a frontier rancher named Stephen. Although the trip would have been hazardous under the most ideal conditions, the danger is magnified by the reports of fresh Indian uprisings, testified to by the absence of any traffic on the trail. Uncle Gideon, who was to accompany Nancy to her new home, fails to appear, and although no one says so, all suspect he has met with some kind of misfortune connected with the Indian wars. In spite of this turn of events, Nancy stubbornly refuses to postpone her trip, and consequently, her younger brother is called upon to shoulder a man's responsibility in taking his sister to Stephen's ranch, a journey of several days through uninhabited wilderness.

The journey itself is a minor epic of hardship and trial. To begin with, a pioneer family encountered on the trail brings news of Indian atrocities and a severe warning to turn back; the youngsters stubbornly push ahead, although they are later filled with horror and dread when they come across the smouldering ruins and mutilated bodies of a pioneer family massacred by the

[44] Ibid., pp. 295-322.

Indians. Nature itself appears to become a hostile enemy: a fierce sandstorm during the night adds its unique miseries and causes the horses to break loose from their hobbles. The younger brother spends the next day tracking down the runaways while Nancy waits alone at the wagon, whiling away the dreary hours by reading her testament and busying herself with domestic activities. When night arrives before the lad returns, her terrors are heightened by the presence of three hungry prairie coyotes who encircle the wagon, piercing the air with unnerving barks and screams. Nancy preserves her sanity by talking aloud and going over familiar scenes, calling to mind such things as the arrangement of furniture in the parlor back home. Rain follows the sandstorm, and when the two reach the Rio Grande, they find it swollen with flood waters, its currents violent and vicious. After this last hazardous crossing, they are met by Nancy's intended husband, who explains that Indian uprisings on his part of the range had prevented his coming to meet her. Nothing is spoken of the dangers encountered on the trip, and the story concludes with the marriage ceremony rudely conducted in the ranchhouse living room. Richter avoids a sentimental ending by having Nancy's consciousness filled with fear for her father back at the lonely outpost in Indian-infested country.

The plot summaries necessary to facilitate discussion of these stories unfortunately call undue attention to the broad outline of action and thus do serious injustice to the integrity and subtlety of Richter's tales. Thematic analysis is crucial, of course, but Richter's real achievement is on the level of technique. As important as physical action is in the narrative structure of each story, the essential power of these tales derives from the sustained underlying tension created by the continual suggestion of violent emotion held in suspense. The human emotional response to the intense strain of unspoken fears elicited by frontier experience is the actual subject of Richter's fiction. His conception of character and his vision of human behavior under the harsh conditions of primitive existence reflected both in thematic resolution and in technique are intimately related to his cosmological and psychological theories.

An intelligible fate, apparent in the autonomy of nature, works through experience to compel men and women to live in organic harmony with the land; this intimate relationship with the land begins with an acknowledgement of its own wild spirit and involves an acceptance of its relentless adversity as part of its long-range benefits to the human race. The more perceptive characters are depicted as sensing intuitively this organic relationship in the discipline of pain. Those who do not attain the clear insight manifested by a Lalla Porterfield in her intuitive understanding that the bitter experience of defeat in war issues in the "strange sweet fruit" of inner strength, "a kind of flowing armour of the blood", nevertheless are made aware that somehow inner resources of energy can be tapped by certain psychological processes which unlock associational memories.

The thematic continuity of the nine tales is readily apparent; however, the casual observer may overlook the significance of Richter's psycho-energic theories on the level of technique. One of his expressed aims in this volume is to present the underlying pattern of authenticities in a "style" suggestive of those times. The style is characterized by a rigid economy of language and understatement; words as well as scenes and episodes are carefully chosen to suggest restraint and discipline in the face of extraordinary adversity. The grim silences and unspoken words powerfully convey volumes of meaning that would be obscured in the unnecessary verbiage of a less skilled writer. This spartan simplicity of language is itself a conscious attempt by Richter to employ his theories of psycho-energics: more energy is released by understatement than by overstatement. The same is true of the narrative structure as well. Each story presents the augmentation of deprivation which finally culminates in some form of release – marriage, reunion, rain, or death.

Not only does the restraint suggested by a terse, laconic style complement and communicate the emotional restraint and self-discipline of the characters, but it enables Richter to avoid the detailed analysis of a state of mind which a less skilled writer might permit to violate the illusion of reality. Only rarely does he permit the characters to indulge in introspective analysis. Gener-

ally, the insight we gain comes not so much from articulated
self-analysis as it does from the dramatization of unconscious
forces that predicate human behavior. This is most evident in the
technique of flashback-reminiscence in which the characters,
either by chance or conscious deliberation, ruminate over familiar
childhood scenes to obtain energy to confront immediate exigencies and the terror of the unknown. The same principle is apparent in the detailed description of routine tasks and domestic
duties; almost invariably the characters are thrown back upon
inner reservoirs of strength which are tapped by engaging in routine behavior. The technical implication of this device is obvious:
it permits Richter to present a fiction well-nourished by the facts
of experience. The authentic details of pioneer life inobtrusively
develop from the action itself rather than being imposed upon it
as forced documentation. The result is an organic interrelation-
ship of action, character, setting, and details.

This is not to imply that some of the tales do not suffer structural and textural weaknesses. Richter's earlier penchant for rosy-
rainbow endings threatens to reappear, but this tendency is
generally checked by the blunt picture of the unrelieved terror
and ugliness of frontier life. For example, the marriage of Laban
and Catherine in "Early Americana" takes place against the background of brutal Indian atrocities, and the marriage certificate
itself, with the original names scratched out, is a grim reminder
of the grotesque turn of fate.

The triumph of romance and marriage against physical and
parental obstacles in some of the tales may be a concession to the
Saturday Evening Post and *Ladies Home Journal* readers, who
comprised the first audience of these stories; however, the fact
that all nine stories deal in one way or another with betrothal and
marriage is not easily dismissed as a leftover from Richter's
apprenticeship days with popular fiction. Marriage is tacitly recognized as one of the most significant experiences of frontier life,
and his preoccupation with it is actually a concession to reality.
Furthermore, the juxtaposition of this gentle and intimate love
relationship between man and woman and the harsh, incipient
violence of the frontier calls attention to the primacy of human

relationships in a lonely environment. The basis for frontier marriage forms such a remarkable contrast to our present modes of courtship and wedlock that Richter could not help having been struck by the immense difficulties frontier life imposed upon an institution so unhampered in the present economy of our existence. And finally, marriage forms the family unit itself, which is recognized as the inevitable mode of transmitting those values and qualities of frontier parents to their offspring; children must be made fit to understand and to survive the polarities of Western adversity and prosperity.

Before concluding this analysis of *Early Americana,* we must note Richter's technique of juxtaposing the past and the present in an implicit criticism of present forms of civilization. This becomes an explicit theme in "Smoke Over the Prairie", but it is subtly suggested by the narrative distance established in the opening of seven of the nine stories. "Early Americana" begins, "It has slipped almost out of reality now, into the golden haze . . . so that today, behind speeding headlights or in the carpeted Pullman, it seems as if it might never have really been." [45] "Smoke Over the Prairie" opens with a declaration of the narrator's difficulty in communicating his sense of the past: "It is ground into dust now . . . And how can I say it so that you who were not there may see it as I did . . .?" [46] Early in "New Home" Sabina is described in explicit contrast to modern womanhood: "Her seventeen-year-old face, framed by the bolster, was of a type not often seen today – the cheekbones strong and resolute . . ." [47] Later, her singing of a familiar but dirge-like song to express her happiness is explained for a modern audience: "Seeing the words today and hearing the strange old tune, full of slurs and minors, a modern might find it sad and melancholy. . . ." [48]

Richter suggests a distance linked by memories in his description of Joanna in "Long Drought": "Lookink back today on the early photographs, you would see a tall, slender, womanly fig-

[45]   *Ibid.,* p. 3.
[46]   *Ibid.,* p. 38.
[47]   *Ibid.,* p. 84.
[48]   *Ibid.,* p. 98.

ure. . . ." [49] "The Square Piano" also begins with a note of nostalgia for an irrecoverable past: "I never thought that it would
ever be gone, or that there would come a time when I would
wish to see it again and could not, the dusty, frontier street of La
Cruz. . . ." [50] Rosalie Potter of "Buckskin Vacation" is introduced
riding in a railroad car westward: "About her in the dim steam
car, less than half as long as coaches today, rode a fragment of
the Western tide of sixty or seventy years ago . . ." [51] And in
"Early Marriage", the rude El Paso trail is juxtaposed to the
modern and convenient modes of transportation and communication to emphasize the remoteness and isolation of Asa Putman's
post: "Far as the eyes could see from his doorway, the rutted El
Paso trail, unfenced, gutterless, innocent of grading, gravel, cul-
verts, or telephone poles, imprinted only by iron tires . . . lay with
dust unraised." [52]

This technique is effective in suggesting the immense rift between two modes of life over a relatively brief span of years.
Those tales which employ a narrator looking back over the span
of half a century to the frontier of his youth achieve an emotional immediacy and authenticity in tension against a nostalgic
tone of reminiscence and sense of chronological distance. In each
story, Richter not only suggests loss of the past but implies severe
criticism of the present which, somehow, is held responsible for
that loss.

5. *THE SEA OF GRASS* AND RICHTER'S
TRAGIC VISION

In his first full-length novel, *The Sea of Grass*,[53] Richter tells the
story of a people and land which are ravaged by years of conflict
and change. It is a story of change, writes Bruce Sutherland,
which destroys and builds at the same time, a story of the past

[49]   *Ibid.*, p. 120.
[50]   *Ibid.*, p. 262.
[51]   *Ibid.*, pp. 228-229.
[52]   *Ibid.*, p. 295.
[53]   (New York, 1937).

which succumbs to the present and of personal tragedy which attends the tide of progress.[54] In conception, the story is midway between the earlier "Smoke Over the Prairie" and the later Ohio trilogy. Although a short novel of some thirty thousand words, it is still long enough for Richter to suggest his philosophical theories more clearly than his short stories allowed, because it enables him to treat a number of specific episodes over a twenty-year span of time. The cause-effect relationship of human actions and their involvement in a transcendental destiny can be traced in specific consequences to specific acts.

Structurally, the novel is in three parts, each of which is devoted successively to the main characters: Lutie, wife of Colonel Jim Brewton; the Colonel, baron of a cattle empire; and Brock, the illegitimate son of Lutie and Brice Chamberlain, a lawyer. The story is told in reminiscence from the point of view of the Colonel's nephew, Hal Brewton, who is involved only peripherally in the central action. As some critics have noted, this "middle-distance" point of view enables the narrator to be sufficiently involved in the action to serve as a center of consciousness and yet to remain safely detached from it to permit an objective reporting.[55]

The first section sketches the story of Lutie's arrival from the East, her discovery that the Colonel and Brice Chamberlain are adversaries, her marriage to Brewton, her desperate attempt to accommodate to the frontier mode of life, and her subsequent affair with Brice Chamberlain, which results in their plan to elope. Part one concludes with a tense scene in which Lutie, having declared her intentions to leave her husband and children, is deserted at the train station by the cowardly Chamberlain, who has reason to fear the Colonel's wrath.

Part two opens with the narrator's reminiscence about Lutie's humiliating departure and her subsequent disappearence in Denver. This section traces the growing conflict between Chamberlain, self-styled champion of the emigrant farmers, and the Colonel. In this middle section, the land itself becomes part of

[54] Sutherland, p. 418.
[55] E.g., Gaston, pp. 51, 77.

the drama, and the triumph of the farmers, who break the sod to plant corn, is turned to ashes when the region suffers a sustained drought, and the parched land becomes an engine of destiny. The concluding section contains the tragedy of Brock's brief, self-destructive career: unable to reconcile the contradictory forces in his nature, Brock becomes a romantic desperado and dies a violent death. His notoriety and the imminence of disaster bring Lutie back after her absence of many years, and the novel concludes with the Colonel's decision to accept Lutie's unapologetic and unexplained return.

Richter's psycho-energic theories are particularly apparent both in the overall structural unity and in the specific textural parts such as selectivity of details and conception of character. The structural pattern will be discussed first since this relates obviously to Richter's intended meaning in the novel. The textural aspects will be discussed later, for we have in *The Sea of Grass* the first important example of how Richter's psycho-energic conceptions are augmented by other levels of meaning, some of which he well may have been oblivious to himself.

On the first level of meaning, Richter clearly intended to suggest the sovereignty of cosmic destiny, which overrules the designs of man. Although Chamberlain, backed by legal authority and the cause of "justice", forces Brewton to permit homesteaders to file claims, the destiny of the people and of the land is not so readily shaped to correspond to man's planning. After two or three exceptionally wet years, the arid Southwestern land returns to its normal climate; hot winds kill the crops and drive most of the settlers off the land, robbing them of their dignity as well as their livelihood, and leaving only a "wasteland of barbed wire and bare ground". The nesters call it a "drought" and resent the evil misfortune that has befallen them; but Brewton and the other ranchers know it is only "normal old-fashioned New Mexican weather".

Brewton's nephew expresses Richter's view of the cosmos as he reflects on the fate of Chamberlain's nesters:

At that time I thought it only the way the cards happened to fall. But when I look back on it now, it seems immutable and fixed as a chapter out of Genesis or Exodus, with the nesters safe on their Promised land; with my uncle pushed back with his cattle on a thousand hills; with Brice Chamberlain in the seats of the mighty: and all the time the red eye of God watched from the burning bush, not to see what was to come would be humane and sweet and according to progress, but it should be cruel and just and true according to the book of destiny which blinds man from properly reading it until those who dictate it are dead and fifty or a thousand years have passed.[56]

Appeal to his absolute cause-effect relationship effectively orders the episodes in the novel and demonstrates clearly the central role Richter's conception of the cosmos plays in the structure of his fiction.

On the second level of meaning, Richter intended to present certain distinguished traits in the major characters which are brought out by the turn of events. The Colonel is depicted in typical Richter fashion as a rude czar or baronial figure, whose long experience in a violent frontier environment has established in him great wells of strength; but he already has by heritage the potentials of strength, derived from his pioneer parents. He is a man whose vital energies are quickly aroused by the prospect of strife or challenge. Although a peaceable man in his own quietly proud way, the threat of struggle or violence is like a tonic. Thus he is able to confront such personal crises as Lutie's departure, the rape of the land, and the death of Brock with composure and stoic resignation, but not defeat. As the years erode away, he even draws strength from his sustained hatred and contempt for Chamberlain. Although the destructive forces of time and change take their toll, the Colonel meets each fresh exigency by drawing upon inner resources of strength and will. The conflict between Brewton and Chamberlain is deliberately contrived to bring into sharp relief the contrast between them. "In *The Sea of Grass*", writes Richter, "the reader may glimpse a nobility of character and practical intelligence of the hard disciplined Colonel over those of the political do-gooder who seduced his wife." [57]

What Chamberlain lacks in strength he makes up in cunning.

[56]   *The Sea of Grass*, pp. 93-94.
[57]   Correspondence to me, March 21, 1962.

He is a devotee to civilization; religiously committed to planned progress, he is stubbornly oblivious to the organic process which unfolds at the will of the cosmos. He shrewdly manipulates political connections to get appointed to a Federal judgeship so that he might force his will on Brewton. He relies on the power of collective will to impose an agricultural economy upon an environment suited only to stock-raising. The narrator reports that more than once he had caught Chamberlain's eyes measuring Colonel Brewton as if to say, "You're of the past generation now. Your time is soon over. We will run the world from now on, not you." And to Lutie he openly and eloquently boasted: "Civilization is moving west fast." [58]

On the surface Chamberlain appears devoted only to "justice" for the nester, and to compelling Brewton to share his land with the farmers, his "unfortunate fellow men". Richter's intention, however, is to show that Chamberlain belongs to that group whose

... vocal interest in the good of certain others was born not from having reached the intermediate class ..., but from a feeling that the world did not readily furnish them with the standard of living, attention and prominence they felt they deserved, and [whose] protests for others might ... readily be protests for themselves.[59]

Undoubtedly his defense of the settlers is partly to compensate for his failure to be faithful to Lutie, and partly to vindicate his own good name from the inevitable scandal that would have attended his leaving.

Psycho-energic principles also inform the characterization of Lutie, a fact particularly evident in Richter's conception of her inner-conflict. Lutie has a sensitive nature; conditioned by an over-protective Eastern society, she recoils in horror at the raw violence of frontier life. This partially accounts for the failure of her marriage to the Colonel. Her attempt to recreate the kind of life she was accustomed to before leaving the East by redecorating the huge, rude ranch house in Eastern decor, by planting trees to

[58] *The Sea of Grass*, p. 36.
[59] Correspondence to me, March 8, 1962.

shut out the sight of the sea of grass, and by energetically throwing herself into a round of social affairs only intensifies her loneliness. To release energy to meet the severe demands of Western life she increasingly turns to Chamberlain, who is associated in her mind with all that is civilized, genteel, and polite in society.

Richter is especially effective in suggesting her delicate and sensitive nature by her quick nervous mannerisms and studied indifference to violence as she fights for composure. For example, upon her initial arrival she observes a corpse still hanging from the train depot water tank, mute testimony of the swift, merciless frontier justice. Psychologically unprepared for this horror, her only recourse is to summon all her emotional strength to ignore it and to activate her mind by chatting gaily to Hal:

With the dead man slowly turning in front of her, she went on chatting to me in slightly incoherent fashion, saying the gayest of things ... all the while her delicate forehead shutting out the water tank and that ring of staring loafers as completely as if she stood alone with me in my uncle's ranch house.[60]

Her reaction here is a foreshadowing of Lutie's inability to cope with harsh reality, and of her need to turn to the unreal for strength and comfort. With the horrible sight of the hanging man and his victim fresh in her memory, she seeks to escape from the ugliness of the raw frontier town by strolling toward the nearby prairie where an emigrant group is encamped. She is flooded with feelings of relief, as sight of the children, mothers, and evidences of a gentler and more stable society fill her with strength (i.e., "releases energy" to meet the severe expenditure of her ordeal). This psychological association of the emigrants with a lawabiding and stable civilization in stark contrast to the evidence of violence she has just had occasion to observe becomes an important factor in her consciousness and explains in part the great appeal Chamberlain has for her, since he identifies himself with their cause.

In the details and minor incidents Richter selects to suggest her temperament, he sets the stage for the inevitable crisis Lutie's

---

[60] *The Sea of Grass*, p. 189.

subsequent marriage to the Colonel is headed for. Her marriage itself is more a matter of determination, pride, and fierce will, for something magic is clearly gone from their relationship even before their marriage. Richter deftly symbolizes this in a diminutive ritual in which Lutie unpins the gay flowers she was wearing upon arrival and tosses them into the dust as she joins the Colonel after the trial. This foreshadows her own fate, for the violent and turbulent West is no place for the gentle, gay Lutie. Either she must accommodate or be withered in the dust and heat of frontier realities.

The most remarkable exemplification of Richter's theories of inherited and acquired "blood consciousness" is that of Brock. As the offspring of the cruel, weak, cowardly, selfish Chamberlain and the gentle, gay, yet proud and impulsive Lutie, Brock is infused with contradictory compulsions and drives. These become more apparent as he matures, and they are responsible for his severe self-estrangement which alienates him from his parents and from society; eventually, they drive him to his death.

These internal conflicts which will lead to Brock's self-destruction only intensify at first the external conflict between the Colonel and Chamberlain. The community divines Brock's paternal parentage by the unmistakable blond hair and striking resemblance to the lawyer. The gossip of village loafers often cruelly turns on the obvious differences between Brock and Jimmy, the legitimate son of the Colonel and Lutie. Hal is aware of the tyranny of heredity, and he often wonders if "this unnameable thing could have been the source of the deep-seated enmity between the two brothers".[61] The internal conflict in Brock's nature becomes increasingly irrepressible, and his moods and behavior are a study in self-estrangement. At times he is gentle, tender, charming, proud, full of laughter, gregarious, courageous and impulsive; at other times, and often in the same moment, he becomes callous, cruel, vindictive, arrogant, bitter, shrewd, cowardly, and reckless. The conflicting compulsions and drives in his temperament eventually force Brock to commit murder and

61   *Ibid.*, p. 226.

to become a hunted, though glamorous, desperado. Unable to resist the antagonistic internal drives, he is driven to self-destruction, and his brief and violent career is ended in a bullet-riddled nester's shack where a posse has cornered him as if he were a wounded animal.

The tyranny of blood consciousness becomes increasingly important in Richter's conception of character and accounts both for the weakness and the strength of his powers of characterization. On the one hand his major characters develop only to the extent that their "inherited" drives permit them. Thus Richter shares with traditional Zolaesque naturalism the notion of being radically limited by internal and external forces beyond control. Heredity and environment are the major keys to unlock human behavior and potential; consequently, the characters are locked into a temperament of "consciousness" which forbids fundamental changes in perception or behavior. To some extent, then, Richter's characters often tend to be static rather than dynamic. The potential for strength or weakness is less a matter of choice and will than a matter of having the traits already in their character. Thus Richter's notion about the invalidity of "moral education" considered earlier in this study has its counterpart in his notion of character development. The tyranny of blood consciousness – an expression of Richter's reductive naturalism – is a debatable and inconclusive doctrine.

It must be acknowledged, however, that within the framework of this dual conception, experience is a crucial determinant – at least on the level of theory. To this extent, experience, in which the living tissue of life becomes part of the psychological substance of an individual, can effect some alteration of man's constitution. Thus, Lutie's unexplained return is made possible, no doubt, only because of the strength and determination she has acquired as the result of suffering and ordeals experienced in her sojourn into anonymity: the isolation of exile, estrangement from her husband, and separation from her children. News of Brock's self-destructive course brings her back to the sea of grass; his tragic death keeps her there. Her staying is not due to her having had her "fling" so much as to her having acquired the necessary subconscious strength to endure and to her having experienced a degree of spiritual growth in which her happiness is no longer self-contained but enlarged to include the happiness of others. Staying on in the face of the inevitable gossip and misunderstanding is a form of atonement – a sacrificial and redemptive gesture.

Fortunately, Richter's intuition of the complexity as well as the immutable limitations of human personality is greater than his theoretical definition of them, and the strength of his characterization has to do with the sense of tragedy which pervades his frontier fiction.[62] The tyranny of blood consciousness is partly the ground of a tragic perception. On the simplest level, it is a "fatal flaw" that irresistibly moves Brock to his starcrossed destiny. Brock's tragedy is his helplessness before his slow discovery or awareness of the self-destructive nature which is his; and his violent career as an outlaw is a desperate rebellion against irresistible forces at the same time that it is carried by those very forces.

In a sense, Brock's dimly understood and bitterly resented inner-self is that of Richter, and Brock's tragic destruction is presented in terms of an anguished protest against currents of existence that seem to conspire against self-identity. This protest is intensified and made more universal and significant by the introduction of another theme which Richter develops in much greater detail in his later fiction: the myth of Cronos which involves the ambiguity of the son's hatred for the father. The insights into human consciousness furnished by this mythical archetype are already operative in Richter's fiction in the mid-thirties although he consciously exploits them later in *The Waters of Kronos*.

The tragic vision in *The Sea of Grass* is on a number of levels, and the tyranny of blood consciousness is one of them. But equally compelling is the theme of the irresistible flux of time, the sense of erosion and permanent loss that becomes part of the emotional aura of the novel, and which is related to the myth of

---

[62] I am indebted to David Young's unpublished study which has helped me to clarify my thoughts about Richter's tragic vision.

Cronos. The machine, said D. H. Lawrence, will eventually emasculate all of modern society; [63] Richter's view of the universe is partially mechanistic (despite the organic metaphor he often implies). The conception of clock time – the measured tread of change and decay – is also mechanistic, and as such, is a force that emasculates. The Cronos myth itself suggests that the alienation of father and son is related to the emasculating effects of time.[64] In the archetypal myth, Cronos (Saturn), youngest of the Titans, dethrones his father, Uranus, at the instigation of his mother, Terra (Gaea). To equip him for this task, Terra gives Cronos a curved sword with which he castrates Uranus (thus symbolically separating heaven and earth in this pagan Hellenic creation myth). Fearing that his own sons (by Rhea, his half-sister) would divest him of his power, Cronos devours them at their birth – (symbolically, time consumes our lives). Jupiter, one of the sons Rhea manages to save from Cronos' destructive appetite, eventually reaches young manhood, rebels, and dethrones Cronos, his father. Cronos is thereupon relegated to the realm of mortality, where he becomes king of mortals and grows famous for making his subjects happy in time. His reign in mortality later becomes known as the Golden Age, but Cronos himself becomes associated almost exclusively with death, the end of consciousness in time.

The myth thus suggests that the age-old hatred of the son for the father is related to the threat of emasculation, in which virile youth inevitably replaces sterile age. Richter makes remarkable use of the myth in *The Waters of Kronos* to give order and meaning to John Donner's moment of awareness and self discovery. Donner comes to understand that what he hated in his father was the inevitable decay and death that his father dramatized and that he subconsciously knew he would duplicate in himself.[65] He had transferred his great fear and hatred for death to his father, who visibly showed the evidence of mortality.

[63]   *Studies in Classic American Literature* (New York, 1930), p. 186.
[64]   *Larousse Encyclopedia of Mythology*, pp. 89-96.
[65]   *The Waters of Kronos* (New York, 1960), p. 161.

Thus time emasculates and confronts mortals with the irresistible sterility of age and the finality which is death.

Tragedy is produced when the human mind is unable to persuade itself that its place in the universe is secure. "It recalls the original unreason, the terror of the irrational", writes Richard Sewall. "It sees man as questioner, naked, unaccommodated, alone, facing mysterious demonic forces in his own nature and outside, and the irreducible facts of suffering and death." [66] The past-present perspective which we have noted in Richter's stories in *Early Americana* is thus related to a tragic conception of time in the Cronos myth. The same perspective is also true of *The Sea of Grass*. Indeed, the opening paragraph of the story is a moving indictment of the tyranny of time and by implication introduces the Cronos myth of time-as-emasculator. Time emasculates and the blood of succeeding generations is increasingly sterile:

That lusty pioneer blood is tamed now, broken and gelded like the wild horse and the frontier settlement. And I think that I shall never see it flowing through human veins again as it did in my Uncle Jim Brewton. . . .[67]

Hal Brewton as narrator is already sensitive to a weakening in himself of the lusty pioneer blood, but he still has personal memory and associations with the frontier to provide him with energy. But the predicament of modern man is tragic because time (process, change) gelds and destroys. Richter brings emasculation and destruction together in his image of a dead and quartered steer and in his image of soil erosion. The erosion of time is in the physical erosion of land, which results from the farmers ripping open the grass-land sod and exposing it to the heat and winds of the arid Southwest. But this erosion is only secondary to the physical erosion of Colonel Brewton.

Although his internal youth and strength remain ("Times might have changed, but my uncle never would change . . . till he died."),[68] the Colonel visibly wears away as time takes its toll.

[66] *The Vision of Tragedy* (New Haven, 1959), p. 5.
[67] *The Sea of Grass*, pp. 3-4.
[68] *Ibid.*, p. 91.

Hal observes that although his uncle's eyes were still pitch-black and strong, his great face "was plowed and harrowed". In one particularly effective symbol, Richter compares the physical ravages of time endured by the Colonel to the ravages of destiny endured by a huge cottonwood tree in Salt Fork:

Of late the nesters had been tying their bony horses to it and the horses had chewed off half its bark. The lightning had struck it, and the woman of the house and her young son had tried to cut it down. And when of a morning I crossed the plaza to my office, I found myself glancing to see if the old tree weathered last night's storm.[69]

The value of this symbol is incremental as specific details are accumulated and augmented into one symbolic whole: the tree's endurance of the destructive forces of settlement (settlers' horses), natural catastrophes (lightning and storm), and imprudent civilization (town woman's attempt to fell it) are symbolic of the Colonel's endurance. Hal is particularly concerned to see if the tree is standing after each storm because as a doctor, he knows that "the winds that blow in my profession usually blow in the night."[70]

The Cronos myth thus helps explain the sense of tragedy so apparent in Richter's fiction. However, it also helps explain, or at least draws attention to, Richter's increasing obsession with themes of guilt, the loss of identity, and the alienation of father and son.

One of the most moving themes in the novel is that of Brock's loss of identity. As we have noted, his contradictory inner forces and his growing awareness and sensitivity to his illegitimacy drive him into a life of recklessness and self-exposure. He becomes increasingly turbulent and detached from the Brewton household. When the Colonel refuses to intercede or unfairly use his influence on Brock's behalf to keep him from going to trial for killing the gambler, Brock repudiates the Colonel as father: " 'No father', he said defiantly, 'would send his boy to prison when the judge got him out of it'."[71] Brock subsequently transfers his loyalties

---

[69]   *Ibid.*, p. 124.
[70]   *Ibid.*
[71]   *Ibid.*, p. 121.

to the judge, takes the name of Chamberlain, and withdraws from the real world of the Colonel and Hal into an unreal – and therefore to him more personal and appealing – world of outlaw romance. His activities are all played off stage as Richter customarily mutes the violence; only vague reports reach Salt Fork and the Brewtons, and even Hal confesses that Brock seems more like a "glittering idea" than a reality.

When Brock is finally wounded and cornered in a deserted nester's shack – itself symbolic of the unrealistic dream that had violated the spirit of the land – Brice Chamberlain is sent for to persuade his son to surrender. Brice, of course, hurriedly leaves town on contrived legal business, and thus Brock is deserted by his real father. He is both physically and spiritually orphaned.

Meanwhile, Colonel Brewton rushes to the scene and pushes beyond the posse, ignoring the warning from Brock within the shack that "the old man wasn't his father anyway", and that he would shoot if the Colonel came closer. Disregarding the threats, the Colonel enters the shack where Brock lies mortally wounded. Richter's description of this reunion – unwanted by the son – is a key which unlocks much of the tragic ambiguity of the novel. The Christian motif of the forgiving father and prodigal son as well as the Christian theology of redemptive reconciliation form the background against which this tragedy is played to its conclusion. The Colonel's involvement here is on both a physical and a symbolic level. Symbolically, the "spiritual" father has set about to rescue his errant son, to initiate a reconciliation. His aim is to help Brock escape from his self-imposed isolation and concealment by affirming the love, sympathy, and communion of a "spiritual" father who is willing to suffer humiliation to restore unto himself a prodigal son, just as the heavenly Father suffered humiliation in the incarnation to reconcile rebellious man to Himself. But Brock is unable to respond; not only is he fixed into his alienation by unalterable forces, but he cannot repudiate the blood consciousness of Brice Chamberlain, his earthly father, who has callously rejected and forsaken him. The sense of being forsaken, of course, is magnified by the earlier desertion of his mother. Brock is therefore capable only of cynical despair.

Finally too weak even to voice his bitter cynicism, he catches Hal's attention and directs his gaze to a newspaper print on the wall:

Only one conspicuous place on the four walls remained untouched by bullets, and I found now that he was derisively drawing my attention to what hung posted by unknown hands to the center of this spot, a faded Christmas newspaper print of Christ in the manger, with the well known words: "Peace on Earth, Good Will towards Men." [72]

The scene of the birth of Christ with its promise of reconciliation and peace is ironically juxtaposed to Brock's own hopeless predicament; his permanent estrangement and "lostness" is associated symbolically with an unconscious rejection of Christ's vicarious atonement. Because of his nature, Brock fails to achieve reconciliation with his "spiritual" father.

The Colonel eventually erects a gravestone within sight of the ranch house on which he declares that Brock is a Brewton; thus he asserts his "spiritual" fatherhood before all the world. However, there is an aura of self-deception about it; the Colonel's intense pride is no doubt involved in his gesture of love and grief. More compelling than the Colonel's willingness to reconcile his son to himself is the son's failure to respond. Brock is himself spiritually sterile, and like T. S. Eliot's J. Alfred Prufrock, he cannot respond to the proffer of spiritual love. He dies in a spiritual wasteland, incapable even of expressing grief.

It is outside the purpose of this present study to explore in great detail those themes of spiritual alienation and the quest for personal identity which make so remarkable Richter's most recent fiction. Inasmuch as they relate both to the view of life he explains in terms of his philosophical and psychological theories and to the increasingly tragic vision which empowers his Ohio trilogy, however, it will be prudent here briefly to summarize this concern and to relate it to another dimension of Richter's biography which explains a partial source of his tragic vision.

Brock's loss of identity and alienation from the Colonel is paralleled in a number of Richter's stories. The youthful narrator

[72]   *Ibid.*, p. 138.

of *Tacey Cromwell* [73] leaves his Kansas home to make a journey to the far Southwest to be reunited with his half-brother. His desire to leave his parental home is related to the hostility between himself and Wickers Covington, his paranoiac uncle who serves as his father after the boy's father was killed in a quarry. The journey West takes on a kind of symbolic significance as if Nugget, who has repudiated his father's name because it is associated with the cruel uncle, is in quest of his spiritual father. The reunion with his half-brother, Gaye Oldaker, a rather weak-willed gambler, does not provide Nugget with any sense of reconciliation; however, he does find acceptance and a mother-figure in Tacey Cromwell, a prostitute who assumes responsibility for the lad, and who forsakes her profession and successfully achieves respectability as a seamstress.

The Light in the Forest [74] also involves a youth with lost identity who is estranged from both his physical and his spiritual fathers. John Butler, a white boy captured and raised by the Indians, leads an idyllic Indian life until he is forceably repatriated to his natural parents as the result of an Indian peace treaty. Unable to be reconciled to the binding captivity of his civilized white parents, he escapes and returns to the wilderness. But when the tribal warriors want him to serve as a decoy to lure white settlers into an ambush, he cannot repudiate the white blood consciousness in him, and he warns the intended victims. This causes him to be rejected by his disgraced Indian father. Thus he becomes fatherless, an orphan in time, and near the end of the novel he cries in despair, "Then who is my father?"

Richter's penultimate novel, *A Country of Strangers*,[75] is a companion volume to *The Light in the Forest* and develops a similar theme. Stone Girl, a white captive of the Lenni Lenape Indians with a child by an Indian father, is repatriated; her reception by her white parents and the white community, however, is in marked contrast to that of True Son in the earlier novel.

[73] (New York, 1942).
[74] (New York, 1953).
[75] (New York, 1966).

An unscrupulous woman has persuaded Stone Girl's parents that her one child is their missing daughter, and Stone Girl has a rival for her true identity. Thus when she is returned to the Pennsylvania settlement, she is regarded as an imposter and outsider. As in the case of True Son, Stone Girl has not wanted to be repatriated, a fact she manages to communicate to her aging grandmother by means of a fable. Torn between her real identity and her loyalty to her Indian upbringing, Stone Girl's conflict is brought to a crisis when the settlement comes under Indian attack and she makes her escape to join True Son. Presumeably they will face together the problem of identity, a New World Adam and Eve drawn together by the bonds of mutual suffering and the spiritual anguish of alienation.

The same question is pondered in a much different kind of novel, *The Grandfathers*,[76] an anecdotal serio-comic yarn of a backwoods family in western Maryland. Here the protagonist, Chariter Murdoch, a strong character reminiscent of Sayward Wheeler of the Ohio trilogy, is in search of the identity of her father and her other grandfather. One of five illegitimate children born to a kind of female combination of Tom Jones and Huck Finn, Chariter's search is complicated by the unrestrained promiscuity of her mother, who is by no means certain herself of Chariter's paternity. After considering and rejecting the possibilities that Morg and Noble Gandy and Lip and Tom Leck are her father and grandfather, Chariter discovers, while working for Squire Minor Goddem, that she is conscious of a curiously intimate affinity with the old man and with items associated with his son. She finally concludes that her real father is Richard Goddem, who had died in Nicaragua while on military duty. It is a tenuous identification, but it seems to satisfy Chariter's quest for identity.

In *The Waters of Kronos* and *A Simple Honorable Man*, Richter turns from the pioneer past to probe the personal significance of the past of his own consciousness. Richter's description of this intended triology suggests that it is the most autobio-

---

[76] (New York, 1964).

graphical of all his novels.[77] In view of the extraordinary self-revelation in these latest novels, it is not unreasonable to read John Donner, the psychic center of the trilogy, as Richter's alter-ego. John Donner is engaged in a quest for meaning and self-understanding. The urgency of his quest turns upon the young and sensitive protagonist's failure to share his father's devotion and complete surrender to the gospel of Jesus Christ. In *The Waters of Kronos*, John's increasing hostility toward Christianity is traced to his father's belated decision to forsake his modest but secure trade as a store-keeper to enter the ministry – a decision that naturally affects the well-being and destiny of the entire family. The novel itself explores the inexplicable hostility that wells up in John's reluctant involvement in his father's "call". Although the novel attempts to establish a reconciliation between father and son in terms of the Cronos myth – i.e., the son's growing awareness that he hated his father because the elder Donner represented the dread but inevitable decay and emasculation of time and mortality – the reconciliation is posthumous and takes place strictly on the level of imagination, for Donner must portentously re-enter the irrecoverable past to effect it. Once the nature of his ambiguous hostility is unveiled, he must resist the return to the consciousness of the present. The conclusion of the novel is not entirely satisfactory.

A Simple Honorable Man continues John's search for understanding of his father and of himself. In this novel, the themes of hostility, doubt, and repudiation are explicitly expressed in young Donner's rebellion against his father and his father's faith. He cannot overcome his personal anger and dismay at the family's enforced poverty, and Harry Donner's response to the ministerial call seems to have uprooted the family from all that young John held dear. Richter's thinly veiled portrait of his father is a curious

---

[77] "The first book lays down the family, and fleshly and spiritual roots of the seeker. The next volume ..., *A Simple Honorable Man*, is the story, life, and spiritual concepts of one based on my father.... The third book, if and when written, will purport to be the life story and progressive concepts of his son, the seeker, the unfolding of hidden processes that torment him, their compulsions, together with the spiritual conclusions of the central character." Correspondence to me, July 4, 1961.

mixture of love, admiration, and resentment; and lurking always in the background is an incipient rejection of Christianity.

John's alienation from his father is further clinched by their distinctively different temperaments: his father is gregarious, a little loud and boisterous at times, ready to greet stranger and friend alike with a smile and cliche-ridden expression. The son, however, is embarrassed at his father's outgoing public manner, and resentful of the dark moodiness his father often reflects at home. To use the terms common to our vocabulary, the father tends to be an extrovert, the son an introvert. Young Donner is painfully shy, given to withdrawal, seeking solitude and relief from painful encounters with society in general and with his father in particular. The clash in temperament, however, only intensifies the initial estrangement, which turns upon the problem of belief.

There can be no doubt about Richter's externalizing his own spiritual history in the story of John Donner. Unable to share his father's spiritual vision, Richter's alienation filled him with a sense of guilt and a foreboding of despair. By repudiating the spiritual vision of his earthly father, he had unconsciously repudiated his spiritual father as well. Only in his most recent fiction has Richter surrendered to his compulsion consciously to confront this predicament. The tragic overtones of his fiction are directly related to this personal history. As we noted above, tragedy is produced when the human mind becomes convinced of its insecurity in the universe. Richter, filled with the terror of the irrational – especially the facts of suffering and death – has assumed the role of the questioner, "unaccommodated, alone, facing mysterious demonic forces in his own nature and outside". The fatalistic and mechanistic view of man which is reflected in his psycho-energic theories is one which attempts to account for Richter's sense of loss, waste, and doom. Richter attempted to erect a philosophical barrier against the spiritual void he experienced in rejecting the way of his father. His view of the meaning of existence is one that admits the possibility of evil and injustice in the world; and it is a view that ultimately affirms the reality of suffering – not physical ordeal only, but mental and

spiritual anguish as well. But it is not a view that can satis-
factorily reconcile Richter to their absolute necessity or to his
desire for inner peace.

The second main source of his tragic vision then has to do
with his deliberate rejection of Christianity. In doctrine, Christianity offers an alternative to tragedy and the mystery of evil
and suffering. But in practice, it confronts man with the age-old
problem of choice – the inescapable decision of whether or not
to believe, a choice charged with anguish and terror. According
to Sewall, the Christian tradition added a new dimension to the
Greek conception of tragedy:

Not to believe meant to face, alone and unaccommodated, a void of
meaninglessness to which the revelation of Christianity has added an
ultimate terror: infinity. One could close the door on it or try to fill
the void with sturdy philosophy, but once it had become a part of
Western imagination it could not be ignored.[78]

The Greeks accounted for human actions in terms of external
forces shaping them; thus the gods alone were ultimately responsible. But Christianity added the dimension of personal and
individual responsibility, and the consequent possibility of anxiety,
doubt, and guilt. Richter's tragic vision is a combination of both
traditions: pagan and Christian.

Early Americana and *The Sea of Grass* clearly reflect the
crucial role of Richter's psycho-energic theories, both on the level
of textural technique in terms of specific details, symbol, and
characterization, and on the level of structural technique in providing a meaningful order for plot narrative. But especially with
the publication of *The Sea of Grass* do we see that Richter's
intuitions reach farther than his discursively expressed theories.
He displays increasing command of form and idea; at the same
time, the complexity of meaning is augmented by the conscious
and unconscious ordering on the level of symbol and myth of
certain questions, doubts, and anxieties which evoke a tragic
vision. *Early Americana* and *The Sea of Grass* provided Richter
with the necessary experience to develop his artistic maturity; the

---

[78]   Sewall, p. 51.

Ohio trilogy provided him with the epic theme and sweep of history sure to engage his greatest sympathies and finest energies.

6. THE OHIO TRILOGY AND THE 'EVERLASTING YEA' OF THE PIONEER

Richter's greatest tribute to the affirmative and constructive values of the pioneers, and his highest achievement in the genre in which he finds his best expression, is the Ohio trilogy: *The Trees, The Fields,* and *The Town.*[79] The pioneers and their descendants whom Richter encountered in his diligent research into historical documents and in his tireless interviews were "unaffected by so-called progress"; his affection, admiration, and appreciation for these people were among the chief motives that prompted him to write the trilogy.[80] Although the trilogy represents in many ways the culmination of Richter's achievement in his fiction of the past, it was actually in gestation long before *The Trees* appeared in 1940. Indeed, its initial conception coincided with his work on the New Mexican series as early as 1933; furthermore, its roots go back even further to Richter's experiences in Pennsylvania.

In a pleasantly reminiscent essay entitled "Valley from the Past", Richter relates the circumstances and significance of his brief sojourn in Clark's Valley, Pennsylvania, a remote, quiet, peaceful, and quaint region whose isolation had caused it to preserve a mode of life deeply rooted in the frontier past. It was like a haven to Richter, who took his family there from the city. He characteristically interprets the Valley's curious impact on his consciousness in mystical psycho-energic terms. Both he and his wife felt something unnameable and undefinable in themselves which the scenes of the Valley evoked:

There are still in us sensations and capacities for sensation unguessed by modern man, and how were we to suppose then that what spoke to

[79] Although Richter has recently retitled his trilogy *This Awakening Land* in a one volume edition, references to the three novels will be made to the first editions which were published in this order (New York, 1940); (New York, 1946); and (New York, 1950).
[80] Correspondence to me, July 4, 1961.

us here in this strange Valley and in what our inner senses gratefully swam was a racial remembrance buried deep within us, a recognition of nameless primal elements we had all but lost today? We know only that we were irresistibly drawn by something unseen and unknown. ... Some blind instinct worked in us ..., but exactly what it was that had called us so powerfully lay hidden from our sight.[81]

The Valley not only awakened in Richter a sense of mysterious, wild instinct, but it furnished him with sensations, experiences, and material which he was to draw upon for over forty years. The remoteness, the occult experiences of living in a "haunted" house and of witnessing a more than will-o-the-wisp night light, the vigorous regional language with its archaisms and preserved figures and patterns of speech, the original and stimulating neighbors, the experience of working out in the open fields with jovial mountain men – all of these formed a matrix for his later fiction. Richter's respect for the "ancient ways and life acceptance of these men grew", as he carefully noted their easy adaptation to nature. The organic harmony of life lived in intimate contact with the primal elements profoundly influenced his thought, and for the first time he truly experienced the sensation of the earth turning beneath him "while in tune with night and day, the seasons, the earth and the planets".[82]

Richter's theories of the discipline of pain and hardship were further formed and confirmed by the life shared with the Valley inhabitants. Adversity and hardship were community affairs shared by all. The residents had learned matter-of-factly to face heartbreak with courage, and they took "the bad with the good, for this was life, this was the way it came to all".[83] Richter believes their everlasting yea to life prepared him for the disaster and tribulation which eventually forced him to relocate his family to New Mexico in exile from his native Pennsylvania. But the impact of his stay here was too profound to be forgotten. "Here is where we lived closest to the heart of man and nature", writes

[81] "Valley from the Past", *Country Beautiful*, II (April 1963), pp. 9-10.
[82] *Ibid.*, p. 11.
[83] *Ibid.*, p. 12.

Richter, "where we drank deepest from the ancient springs that nourished the race." [84] He is convinced that some essence by which the pioneer fathers lived still flourished in this isolated region, and that it evoked "felt intimations" of roots which reached deeply into "his own inherited being". Although its ultimate spiritual significance is still obscure, Richter declares that the Valley "has left its mark on most of the books that I have written".[85]

Several of the prototypes of the pioneers who people the trilogy lived in Richter's beloved Valley, and one of the compensations of the economic disaster and ill health in the family which caused him to resettle in New Mexico was the experience of encountering people in remote and isolated regions of the New Mexican deserts and mountains whose character and views of life resembled in every way the originals in Clark's Valley. Even as Richter interviewed New Mexican pioneers and their descendents to gather authentic material for *Early Americana* and *The Sea of Grass*, he was laying the groundwork for the trilogy. The sense of being in intimate contact with the natural rhythms of the earth begun in the Pennsylvania Valley was rekindled as Richter developed a love for the New Mexican environment – a love which he insists the land returned in kind.[86] Taking a cabin in June on the eastern slope of the Sandia Mountains, Richter and his family stayed until Christmas and returned in the spring. Not only did the remoteness and strange beauty of the mountains pay dividends in mental health and authentic Americana, but it provided him with the occasion to begin in earnest research for the Ohio trilogy. A neighbor at Sandia Park brought Richter two old and tattered books to read – Henry Howe's monumental historical collections of early Ohio, published in 1840.

I read them by gasoline lantern light to the sound of wind in the pines. A new world of life in the deep forests of the early Midwest was opened to me. Out of it came my Ohio trilogy, first conceived and planned at 7200 feet in the big timber of the Sandias which, I

[84]   *Ibid.*, p. 13.
[85]   *Ibid.*, p. 13.
[86]   "New Mexico Was Our Fate", p. 45.

think, helped me to understand the big timber of a life 150 years and 1500 miles away.[87]

As we shall have occasion to note later in this study, Howe's collections represent the major source of episodes and authentic detail in the trilogy. But equally important, the stories of the New Mexican frontier formed a kind of experimental basis for Richter's craftsmanship, and for the task of weaving philosophical and psychological theory into the warp and woof of his fiction. The breadth and range of the trilogy at last provided a structural vehicle equal to the epic story of frontier settlement and the growth of community – the nomadic penetration into a primeval forest, the clearing of the fields for stable agriculture, the eventual growth of a well-defined town, and the ultimate development of an industrial complex whose values and mode of life represent a radical reversal of those of the pioneers. Not only does the greater sweep of the trilogy enable Richter to dramatize the fact that steady conflict with wilderness adversity and rigors incessantly annealed mind and body and acted as a stimulant for the development of character potential and the revelation of a cosmic destiny operative in even the smallest detail of life; it also enables him to trace the history of three generations of one blood line and to suggest the tragic erosion of energy and powers of endurance as well as the acceleration of alienation and self-estrangement which have accompanied our cultural shift from an agrarian to an industrial society.

The psychic center in the trilogy is Sayward Luckett Wheeler, the archetypal "earth woman" or eternal mother figure; Sayward is the most memorable character in the trilogy and the most remarkable protagonist of all of Richter's fiction. Her strong personality and presence dominate in all three novels. Since Sayward is the main character of the trilogy, and since Richter's use of women as protagonists is significantly related to his psychological theories, it will be useful here to reflect briefly on this characteristic of his fiction.

Five of the stories in *Early Americana* feature women as

---

[87] *Ibid.*, p. 45.

protagonists; and in the other four stories, strong and forceful women play prominent roles. One third of *The Sea of Grass*, of course, is given over to the unforgettable Lutie. After Sayward appeared in *The Trees*, Richter set aside his trilogy to write *Tacey Cromwell*, the story of a reformed prostitute about whom Richter wrote, "more intelligence in bringing up children is found in the once Western sporting house woman than in the soft loving mother brought up in luxury and ease".[88] After completing *The Fields*, Richter again turned his attention away from the trilogy, this time to write *Always Young and Fair*, the central character of which is Lucy Markle.[89] Seven years after winning the Pulitzer prize for *The Town*, which concludes Sayward's story, he published *The Lady*, the narrative of Doña Ellen Sessions, a memorable Southwestern heroine.[90] The story of Chariter Murdoch's search for her identity in *The Grandfathers* is yet another novel featuring a woman protagonist; and Richter's penultimate novel, *A Country of Strangers*, tells the story of Stone Girl, a white woman returned from Indian captivity but rejected by the white community.

Richter's continued use of the woman protagonist cannot be explained merely as a habit acquired from writing for popular magazines read chiefly by women. His alienation from his father may have contributed to his lack of confidence and reluctance to handle male characters; when he does choose to feature a male character, the more effective ones are the onlookers and questioners, the weaker and insecure, rather than the larger-than-life protagonists such as Colonel Brewton. But the most important reason for his proclivity for female protagonists is because of their powers of endurance, a fact Richter is careful to note in

---

[88] Correspondence to me, March 21, 1962. N.B. Richter adds, "In this connection Will Keleher, the most authoritative historian of New Mexico, once told me this was the book he would have written if I hadn't, not in fiction but a document on the character of such women who later became respectable wives and mothers all over the West. Having seen the worst, they turned out to be the most careful and successful mothers of their children."

[89] (New York, 1947).

[90] (New York, 1957).

light of his psycho-energic theories. In *A Simple Honorable Man*, Harry Donner makes an observation that provides a clue to Richter's attitude toward women:

Of all God's creation, the preacher thought, His finest work had been woman. She was, when you reflected on her, a most divine and marvelous invention, one that could feel tenderness for the weak, pity for the suffering, could delight man, make his bed and supper, not to mention her astounding gift to conceive and perpetuate her kind . . .
There were exceptions, of course, but all through life Harry Donner had noticed that women could endure more than their husbands.[91]

Although this observation is set off against John Donner's feeling of anger and resentment against his father and pity for his uncomplaining mother in seeing her uprooted from her genteel society and forced into a life of grinding poverty, the observation is nevertheless consistent with Richter's psychological theories, a reluctant concession to reality. Something about the nature of woman fits her to be the exemplar of the eternal stoic virtues of self-restraint, self-control, self-discipline, and self-reliance. Like the "iron lady" in a story with that title, the example of enduring woman puts "iron" into the soul of those who respond to the wisdom Mary Harris expresses in this simple declaration: "You always got to fight something in this life. If it ain't Injuns, it's something else." [92]

The prototype of Sayward herself is an ageing grandmother in the story, "The Rawhide Knot", an account of an old woman's dissatisfaction with modern life and her reminiscence of her strange frontier wedding.[93] The story, which appeared two years before *The Trees*, introduces us to Sayward and Portius Wheeler and sets forth in broad outline the thematic structure of the Ohio trilogy. Indeed, the episode of the frontier marriage itself reappears in slightly altered form in *The Trees*. The main significance of the short story is that it suggests clearly Richter's inten-

[91] *A Simple Honorable Man*, p. 159.
[92] "The Iron Lady", *Saturday Evening Post*, CCXXX (July 13, 1957), p. 90.
[93] "The Rawhide Knot", *Saturday Evening Post*, CCX (Jan. 1, 1938), pp. 18-19.

tion to make Sayward Wheeler the central character in the trilogy and to construct the trilogy around the theme of the growth and loss that attends the tide of progress as a frontier town becomes an industrial city.

Whereas "The Rawhide Knot" is told in Richter's customary reminiscent point of view, the trilogy is narrated from the omniscient point of view in the unforced vernacular of the pioneers. The action and time-change of a shift from frontier to industrial city provide the past-present perspective that Richter's reminiscing narrators typically bring to their stories; and Sayward as psychic center provides the growing consciousness of the configuration of life's pattern and thus provides a developmental unity in the narrative structure. Richter's philosophical and psychological theories are adumbrated in Sayward's development to physical and emotional maturity.

Although an unschooled and isolated "Woodsy", Sayward is an intelligent, sensitive woman who draws forceful conclusions from her experiences with the living tissue of life. The most significant discovery she makes about the mystery of existence is that nothing can substitute for the wisdom and sympathetic understanding gained through experience. Slowly and painfully through the years she catches a glimpse of the cosmic destiny that reveals a benevolent force behind the apparent hostility symbolized by the forces of the wilderness itself, and by the operations of fate in pestilences, famines, and personal tragedies.

The setting of the trilogy is a frontier region in the old Northwest Territory west of the Alleghenies and north of the Ohio River. The first two novels lay down the fleshly and spiritual ties of Sayward Luckett Wheeler; the last novel turns on her conflict with the new order ushered in by the great industrial expansion of the mid-nineteenth century. The novels are largely episodic in structure (several of the episodes having appeared earlier as short stories), with each episode describing in realistic and compelling terms some revealing situation or crisis in the lives of the settlers, and thereby compressing, suggesting, and illuminating so much of the meaning of life in the affairs of ordinary men and women.

The Trees describes the coming of the Worth Luckett family, the first to settle in this part of the great Ohio Forests. Worth, Sayward's father, is a Leatherstocking figure without Leatherstocking's nobility. In short time, his ailing wife dies, overcome by the ocean of trees beneath which she feels trapped. Worth, usually away on hunting trips, eventually drifts westward leaving his three daughters and one son in the charge of Sayward, the oldest. Various episodes of the novel deal with the Luckett children as they come to maturity under Sayward's care. One sister, Genny, marries a renegade white who mistreats her and runs off with her sister, Achsa. The son, Wyitt, a natural born hunter like his father, is restless and anxious to be off to the West. Only Sayward sends down roots; in a curious and unromantic wedding ceremony, she marries the drunken, aristocratic Massachusetts lawyer, Portius Wheeler, who is in self-imposed exile in the wilderness. Her strength, common sense, and desire for stability, coupled with his learning, wit, and ambition, make the union a strange but satisfying one.

The Fields continues the story of the settlement. The monstrous trees are cleared away to make room for fields and farms. Portius, stabilized by Sayward, assumes an increasingly prominent position as a lawyer, and Sayward's family grows. The territory becomes a state, and the community of settlers forms a township. Sayward's daughter, Sulie, named after her aunt who had disappeared as a child into the forest, is burned to death in a soap kettle fire. The settlers drive out the wild game, and nature retaliates by sending drought and famine, forcing some of the men to march to Kentucky for food. A church meeting house is raised, and Portius organizes the first school. An attractive but weak and romantically inclined young woman is hired to replace Portius, and eventually Sayward is humiliated and shamed to learn that Portius and the young lady have had an adulterous affair. The school teacher, finding herself with child, is forced to marry the unsavory Jake Tench, and the child, Rosa Tench, is given a name. The novel ends with a celebration of Jake's new keelboat service, and Sayward realizes a town has sprung up in the community of Moonshine Church.

The Town, longest of the novels, traces the growth of the

settlement, renamed Americus, and records the appearance of a younger generation unsympathetic to the pioneer's notions of the necessary discipline of suffering and hardship. Sayward has another boy named Chancey, a weakly, spindly child who is overprotected and mollycoddled by the others. Her other children develop to maturity: Resolve, the oldest, studies law and becomes an early governor of Ohio; Huldah, a tempestuous wench, disgraces the family by presenting herself nude before the man she hoped to marry; and Guerdon, the next oldest son, marries a waterfront wench whose promiscuous behavior enrages and provokes Guerdon to murder her lover, an act that banishes him from Americus. The other daughters make satisfactory marriages.

Of all the children, Chancey is the heaviest burden on Sayward's heart. Ironically, he and Rosa Tench fall in love, both oblivious to their blood kinships. Fearing their relationship will lead to incest, Rosa's mother brutally tells her the truth; overcome with grief, Rosa commits suicide. This tragic turn of events embitters Chancey, who takes his rage out on those who philosophically vindicate the necessity of evil. Chancey becomes the questioner, unaccommodated, alone; in his rage, frustration, and grief, he holds society responsible for social evil, becomes a radical socialist, and organizes a newspaper specifically to attack all traditional values and pioneer norms as anachronisms. His chief aim is to destroy the source and manifestations of evil. The trilogy concludes with Sayward's death in the once beautiful mansion, now surrounded by shops and factories. At the very close of the novel, Chancey is filled with doubts and fears that, inadvertently, he has rejected a great heritage in repudiating his mother's affirmation of the meaning of life.

This plot summary of the trilogy calls attention to the importance of Sayward's vision of existence, and the various episodes in all three novels chiefly turn on her gradual awareness of something mysterious and unseen in herself which responds to a mystical order of meaningful conflict in nature. In the very beginning, her conflict with the trees takes on the proportions of an intensely personal spiritual battle. She is equipped with a "woodsy's" mind and imagination, sensitive to preternatural forces. In her early years beneath the sea-green ocean of trees, she perceives a power in the woods that seems subtly hostile and predatory. The settlers, and particularly Sayward, initially regard the trees as dark and sentient beasts. Jary is the first "victim" to the forest, and Sulie, who is swallowed by the "cruel trees", is the second.[94] Genny, during her harrowing night-long ordeal in preventing a hungry panther from descending the wide chimney on her lonesome cabin, temporarily loses her mind and insists it was "the night trees" trying to get her. Even Sayward believes the wild trees "hated to see Genny get pulled out of their clutches. They thought they had had her fast like they had little Sulie".[95] The battle against the unnameable and omnipotent "evil" in the forest is waged constantly, always near the surface of Sayward's mind. "Oh, it had evil things in the woods that were older than the oldest man", she observes. "The woods shut you in and fought you while you lived, and sucked up your flesh and blood with its roots after you died." [96]

This near-sentient power – "the Wild Thing without a name that followed you in the deep woods, and no man knew whether it was flesh or spirit" [97] – gives mystical overtones to the conflict between Sayward and the "everforest"; in her imagination the battle against the monstrous butts is in some inexplicable way a battle between the forces of good and evil, and she is constantly summoning up strength and energy, both morally and physically, not to be overcome by her adversary, fearing yet respecting her foe:

Oh, the big butts were a hard foe for humans to fight, a race of giants with arms thicker than any other beast around, and body weighty as the river bed. There they stood with their heads in the sky, never even looking at you or letting on you were there.[98]

Years later when the forest has been felled to make way for fields and eventually a city, she is compelled by some strange and

[94]   *The Trees*, pp. 65, 179.
[95]   *Ibid.*, pp. 257-260.
[96]   *The Fields*, p. 35.
[97]   *The Town*, p. 152.
[98]   *The Fields*, p. 107; see also, pp. 12 f., 30, 33, and 107 f.

mystical urge to plant around her town house trees which she had once "hated like poison"; her act is more than a gesture of nostalgia, for the trees come to stand for a vanished way of life that has succumbed before merciless change. The tremendous energy expenditure built up over the years in her personal conflict with the trees and the Awful Presence they stood for has now found "contraction", and her hatred gives way to love. What she had once thought "evil" is now, from a later perspective, seen to be part of a general benevolent plan.

Not only have the trees become for her a symbol of mysterious plan inherent in the natural order, but Sayward's change of attitude toward them is instrumental in causing the extremist Chancey to consider seriously the merits of his mother's philosophy. At her death bed he discovers her now great love for her one-time enemy, whose leaves she can faintly hear rustling at her window, and Chancey is moved to reflect:

Was there something deeper and more mysterious in his mother's philosophy than he suspected; something not simple but complex; something which held not only that hardship built happiness but which somehow implied that hate built love; and evil, goodness? [99]

The theme of cosmic destiny runs throughout the trilogy, helping to unify the three novels into a continuous whole. Like the surface ripples that reveal a swift undercurrent, it suggests that what happens is *permitted* to happen by a controlling power in the universe, a natural ordination, which is ironically set off against the frustrated efforts of man to have final control in the destiny of things to come. And when man does interfere in the destiny of others, Richter shows us, the results can be tragic.

Sayward learns this lesson painfully, and as she does, she gains increasing respect for that power in the universe ordering the affairs of men. Even death, the most hated of "evils", must be accepted as a natural process of being; but even death is meaningful and ordered rather than capricious and arbitrary: "There was one thing, it looked like, that could stand off Death. If your time

[99]   *The Town*, p. 432.

hadn't come yet, it made you slick as an eel and Death couldn't hold you." [100]

Related to the theme of cosmic destiny, and Richter's injunction against interfering in this destiny, is his theory of "blood" consciousness in inherited traits and drives ("rate flows" and "energy deficiencies") which play a leading role in that "which secretly governed man and determined his destiny". Sayward discovers she must accept man for what he is naturally, for *what he must be because he is what he is.* Although in possession of a will to order certain parts of the whole, man will think and act in correspondence to the essential and unique nature that is his by inheritance; although always susceptible to being tempered by experience, it nevertheless accounts for his compulsions and drives. In *The Town*, Rosa, the bastard child of Portius and Miss Bartram, comes to her own realization of this truth:

Wasn't it a strange thing about people in this world why they were themselves and why you were the person you were? When she tried to think who it was that stood here in her flesh living and thinking she seemed to be blown away and lost far back in her mind . . . Wasn't it the saddest thing in this world that you always had to be yourself, that you couldn't be somebody else? [101]

In the trilogy Richter can trace the recurrence in three generations of certain racial and familial traits peculiar to Sayward's blood line. The hunter strain runs deeply in Worth and Wyitt and reappears in Guerdon and even Chancey, although with each generation it is thinned and manifested differently. The same strain predicates the dark, primitive, and impetuous behavior in Achsa and later in Huldah. Worth himself has Monsey Indian blood, which accounts for his primitive nature, his restless spirit, and his hunter instinct.

The same drives reappear in his son Wyitt. Sayward stoically accepts the inevitability of Wyitt's someday following his father into the forest. "He'd grow up a hunter like his pappy, following

---

[100] *The Trees,* p. 132.
[101] *The Town,* p. 221.

the woods, moving on with the game. If it was in him it would come out. There was no stopping such kind." [102] Wyitt himself had fought the instinct, trying to accept the life of the settled and established. "He'd knock the wildness out of him, he said, if it was the last thing he did. He had done his dangest to kill the ever-hunter in him, but it wouldn't stay killed. It was his Monsey blood, he reckoned. It would never say die." [103]

The same inherited characteristics Sayward sadly observes reappearing in some of her own children, and her motherly desire to protect causes her at times foolishly to interfere. The son most like Wyitt is Guerdon, who hated schooling and restlessly flitted from job to job. "Oh, Sayward knew what was the matter with him. It was his Monsey blood that wouldn't let him be, the same as Wyitt and Worth before him." [104] When Guerdon announces his intentions of leaving home to work at "bridging" in a distant town, Sayward foolishly acts to keep him home. She convinces Portius that Americus needs a bridge to replace the ferry and thus she is instrumental in providing Guerdon with his "bridging" work right in Americus and near her protection.

She is repaid harshly for interfering in his destiny, however, for Guerdon meets a cheap waterfront girl while working on the bridge and secretly marries her. Guerdon, prior to the birth of Chancey, is the least fitted of Sayward's children to stand up for himself in life; he would let others impose on him until "something in him would snap. He lacked the staying part and balance the others had." [105] Guerdon's murdering of the man he finds sleeping with his wife and his subsequent forced exile from Americus is a graphic lesson to Sayward; the rhetoric of experience argues the danger of interfering in the fixed order of destiny no matter how benevolent or honorable the intentions:

Well, she was getting paid back for pushing the bridge before its time, she reckoned. In her heart she knew she had done it mostly for spite and cowardice, spite against King Sam and cowardice to let her

[102]   *The Trees*, p. 236.
[103]   *The Fields*, p. 82.
[104]   *The Town*, p. 91.
[105]   *Ibid.*, p. 99.

second boy go off from home a bridging. Now she could see what you got for putting your nose where it wasn't wanted.[106]

Wiser from the painful experience, Sayward later reluctantly refrains from interfering when her daughter, Sooth, plans to marry a much older Frenchman. Sayward's first impulse is to forbid the marriage, recalling the tragedy of Genny's union with Louie Scurrah. But when it comes to mating, she has learned, the human will cannot be counseled: "Humans were free as wild pigeons in the woods.[107] She later concludes, as she reluctantly faces her own daughter's wedding, that marriage is directed by some power above man. "Why always had opposites to pull each other? She reckoned it some wise plan of the Lord to keep the pretty from getting prettier and the homely homelier, the sweet sweeter and the mean meaner." [108]

Sooth, one of her most innocent and naive daughters, has never yet faced any real sadness or tragedy, but Sayward fears that her interference in the marriage may result in even worse hardship, if not retardation of Sooth's natural education: "What sort of ma would she be to try and stop her? Not always could she be here to fend for her child, to try and save it from harm and hardship. Better had it find out about life at the beginning than at the end." [109] Although Sayward seeks guidance in prayer, she knows she will in the end rely on her common sense respect for Providence and fear of interfering to the detriment of the one she would protect:

No, unless the Lord spoke to her strong and plain, she would fall back on her own good sense. That sense told her that the hand of the Almighty might be a little slow but it was more knowing than hers. Once she had reckoned to save Guerdon from life by tying him close to her. All that came out of it was spilled blood, and sending him away from home for good.[110]

Other incidents show in good light the theme of cosmic destiny

---

[106]   *Ibid.*
[107]   *The Trees*, p. 154.
[108]   *The Town*, p. 170.
[109]   *Ibid.*
[110]   *Ibid.*, p. 171.

and the danger of interference in the inevitable order of things. For example, Sayward makes an ill-fated attempt to reestablish family connections with Sulie, who, forty years after her disappearance, is reported to be alive and married to an Indian. At the unhappy reunion Sayward realizes it was a mistake to seek Sulie out; providence had had a destiny planned for Sulie, and she was no longer a member of the family but an Indian. Sayward sadly concludes that one had to take the life one got and live it the best he could. Chancey's own immaturity, weakness, and self-pity, his vindictive and soured nature, can be traced to the family's interference in his natural growth – by their good-intentioned but ill-advised coddling and over-protection. Sayward particularly carries a burden of guilt for her part in this interference, for her too compassionate resolution to "be strong for him" and make up the deficiencies in his strength with strength from herself.[111]

Not only individual human destiny but the founding of towns is ultimately out of the hands of man. The speculator, Major Tate, in order to attract settlers to his land to increase its value, lays out a complete townsite and attempts to attract Sayward to the growing village since he wants no competition from her own attractively situated land. Although she is tempted to move to an easier and more secure life in the village, she refuses, knowing she would "feel ashamed to run off and be licked by the trees".[112] The town of Tateville does attract settlers, but on Sayward's own property emerges a settlement which eventually grows into a town (becoming in time the county seat and a greater and larger industrial city than Tateville), and Sayward learns to respect the slow pace of providence:

Now who would have reckoned, Sayward asked herself, that all the time this dark, choked-up river bank under the big butts and tangled vines here by the Moonshine Church was townsite just waiting for its time in God's Almanack to come around? [113]

[111]   Ibid., p. 307 f.
[112]   The Fields, p. 177.
[113]   Ibid., p. 288.

The growth of the town brings a new and disturbing tenor into the trilogy, for it is inhabited by a different type of man than was the village settlement. A new spirit of change and of progress envelops the village as its residents, on a vigorous quest for affluence, become more and more conscious of "bringing civilization", and as late-comers, merchants, and speculators begin to exude an air of propriety and decorum along with a disapproval of the crude and primitive.

Richter's protest and warning against the cult of comfort becomes much stronger as the grist for his mill increases. The protest is manifest in two main threads that weave together the plot of *The Town*. The one is Sayward's growing awareness and uneasiness at the unhealthy spirit being fanned by the growth of the industrial city, and her general distrust of it which solidifies ultimately into open protest against the assumption that any change which makes for a higher standard of living, and which makes for economic prosperity, is progress.[114] The second thread is the career of Sayward's youngest son, Chancey, and particularly the barrier between Chancey and Sayward, which dramatizes the cultural conflict between the old spirit and the new. Both threads constantly interweave in the novel.

Chancey himself is a dreamer, longing for and indwelling on the level of imagination "The Effortless Place, the Unencumbered World". Like Brock of *The Sea of Grass*, he finds reality too confusing and complicated; thus he seeks escape to the realm of the unreal. For example, on one occasion he finds his dream so compelling that he convinces himself it is a factual experience. Later, when trapped on a bridge that collapses during a flood, his real experience is so strange he concludes it is only a dream.

The scenes in which Sayward and Chancey are brought into direct conflict are the most contrived in the novel. Chancey grows to maturity unable to understand or accept his mother's interpretation of life. He stands for what Richter regards as the typical modern attitude of contemporaneity, which regards its problems uniquely of the present and which can see no continuity between

---

[114]   *The Town*, pp. 52 f., 183, 238 f., 271 ff.

past and present. Consequently, Chancey rejects the wisdom of the past; specifically, he ridicules the pioneer penchant for hard work and self-discipline. He concludes that his mother and her generation venerate the past only because of the inevitable nostalgia attached to the "good old days": he believes the good old days to be legendary, "a dream, the self-made illusion of a rude and primitive race back there in the twilight of the forest".[115]

Chancey warmly embraces Robert Owens' theories of relieving mankind of evil and unhappiness through a philosophy of benefaction. He comes to believe that through conscious and deliberate planning, the future can be determined and that society can progress until it does away with all toil and painful labor. Sayward on the other hand can only argue from common sense and the wisdom of experience. All humanitarian theory is on the side of Chancey, but all experience supports Sayward. Work and hardship, she insists, can never be avoided; and the "good Lord lets man sink or swim in his own troubles".

Chancey's rebellion against what he feels to be the senseless and dehumanizing pioneer ethic of labor is intensified by his horror at the irrational evil of Rosa's death – an occurrence which causes his rupture from the family. In an effort to resist hardship and evil he goes to Cincinnati to become editor of *The New Palladium*, which advocates radical social reform. His sensitivity, of course, is one mark of evolutionary growth; but, writes Richter,

he was not intended as the most advanced of characters but rather one of those who, given a sensitive nature and lack of understanding of the facts of life, suppose the world can be turned into paradise and its people into saints or at least worthy and happy citizens by the elimination of hardship and the administering of largess and plenty. What such see are present troubles, not the greater troubles their easy prescriptions could bring on, since they do not attempt to change inequalities in evolution in the people except by education alone which, if it could be successful of itself we would suppose the Higher Intelligence to have employed instead of the tool of suffering.[116]

After years of rebellion, Chancey is brought up short by the

[115] *Ibid.*, p. 424.
[116] Correspondence to me, March 8, 1962.

specter of Civil War, which makes him realize that man, despite his modern enlightenment, could not avoid adversity. "Does it mean", he wondered, "that the need for strength and toughness was to be always with them; that the farther they advanced, the more terrible would be the hardship that descended upon them, and the more crying the need of hardihood to be saved?" [117] In the moral context of the novel, Chancey has taken the first step toward answering the question by his willingness to face it. The novel ends before he repudiates his earlier convictions, but Chancey is at least willing to ask questions which his mind had previously rejected as even worthy of consideration.

The repeated recurrence in Richter's trilogy of the conclusions he derives from his cosmic scheme shows how important his philosophical and psychological theories are to his conception of order in the three books. This is not to say that Richter's theory of emergent evolution and purposeful destiny as it gives direction to his trilogy makes of it an ideological tract disguised as fiction. René Wellek and Austin Warren have shown that art and idea are not really opposed to each other. "Serious art implies a view of life which can be stated in philosophical terms, even in terms of systems. Between artistic coherence . . . and philosophical coherence there is some kind of correlation." [118] It is neither necessary nor accurate to regard Richter's system as having no crucial relationship with the structural unity of the trilogy.[119]

Part of the novelist's art, Richter well realizes, is to associate a truthful disclosure of reality with its moral significance. The moral purpose of the Ohio trilogy is, broadly speaking, to suggest the workings of a cosmic destiny, and to disclose the role of hardship and discipline as a means of grace. Thus the surface narrative of the trilogy is connected with a background meaning. He is interested both in the broad outline of human destiny, and in the source of man's desires and compulsions, his strengths and

---

[117] *The Town*, p. 431.
[118] *Theory of Literature* (New York, 1949), p. 27.
[119] David Young's notion that since the novels are episodic, Richter's "philosophy shows up less in total plan than in particular scenes" is simply not tenable in view of the consistent and sustained view of destiny that laces all episodes together into a coherent whole.

weaknesses of personality. The pattern of life he has discerned imposes order on his fictional world. It gives the Ohio trilogy unity of theme and determines the selectivity of details, enabling Richter to co-ordinate structure and moral meaning.

Although the Ohio trilogy is thus enclosed by the framework of order Richter sees in the universe and in the details of human experience, its emotional power derives largely from the tragic overtones of his apprehension of the eternal enigmas – particularly the inevitable conditions of existence such as suffering and pain, evil and death. This tragic sense qualifies the more optimistic aspects of his cosmology. As in the case of his Southwestern stories, the discovery that man's individual path is fixed by immutable laws operative both in nature and in his racial consciousness is not without its tragic implications. David Young, in his very helpful study of Richter, observes that a conception of man fated to be what he is and determined by his "blood" is essentially tragic, and that the power of Richter's best fiction depends on the tragic implications of fixed character and certain ironic reversals.[120]

The tragic overtones in Richter's view of man and the cosmos are adumbrated early in *The Trees*, perhaps most graphically in Jary's death from internal hemorrhaging just at the moment she is given the wheat bread she has craved and for which Worth has made a long and arduous trip. Death thus visits the Luckett family the first months of their residence in the dark forest and sets the tone for that which is to follow. Sayward's constant battle against the "evil" thing in the trees is accompanied by portentous omens, a sense of forboding and impending doom that precedes various disasters. Her awful intuitions about imminent and unavoidable sorrows and sufferings – such as Genny's ill-fated marriage and temporary insanity, Sullie's disappearance into the dark forest, little Sulie's horrible death by fire, Guerdon's becoming a murderer and fugitive, and innocent little Guerda's inexplicable death, to name but a few – suggest her prescient knowledge of the order of fate. But this prescient knowledge is terrifying in that Sayward is virtually helpless to alter the funda-

120   Young, pp. 151-156.

mental conditions of human destiny. The crucial events of life in the trilogy are essentially tragic because they seem to violate our feelings of moral congruity and fitness; the discovery that tragic occurrences are the inescapable substance of life, the *sine qua non* of spiritual growth, does not relieve them of their immediate horror.

Chancey is the one character most sensitive to the tragedies of existence – especially the problem of why the innocent must suffer. If we recall Richter's admission that Michael's grief at witnessing suffering and his prayer for a gentler evolutionary system, in *The Mountain on the Desert*, are his own, then it is not unreasonable to infer that Chancey's attitude toward evil reflects some of Richter's own rage and sense of injustice, despite his stubborn insistence that the end of suffering and pain is good.

Although Rosa Tench's suicide is the most intensely tragic of the crises Chancey endures, it is by no means the first. His sheltered life, his preference for a dream world of escape from reality, and his sensitivity to apparently irrational evil are all of a piece and consistent with his fundamental nature. His desire to escape from the harsher realities of existence forces him even as a lad of six to withdraw from life and to become introspective and reflective. His first painful sense of universal injustice has to do with Portius' failure to be named a judge when the township is accepted as a legal county. Portius, who had drawn up the bill and was the one chiefly responsible for its passage, is the most likely candidate; but because of his agnosticism and the bigotry of his neighbors, he is ignored and the judgeship granted to Zephon Brown, a merciless skinflint tax-collector and farmer, who is appointed because he is a church elder.

The crowning insult to Chancey's father is Zephon's insistence that Portius buy a load of the hay the lawyer had ordered even though Portius in the meantime had sold his horse in his disappointment at being deprived of the judgeship. Chancey's reflections are a bitter indictment of God:

His mother claimed that God was good and kind, but it looked like God was cruel, playing with his father like a cat with a mouse. First He had given a fine new horse to his father as a judge to ride on.

Then He took the judgeship away, and now when the hay for the fine horse was coming, He had taken the horse away ... How [Chancey] hated the sight of the triumphant Zephon driving the best pair of horses. God had not taken Zephon Brown's horses away.[121]

The fact that Portius shrewdly and ironically bests Zephon in the hay-buying incident and that he eventually becomes a judge in the county fails to alter Chancey's ingrained sense of injustice. Chancey sees life as a series of apparent contradictions to the standards and values of a supreme equity. He resents a world of inescapable disproportion in rewards and punishments, which apparently fall mysteriously to the deserving and undeserving alike. This incongruity shakes his confidence in the moral order of the universe.

The relationship between Chancey and Rosa Tench sets the stage for the most calamitous episode in Chancey's long encounter with universal injustice. Rosa's plight is immensely touching to Chancey. The chief attraction he feels for Rosa has to do with the similarity of their natures and predicament. Both are sensitive, slightly ethereal characters, given to introspection and withdrawal. Chancey can see no justice in her suffering; he is especially drawn to her because of his belief that she was "like he, wronged by the stars, caught in the blind machinations of birth and life".[122]

The events leading to Rosa's suicide are admittedly a tragic commentary on the cruelty of life. Rosa, who has felt no identification with her coarse, rough, and boisterous legal father, Jake Tench, has experienced a longing for and inclination toward the Wheeler mansion. She has heard rumors of her true paternity, and cannot resist being with Chancey in spite of the ban placed on their meeting. She continues to see Chancey during the fatal summer, wandering with him through the countryside, drinking in the "wild beauty of God" in nature. Filled with a sense of dread at the omen of a falling star, she attempts to free Chancey and herself from the stifling limitations of a predestinate life in Americus by releasing a ballon the two are riding in during a

---

[121] *The Town*, p. 37.
[122] *Ibid.*, p. 302.

summer exhibition. The attempt to float away from the ever-present cruelty of life in Americus fails, and the malicious town gossip which wrongly connects her with the dead baby found in the canal – along with the cruel revelation of her actual relationship with Chancey – forces her into a terrible and grotesque suicide.

This event precipitates Chancey's earnest quest for evidence of a moral order in the universe, but he is enraged by what strikes him as the smug and complacent platitudes of philosophers, of ministers, and especially of his parents. He feels a "sense of anger against his father and mother, against preachers and priests, philosophers and pioneers and all the rest who saw any good in the unjust and meaningless torment of life".[123] The breach between Chancey and his parents is now irreparable, for he holds Sayward responsible in general for the philosophy of hardship in the anachronistic pioneer ethic, and Portius responsible in particular for Rosa's fate. In his confused and distraught state of mind, he briefly finds peace in the strange and incoherent utterings of the itinerant Johnny Appleseed, who indiscriminately quotes from Swedenborg's *Heaven and Hell*. But the Swedenborgian balm cannot heal Chancey's heart wounds, and his quest ends finally in a kind of desperate and self-pitying cynicism mixed with an impossible idealism.

Professor Hall Frye distinguishes between the art of tragedy and the "tragic qualm" caused by those senseless and incongruous occurrences of life which form the substance of the tragic view. Frye defines this tragic qualm as a

feeling of insecurity and confusion, as it were a sort of moral dizziness and nausea, due to the vivid realization ... of a suspicion which is always lurking uncomfortably near the threshold of consciousness, that the world is somehow out of plumb.[124]

Although Frye is here describing the affective response of the audience as it apprehends the tragic qualm in tragic drama, his description well expresses Chancey's state of mind; and again,

---

[123] *Ibid.*, p. 370.
[124] *Romance and Tragedy*, rev. ed. (Lincoln, 1961), pp. 96-97.

the sensitivity of Richter's insight suggests more than a little of his own occasional emotional response to the laws of necessity. The tragic vision has to do with the apparently terrible incongruity between inevitable power or necessity and the moral imperatives of justice and equity. Victory, of course, always goes to the powers of necessity, and as Richter's sensitive characters confront the fearful symmetry of a mechanistic universe, they are faced with the need to reconcile experience with conscience, to resolve the conflict between the certainties of experience and the demands of conscience for ultimate justice.

Although the Ohio trilogy is no tragedy properly speaking, Richter's dramatization of the human encounter with the inexplicable mystery of evil is essentially tragic. The tragic vision we have inherited from the Greek tragic poets is one in which tensions between apparent lawlessness and underlying law, between a chaotic and a patterned universe have always been fiddle string tight, and charged with the terrors of potential rupture. But the vision of tragedy as such has always been affirmative of a moral order, of a divine justice, and has argued that man is mysteriously both predestinate and free. Despite the decrees of necessity, his freedom is real, if precarious. According to Henry Myers, Aeschylus "regarded himself as a teacher of personal freedom and responsibility", and his tragedies illustrate the final triumph of divine justice in human affairs; Sophocles taught a religious acceptance of ordained events no matter how terrible or frightening they appear to be; the rebel and skeptic Euripides was compelled to demonstrate the justice of strange dooms: in each case, the tragic poets demonstrated "the justice of the unalterable conditions of human experience".[125]

There is no evidence that the Greek tragic poets were especially pleased with the operations of fate in the order of the events they dramatized; nor is it logical to assume that Richter is entirely satisfied with an arbitrary order in the universe that necessitates suffering. Part of his appeal is his honesty in attempting to come to terms with the harsher side of reality. In setting forth the idea

---

[125]   *Tragedy: A View of Life* (Ithaca, 1956), pp. 52-53.

that we are eternally fated to encounter struggle and hardship in this universe, Richter follows the notions of the Greek tragic poets in general and the assumptions of the Stoics in particular that we cannot reject destiny. If man is to triumph, he must first submit to the demiurge that controls his fate; he cannot triumph *over* destiny, but by an act of will he can be triumphant *in* it. The necessity of the historical situation does not capriciously and mercilessly determine man; however, it does radically limit the number of possible alternatives from which he can choose. Thus man has the power and the freedom to work within the limits of destiny, to shape the single day and the single event. Richter tacitly recognizes that, in this view of existence, free will is limited by causal necessity both in the events ordained by destiny and in the determinants of racial consciousness. However, in his most expansive moods, he insists that free will extends so far as to enable man to bargain with Fate. "I do not hold with Euripides when he writes of Fate, 'Thy heart is cruel and never came pity nigh unto thee,' " Richter has said, "and I do hold that the humble and willing can intercede and perhaps even bargain with Fate by intelligent discipline for that laid down for him. . . ." [126]

It is confidence in man's power to bargain with Fate that prompts Richter to dramatize the possibilities of life in which ultimately a sense of injustice and determinism is balanced with a sense of ethical purpose in necessity. This balance is attained in the vision of Sayward, who finds reconciliation in terms of good-out-of-evil, in submitting to the mysterious unseen presence and in choosing to let the Chosen things come. Her discovery of some fundamental universal law whose operation justifies or compensates for the suffering and catastrophes of existence is the only real heritage she can leave for Chancey; it is the only real heritage, Richter argues, that we can claim from the pioneer past. But in spite of this affirmation and resolution, the trilogy ends on a note of doubt and fear; Chancey, representative of a modern generation emasculated by the Cronos knife of time, is still filled with self-absorbed anxiety and a sense of standing alone and un-

[126] Correspondence to me, March 8, 1962.

accommodated. Chancey, is the "woodcutter" of the present who has cut down the tree of the past (Sayward) which "casts its shade upon all, even upon the woodcutter".[127]

Perhaps one aspect of this tragic note can be clarified by comparing Chancey's troubled glimpse into the mystery of life at the dying Sayward's bedside with John Donner's revelation on the precipice of his self-discovery in *The Waters of Kronos*. As Donner reflects on a hymn his father had favored and had often sung, he recalls the powerful and disturbing images in the lines, "the old wayside cross, like a gray friar cowled / In lichens and moss".[128] The song had always troubled John as a boy, but only in his maturity when he had had occasion to read Sophocles had he "recognized a fellow doomsman in Oedipus". John believes Oedipus would have understood his inexplicable inner terror and dread at "the omens of the unfavorable words, the foreboding chorus, the fateful way his father drew it all out, the inescapable doom that lay close ahead . . .".[129] Donner's ultimate discovery that the dread and terror which he associated with his father and which had alienated him were really the felt intimations of his own inevitable decay and death as he followed in his father's footsteps to the grave enables him to understand his sense of estrangement.

The revelation scenes of both Chancey in the trilogy and John Donner in *The Waters of Kronos*, however, have in common an underlying tragic note of despair that self-revelation has come too late, that terrible losses have been suffered which can never be recouped. In each case, son and parent fail to be reconciled before the parent dies. In John Donner's trip into the past of his consciousness, he confronts himself as an untried, innocent lad; the man the boy has become yearns to teach the youth to appreciate his mother, his youthful vitality and the rhythmical mystery of life, to "beat the ancient method of the Zodiac, the slow unwieldy scheme of awareness after deprivation, the cruel system that taught you most beautifully and effectively when it was too

127 *The Town*, p. 420.
128 *The Waters of Kronos*, p. 158.
129 *Ibid*.

late".[130] But he knows that only experience can bring the sad knowledge of inevitable suffering.

Chancey, too, has made his discovery "too late". Sayward's death has brought the odor of grave clothes into the decaying Wheeler mansion, and Chancey's spirit has already suffered the tragic erosion of time. Richter's own sense of the failure of the present to apprehend the crucial lessons of the past – indeed, of the impossibility of learning these lessons second hand – portends the inevitable struggle with pain, hardship, and torment necessary to strip away the false values of modernity, to heal the disease of contemporaneity. The everlasting yea of the pioneer is muffled by the low rumble of impending doom. Richter's vision is essentially tragic, and a dark stain of pessimism tinctures the conclusion of the Ohio trilogy.

130   Ibid., p. 151.

IV

RICHTER AND LITERARY TRADITION: PRIMITIVISM, TRANSCENDENTALISM, THE NOVEL OF THE SOIL, AND THE HISTORICAL NOVEL

1. PRIMITIVISM AND PROGRESS

Richter's commitment to primitivism – derived both from his psycho-energic principles and from a deep strain of nostalgia inherent in his view of the past – is the clue to his relationship with transcendentalism and the tradition of the novel of the soil, both of which share a common attitude toward progress. It is important in understanding Richter's fictional world to assess his attitude toward progress and his commitment to primitivism, both of which may seem incongruous in one who holds forth a doctrine of evolutionary growth. For a doctrine of emergent evolution implies above all else a faith in the desirability of a future state of being, a movement from imperfection toward perfection.

The evolutionary naturalists, with whom Richter has been shown to have a great deal in common, had rationalized historical change through the idea of progress into a benevolent developmental process. They assumed that social, political, and economic institutions were naturally evolving in a desirable direction. Such a pleasantly deterministic view of progress, the assumptions of which were widely held by most Americans in the middle and late nineteenth century during the great eras of westward expansion and economic growth, has in the twentieth century been considerably vitiated; progress, in the nineteenth century sense of the word, is no longer an inevitable law to those who think seriously about it at all.[1]

[1] Arthur P. Dudden, "Nostalgia and the American", *Journal of the History of Ideas*, XXII (October-December 1961), pp. 515-530.

Western man of the twentieth century, Arthur O. Lovejoy has pointed out, has become increasingly skeptical concerning the myth of progress and "increasingly troubled with misgivings about the value of the outcome of civilization thus far, about the future to which it tends, and about himself as the author of it all".[2] Although basically embracing a teleologically optimistic philosophy of growth, Richter has consistently called into question certain popular conceptions of the inevitability of progress. So strong is this current of thought in his writings that the temper of his fictional world is generally more regretful than hopeful, more backward-looking than forward-looking, despite the theoretically inevitable triumph in his cosmology of natural law in its task of bringing mankind up the scale of being and toward "the source". One of the dominant keynotes in his philosophical observations we have seen in chapter three is his protest against certain aspects of modern civilization – i.e., the welfarist intellect and "so-called progress", or the equation of progress and economic growth – for their betrayal of the evolutionary growth of man.

It is not necessarily a contradiction in terms to hold to a theory of evolutionary growth while at the same time to attack prevailing notions of progress, however, since organic progress in the human condition and what passes for progress in our institutions and more advanced way of life need not be the same. At the same time it must be admitted that Richter's nostalgia for the past, his regret for the passing of the established and the traditional, when yoked to his trust in natural and ordained organic growth is at best ambivalent.

On one level this co-existing belief in progress and an intense nostalgia for the past relates Richter to what Arthur Dudden has described as a peculiarly American view of historical change. Dudden has convincingly suggested that in the history of the American people there has lain adjacent to the idea of progress a deep-running tide of nostalgia, a welcome vision of the future with an underlying feeling for popular resistance to novelty and uncertainty, a not-to-be-denied preference for stability and a

[2] Arthur O. Lovejoy et al., A Documentary History of Primitivism and Related Ideas, I (Baltimore, 1935), p. xi.

yearning to "recapture fleeting conditions and former circumstances".

Such a longing for the past, Dudden continues, can "easily be disguised paradoxically as a forward-looking restorative impulse".[3] This retrospective homesickness and restorative impulse is often reflected in our literature as dissatisfaction with the present and preference for the past. "We find ourselves as Americans", wrote Robert Gorham Davis, "by seeing ourselves imaged in a kind of past which – in the character we give it, at least – is largely denied by the material and social circumstances in which we live." [4] Such literary expressions of a belief in the superiority of a past era or condition to what now exists or lies ahead we have come to identify as one of the impulses of primitivism.

Primitivism is a recurring idea in the history of thought that can be traced back to Greco-Roman antiquity.[5] As reflected in literature, philosophy, religion and ethics, it begins with serious misgivings about the direction of civilization, misgivings which characteristically are accompanied by wistful backward glances in time to a better age in which the most ideal conditions of human life supposedly must have occurred (chronological primitivism), or wistful glances from a highly complex and "overcivilized" level of acculturation to a far simpler and less sophisticated life, i.e., a culturally primitive phase of human society (cultural primitivism). To these two traditional varieties may be added a third – modern or psychological primitivism, whose idealized domain is the natural processes (drives or needs) of the human psyche as imbedded in the unconsciousness of man.

Primitivism has found philosophical justification in the concept

[3] Dudden, p. 517. N.B. "From the anthropological standpoint, both the withdrawal impulse of nostalgia and the hopeful vision of progress represent conceptual structures erected and extensively entertained by the people in the United States amidst fluid social conditions in the face of the certain passage of time. From the standpoint of history, both the idea of progress and the mood of nostalgia reflect underlying theoretical explanations for the historical process itself", p. 528.

[4] Quoted by Dudden, p. 526.

[5] E.g., Lovejoy; George Boas, *Essays on Primitivism and Related Ideas in the Middle Ages* (Baltimore, 1948); Chauncey Tinker, *Nature's Simple Plan* (Princeton, 1922).

of "nature" as the expression of the standard of human values, in "the identification of the good with that which is 'natural' or 'according to nature' ".[6] The primitive life is thus extolled as more amenable to the state of nature, or things as they *should* be, as the medium in which nature is permitted its most unrestricted function. Inherent in this concept of nature is a practical anti-intellectualism, "the view that intellectual pursuits are in themselves a sort of abnormality and that the progress of knowledge has not made man happier or better, but rather the reverse".[7]

2. THE PROBLEM OF NOSTALGIA AND THE AMERICAN EXPERIENCE

Before Richter's relationship to the three varieties of primitivism is clarified, particularly with reference to the Ohio trilogy, it should be shown that his own human emotional nostalgia and tragic sense of the erosion of time, quite apart from ordered primitivistic notions, does much to heighten the nostalgia inherent in a primitivistic philosophy. It is probably impossible to say just how much a primitivist's views are born of his wistful desire for the good old days and his regret at the loss of his youth and vitality. Certainly there is a suggestion in Richter's novels that his keen sense of nostalgia threatens to carry him to an *uncritical* preference for the past; only unwillingness to flinch from the uglier aspect of reality in his dramatization of suffering prevents his novels from lapsing occasionally into sentimentalization.

One of the chief motives behind Richter's fiction, and this is restated time and again, has been his desire not so much to recapture, as to pay tribute to a way of life vanishing before the apparently inevitable spread of industrialism, which has attended the twentieth century, and the increasing reliance on centralized government to order the affairs of men at greater cost to their individuality and independence. This is sincere regret at change, a funeral oration for a way of life that must give way before the crushing logic of increasing population and limited space.

[6] Lovejoy, p. 12.
[7] *Ibid.*, p. 14.

The passing of the West, the last great frontier now fenced in, domiciled, and domesticated, is feelingly lamented in *Early Americana, The Sea of Grass, The Lady, The Light in the Forest, A Country of Strangers*, and of course the Ohio trilogy. Scenes from small town life of the 1900's are affectionately preserved in *Tacey Cromwell, Always Young and Fair, The Waters of Kronos*, and *A Simple Honorable Man*. His motive in writing *Always Young and Fair* holds equally true for the others; in it, he tells us, he has attempted to show his "feelings for a vanished way of life" in his home town as he knew it in his youth – a place he recalls as an ideal village, full of "individualists refreshingly different from each other", a town once sought out as a refuge by harassed city dwellers from Philadelphia. Now, he relates sadly, the "beautiful trees have been cut down to make way for progress", its "peace daily broken by the roar of coal from the mines to the north", its charming covered bridges torn down to make way for common concrete ones, its once beautiful creek now "black as the hinges of hell" with industrial soot and filth.[8]

Regret at rapid change has been, in one sense, a peculiarly American reaction to the enormous acceleration in the rate at which the present is superannuated and retired as the past. Born late as a nation, America lacks the sense of continuity with the past and tradition that has acted as a stabilizing force in the cultural norms of Europe. The sense of continuity from one generation to the next has always given way to a feeling of alienation, for the differences in the way of life between generations are too vast, too graphic, too closely tied to the swift changes in this growing country. This underlying regret at rapid change has not been strong enough to try to decelerate the rate of change; however, it has become what one might call a conservative impulse in the American psyche.

A large part of the appeal of the Ohio trilogy lies in just this masterful recreation of the pace of change. During the life span of one woman, a savage wilderness is settled, the wild game wiped

---

[8]   "This Once Ideal Village", *Saturday Evening Post*, CCXIX (Oct. 12, 1946), p. 4.

out, the trees removed, farming country established, a town born, an industrial city raised, and – naturally enough – one generation alienated from another (apotheosized in Chancey's alienation from Sayward). It is the story of the American experience, enacted and re-enacted on a continuously westward moving frontier, its last scene not closed even today as industrialism confronts the remaining predominantly rural regions west of the Mississippi. It has always staggered the American imagination. In the trilogy, Portius reflects this in his speech at the coming of the railroad: "When I think of all these stupendous and undreamed of changes, all within the span of one short life, speech fails me and my power of astonishment is almost exhausted"; and Sayward, too, senses this quickening pace of change when one day she "could feel for the first time in her life the old earth rolling to the eastward, turning under her, pushing against her feet and carrying her along".[9]

The Ohio trilogy, then, is not only an autobiographical expression of Richter's anguished regret at the rapid pace of change and the erosion of time; it is a biography of the American experience, a record of our astonishment when we behold the bewildering speed at which we descendants of the nineteenth century are carried down the stream of time. In the hands of a less skillful novelist, this acute sense of nostalgia might well have emerged as maudlin sentiment; in the hands of Richter, it is an accurate record of our sense of loss, an explanation for that underlying nostalgia and restorative impulse in the American consciousness.

3. PRIMITIVISM IN RICHTER'S PHILOSOPHY AND FICTION

In clarifying Richter's specific commitment to primitivism, one should begin by acknowledging a certain obliqueness in his attitude toward cultural and psychological primitivism. He shares with the modern primitivists (e.g., Eugene O'Neill, Sherwood Anderson, or D. H. Lawrence) the conviction that the impetus for being and doing is the primal self, the inner man, the buried

[9] *The Town*, pp. 378, 380.

thing within the mind (what Richter calls the inherited and developed psycho-energic instrument).

According to this view, mind conscious of itself is really only a small part of our psyche; beneath or within (it is difficult not to use spatial metaphors) the dark recesses of our mind is the unconscious, whose impulses not only trace back to racial and familial memory, but are also connected to a vast storehouse of experiences that have been accumulating since birth. Since the unconscious mind represents the natural and instinctive processes which govern and control thought, it should, so goes the argument, be given its proper freedom to direct and order that which is in its domain.

Implied in such a view is the concept of "nature as norm" with its implications for human conduct, as well as underlying assumptions that intellectual pursuits and the progress of knowledge have little to do with the real stuff of life. If the primitivist holds forth a rigid teleological doctrine, as does Richter, this concept may give birth to a fear that the conscious mind with seemingly rational good intentions may actually interfere in the domain of the unconscious (inhibit, warp, deprive of energy, and so forth) – in short, may interfere in the destiny of the individual as set forth by the powers in the universe working through natural, instinctive, or "mechanical" law.

With the exception of Richter's teleological doctrine, up to this point he and the modern primitivists may be said to share a common ground. But in their interpretation of the basic energy impulse in human nature, they differ radically. The modern psychological primitivist owes his start to Freud. "It is the primitive that Freud found in the realm of the unconscious", writes G. A. Borgese, "in endless conflict with the later impressed and repressing patterns of society and law." [10] Conventional psychological primitivism inevitably becomes tinged with nihilism, ranging from the self-destructive urges noted in D. H. Lawrence to the downright cosmic pessimism of Robinson Jeffers.

Jascha Kessler has defined modern primitivism as a

[10] G. A. Borgese, "Primitivism", *Dictionary of World Literature*, ed. Joseph T. Shipley (Paterson, N.J., 1960), p. 319.

philosophical derivative of the strife in man's mental constitution between what Freud called the forces of Eros and Ananke. Perhaps the best way to differentiate the modern from the various historical forms of primitivism is to note that while masquerading as social criticism it is actually speaking for those impulses in humans which seek to compass only self destruction. For this reason ... it attacks historical truth and manifests a tendency to psychological retrogression ...[11]

Psychological primitivists denigrate modern civilization because of the "artificial" limitations and inhibitions (or "taboos") it has imposed upon the nature of man. And since the edifice of their thinking has been built on a foundation laid by Freud, their protest is largely against those ethical inhibitions carrying over from Puritanism that have frustrated the natural sexual drives in man to the perversion of his personality. To remedy this maladjustment they call for a return to a "healthy" life yielding to the natural impulses and for a "realistic" reappraisal of ethical standards.[12]

Richter, of course, repudiates the basic concept of Freudian psychology and its implications for relaxed codes of personal and social morality. The popular acceptance of Freudian notions, he fears, may account for the common lack of restraint and the sexual license of today. His dissatisfaction with Freudian theory is due specifically to his rejection of Freud's insistence on the necessity of interpreting behavioral patterns pretty largely in terms of instinctive sexual and aggressive drives. To locate the psychical source of energy in the "blind sack of the genital gland" seems to Richter much too reductive and restricted to account for the innumerable behavioral responses to be observed in the human psyche.

[11] Jascha Kessler, "Ashes of the Phoenix: A Study of Primitivism and Myth-Making in D. H. Lawrence's *The Plumed Serpent*" (unpublished Doctoral dissertation, The University of Michigan, Ann Arbor, 1957), pp. 67-68.
[12] Such a view relates the psychological primitivists to "soft" cultural primitivism. They would be sympathetic to escaping from the demands of a highly civilized society to an easier, more leisurely primitive existence, a life less burdened with civilized apparatus, the innumerable restrictions, sexual taboos, rules, regulations and conventionalities that attend a high level of acculturation.

The popularized interpretations – and misinterpretations – of Freudian psychology which we associate with the modern psychological primitivists strike Richter as an evolutionary regression, a lowering of evolutionary standards and evolved ethical requirements to a more savage view of life, primitive in the brute-like sense of the word. For according to psycho-energics, the ethical requirements that have emerged in the course of evolution are instrumental in building up higher energy rates for those moving upward on the scale of being:

We know that civilized life calls for a great deal more expenditure of energy than animal life. Civilized man must furnish energy to be spent in inhibitions, in religious obligations and those of conscience, in sex restrictions, in permanent duty to parents, family and many other requirements that the animal does not know. We call them standards.[13]

On Richter's conception of the scale of being, it will be recalled, those at the bottom are the strong egos with simple, primitive energy needs easily met. In the Ohio trilogy, the most primitive types are not the most admirable; rather the most primitive are more likely to be brutal or selfish and deficient in their sense of moral responsibility. For example, those with the hunter instinct are too primitive to have developed a sense of social responsibility that transcends their own selfish desires. Worth Luckett blithely sheds all parental obligations when he "lights out" for untamed country; Jake Tench finds enjoyment in sadistic jokes and once won the admiration and respect of the Settlement Indians by gleefully skinning a live wolf; Louie Scurrah, after maltreating his wife, Genny, abandons her and runs off with her sister, Achsa, who is herself a primitive type. The primitive acts from the most selfish impulse.

Although Richter accuses the Freudian primitivists of betraying the grand plan of evolution by their deliberate retrogression to a more primitive energy level, and thus fostering primitive types, he has his own serious criticism of the debilitating effects of civilization's restrictions on the physical and spiritual well-being of man. But where the psychological primitivists rebel at ethical standards

13   *The Mountain*, p. 119.

which to them seem artificial and inhibiting, Richter is chiefly critical of materialism fostered by an energy-wasting preoccupation with trivialities detrimental to modern man's evolutionary growth and spiritual health.

To offset the increasing love for comfort Richter champions "hard" cultural primitivism, which accounts for his admiration for certain aspects of Indian life, chiefly its spartan simplicity and stoic values elicited by a hard environment. In *The Mountain,* Michael gives expression to this view:

Civilized man feels superior to the savage. . . . But when some of our civilized explorers live the savage life, they tell us that the savage knows life more fully and feels it more richly than we do. One reason is that his energy is less diffused over the wide range of civilization's knowledge and experience. Instead, it's concentrated on simple things: on just living, seeing and feeling. His energy isn't dissipated, wasted by so many pawns. In psycho-energics we know what counts is never pawns, what we call things, but the energy connected with them in our nervous system.[14]

The nearest Richter comes to finding an ideal in the noble savage is in his small novel, *The Light in the Forest,* in which he treats with great sympathy and insight the Indians' point of view and attitude toward white man's civilization. "In *The Light in the Forest*", he writes, "may be found the superior appeal to youth of the hard primitive Indian life and character over the civilized and artificial of the white man".[15] Although one of the main purposes in writing the novel was to present an historically accurate and objective picture of the forced repatriation of a white boy to his real parents after having lived for a decade with the Indians, a more significant motive was "to point out that in the pride of

---

[14] *Ibid.,* p. 152.
[15] Correspondence to me, March 21, 1962. N.B. An interesting autobiographical comment illustrates how Richter's own experience and romantic temperament color the primitivistic thrust of the novel: *The Light in the Forest* "really came out of my own painful experience as a boy, having to give up at an early age a boy's world and take on the joyless toil and responsibilities of civilization as the Indian captive in the narrative had to submit to the same after the wild joyous freedom of the natural world" (from John K. Hutchens, "Pine Grove to Pulitzer and Back", *New York Herald Tribune Book Review*, April 22, 1962, p. 11).

our American liberties, we're apt to forget that already we've lost a good many to civilization".[16]

In his attempt to tell the story from the Indian's point of view, Richter overdraws the primitivistic virtues of the Indian's life, a tendency he fails to avoid even in his most recent story of Indian life, *A Country of Strangers*. His treatment of the Indian in the majority of his narratives, however, is less idealistic. Several of his best short stories describe or intimate the brutal atrocities committed by Indians against the pioneers.[17] In the Ohio trilogy, the Indian, although he plays an exceedingly minor role, is transformed from a potential and terrifying enemy to a subdued, pitiful, and often ridiculous figure, as completely tamed as the forest, easily beguiled and victimized.

There is, then, in Richter's commitment to cultural primitivism – with the exception of *The Light in the Forest* and *A Country of Strangers* – no sustained idealistic vision of the noble savage *per se*. What Richter idealizes is the hard environment. He sees clearly that a primitive environment is instrumental in eliciting those stoic virtues necessary for survival. In the Ohio trilogy he repeatedly permits Sayward to recognize the importance of primitivistic values for desirable character development.

On one occasion, to cite an instance, Little Turtle, who is being represented in court by Portius, offers to take the sickly Chancey, raise him like an Indian, and thus restore his health:

Little Turtle make um run. Take um long march. Make leg hard. No um sleep on ground summer time, winter time. Make um sleep on snow. Him get hard then hah. Like iron. ... Make um heart like stone. Won't die. But if die, go to Great Spirit. Great Spirit make him over better next time.[18]

Portius is amused at the Indian's naiveté, but Sayward, having overheard, is profoundly influenced by Little Turtle's proposed

---

[16] *The Light in the Forest*, p. viii.
[17] It is True Son's realization that his own tribe would scalp innocent children to get revenge which unsettles his loyalty. His inability to go through with the decoy ambush alienates him from the Indians' scheme of values and brings about his banishment from the tribe.
[18] *The Town*, p. 64.

regimen for her son. She can see both the good and the bad in the primitive life, and she endeavors to make part of the Indian philosophy her own despite Portius's scornful remark that "the Indians practiced the philosophy you mention, and you know how far they got with it".[19]

Richter's commitment to chronological primitivism is predicated by the same psycho-energic principles that lead him to endorse cultural primitivism. The wistful backward glances he casts toward the era of frontier expansion indicate, from his point of view, a forward-looking restorative impulse. In Richter's theory of growth the emphasis is on ascent. Thus, the least excellent time of being was at the beginning. There is a line of continuous progress, but this is offset by recurring periods (although not necessarily cyclic) of decline. The ascent is often arrested when man, in an attempt to outwit the harsh realities of natural law, avoids – or tries to avoid – the painful and the difficult. Some cruel event, however, inevitably makes it clear that pain and discomfort cannot ultimately be avoided; man therefore will see the wisdom of embracing a regimen calculated to help him withstand adversity, and he will voluntarily – or by nature be forced to – return to the enduring stoic values inherent in the primitive life.

4. RICHTER'S RELATIONSHIP TO AMERICAN TRANSCENDENTALISM

Richter's teleologically oriented primitivism relates him to the tradition of American transcendentalism. Indeed, he cites Emerson and Thoreau as among those American writers he has read with pleasure and profit.[20] He was doubtless attracted to them by their mysticism and moral philosophy, and although he tried when quite young to imitate their style, he soon gave it up in the best spirit of transcendental independence. This conscious imitation of Emerson and Thoreau, however, suggests that they played an important role in helping Richter to shape his thought.

---

[19] *Ibid.*, p. 311.
[20] Gaston, p. 48.

If Richter is less overtly and self-consciously mystic than the Concord idealists concerning the operation of the Divine Spirit in man and nature, he is nevertheless a mystic, and certain that every movement of man is made in accordance with teleological law; for in Richter's cosmology, natural law represents the constant attendance of immanent spiritual forces in the universe whose purpose it is to raise man's spiritual consciousness to a higher relationship with the creative power behind the universe. He can with Emerson say every trifle bristles "with a polarity that ranges it instantly on an eternal law . . .; there is no trifle, there is no puzzle, but one design unites and animates the farthest pinnacle and the lowest trench".[21]

This view of the universe, which sees the direct role of Divine Consciousness reflected in both the microcosm and the macrocosm, is necessarily obligated to account for the mystery of evil. Idealism asserts that all phenomena are effected by an Absolute Cause. If the Divine Mind is all-good, and if nothing exists but by the will of the Divine Mind, then only absolute good is willed into being. In view of these assumptions, the problem of evil is immediately apparent, for two kinds of evil in human experience must be taken into account: physical evil, or the evil that happens to man, and moral evil, or the evil that he does or that he is. Richter's philosophical attitude toward these problems is essentially the same as that of Emerson and Thoreau, although his emotional response to evil is a somewhat different story.

Emerson argued that evil in the sense of pain or personal misfortune is unavoidable; but evil in this sense is merely instrumental and effects good. In the words of the young god, Uriel, "evil will bless, and ice will burn". However, evil as an absolute is non-existent, a notion Emerson expressed explicitly in "The Divinity School Address". Only benevolence is absolute and real, and evil as an active malignant force has no objective reality. Physical evil, or that which happens to us, and evil in the sense of man's moral imperfection are merely words which describe the inescapable conditions of mortality.

[21] "The American Scholar", *The Complete Works of Ralph Waldo Emerson*, I (New York, 1903), p. 111.

Richter realized even in his first philosophical essay that his system, based as it is on a transcendental conception of the necessity and efficacy of pain and suffering, must confront the concept of evil. "There is no universal thing such as evil", he writes, "only a relative evil. That is, it appears evil to us individually because it is not harmonious to our individual organisms." [22] To support his contention he appeals to the evolutionary naturalism expressed in John Fiske's declaration, "Moral evil is simply the characteristics of the lower state of being as looked at from the higher." [23] Richter was once asked if his persistent attempts to explain and justify the role of evil in the universe and to attribute pain to a benign plan of the Creator did not make of *The Mountain on the Desert* a theodicy. His reply is worth noting.

The Mountain . . . may well be a theodicy although I would not go so far as to assert that God can be the author only of goodness – let us say eventual goodness – or that my attempt was to prove his divine attributes. I hope the former may be true; I believe it but I do not actually know except in part. In my case the explanations, the theories came first and the removed goodness of God followed as the evil dissipated, became unreal, a contrived illusion.[24]

We are speaking here, of course, of Richter's theories; as we noted in Chapter three, Richter's rationalization of the role of pain and apparent evil does not always convince his heart, and his emotional response to the problem of pain invariably issues in a pervasive sense of tragedy. In this respect, Richter could never effect the studied indifference to pain or private tragedy that caused Emerson to be regarded by his contemporaries as a man of cold temperament.

Nevertheless, Richter's dogged persistence in appealing to his theory of the relativity of evil to justify the forces of historical necessity and to set forth the proper role of the individual with reference to society causes him to regard the problem of social evil in much the same way Emerson and Thoreau did. The social implications of the transcendental attitude toward evil are at once

[22] *Vibration*, p. 159.
[23] *Ibid.*
[24] Correspondence to me, September 22, 1961.

apparent. It is the kind of attitude which tempered Emerson's social vision with the hammer of fatalism and which caused him to take such a bemused and detached point of view regarding the numerous reforms described in "New England Reformers". In a journal entry for May 28, 1839, Emerson wrote, "Nature will not have us fret or fume. When we come out of the Caucus or the Abolition Convention or the Temperance meeting, she says to us 'So hot my little Sir!' " Social altruism in the rage for reform struck him as simply another symptom of the tyrannical societal pressure of conformity. "Do not tell me", Emerson said indignantly, "of my obligation to put all poor men in good situations." [25]

Thoreau also looked upon most social reform as a form of philanthropy, a fashionable altruism. His life of rugged self-reliance, self-imposed poverty, spartan simplicity, and stoic self-discipline obviously did not incline him to be sentimental about the poor. It was, after all, the rich who were most miserable, being possessed by their possessions. Thoreau likened the reformer to a man who, having caught a belly ache, assumes the "world has been eating green apples" and who therefore takes it upon himself to keep others from eating unripe fruit until he cures himself of his own dyspepsia. The reformer or philanthropist "who bestows the largest amount of time and money on the needy is doing the most by his mode of life to produce that misery which he strives in vain to relieve".[26]

Emerson and Thoreau's apparent indifference to what mid-nineteenth century reformers called social evil does not mean that they were unaware of the disturbing presence of social injustice. Both were incensed at the institution of slavery, for example, and both repudiated the Fugitive Slave law of 1850 as a "filthy enactment" which they vowed not to obey. Slavery was clearly a flagrant affront to the infinitude of man because it failed to recognize that every man has within him "somewhat really divine". Thoreau was much more inclined to be involved in support of

---

[25] *Works*, II, p. 49.
[26] *Walden and Other Writings of Henry David Thoreau*, ed. Brooks Atkinson (New York, 1950), p. 68.

abolition than Emerson, and his famous act of civil disobedience
was a symbolic rejection of a government capable of such abuse
as the prosecution of the Mexican War, the unjust treatment of
the American Indian, and the institution of slavery. The problem
was not so much a case of bad government, however, as it was of
government at all, and Richter would certainly have applauded
Thoreau's conclusion that, "That government is best which
governs not at all." [27]

Despite their hatred of slavery, Emerson and Thoreau were
reluctant to share the reformers' zeal to secure justice simply by
altering the social structure, primarily because of their transcendental resignation to the law of organic renewal. This transcendental conception held that reforms of social institutions were
useless until the individual had been "renovated" by Reason to
enjoy an "original relation with the Universe". Moreover, one
could never be sure that what appeared to be evil might not be
friction from the mills of a Divine Fate inexorably grinding away
toward some ultimate good. Indeed, this is the very answer Emerson sent in the form of an "Ode" to William Henry Channing,
who had criticized Emerson's indifference to abolitionist causes.
The "Ode" warned that the inevitable bloodshed and warfare
which would attend the clamour of abolitionism would destroy as
much as they would gain in human freedom and deliverance from
injustice and pain. In the concluding lines, Emerson explicitly
argues that a benevolent cosmic destiny brings good out of evil.
"The over-god / Who marries Right to Might, / Who peoples,
unpeoples, / He who exterminates / Races by stronger races, /
Black by white faces, / Knows to bring honey / Out of the lion /
Grafts gentlest scion / On pirate and Turk."

An equally obvious relationship between Richter and the
transcendentalist can be observed in Emerson and Thoreau's
complaint against trends in the society of their own time. The
transcendentalists accused their contemporaries of emasculating
the human spirit, of discarding manhood. "Man is timid and
apologetic", wrote Emerson, and "society everywhere is in con-

---

[27]   "Civil Disobedience", *Ibid.*, p. 635.

spiracy against the manhood of every one of its members ... The virtue in most request is conformity. Self-reliance is its aversion." [28] The ideal that Richter shares with the earlier transcendentalists is that of self-reliance, and self-reliance to a transcendentalist means reliance on the indwelling over-soul or God-consciousness within; in Richter's case, it is reliance on the intuitive revelation of the ordained destiny of man as it is reflected in the inherited and developed psycho-energic instrument's response to natural law. Practically, self-reliance means to reject the mediocrity and standardization of massmorality; it means to rely on common sense, self-initiative, and an intuitive sense of man's organic relationship with the universe.

The signal spiritual failure in modern times, therefore, is the corrosion of the intuitive sense of man as one with nature, a corrosion brought about by his total preoccupation with material things. Men are slaves to what they own, and they fill their lives with anxiety and trouble because of their failure to discover what is really essential among the myriad inessentialities offered by life. "It would be some advantage to live a primitive and frontier life, though in the midst of an outward civilization", wrote Thoreau, "if only to learn what are the gross necessaries of life. ... For the improvements of ages have had but little influence on the essential laws of man's existence." [29]

The ugliness of modern life, said Emerson, is its "dislocation and detachment from the life of God".[30] Since the transcendent power of the Supreme Being is immanent in nature, man may regain his spiritual sensitivity by living in proximity to it; one of the healthiest influences on the mind and spirit of man, therefore, is that of a natural environment as the unrestricted function of the Creator's purpose. When one voluntarily places himself in a primitive environment, he can return to reason and faith, and nature can repair the disgraces and calamities of life. Richter's love for, and twenty years' sojourn in, the hardy climate of New Mexico was predicated partly by this desire. To live in a hard,

[28] "Self-Reliance", *Works*, II, pp. 49-50.
[29] *Walden*, pp. 10-11.
[30] "The Poet", *Works*, III, p. 18.

primitive environment is "to escape to reality from the standard-ized American scene". In the New Mexican mountains and desert places, celebrated by Michael in *The Mountain on the Desert*, men can "shake the contaminations of civilization from their souls" and "hide from everyone except God". The primitive en-vironment with its unconquered primeval elements helps the sensitive man to "shed his false, modern artificial self" and be-come once again a "creature of the mesas and deserts". The ancient land with its primeval soul, writes Richter, restores a "primitive delight in being alive", and stirs up man's slumbering vitality, releasing energy for full enjoyment of life.[31]

Richter's life and work are of a piece, and his reverence for the primitive setting is reflected in all his works, but especially in the Ohio trilogy. It is not until the hard primitive environment has disappeared as the great Ohio forests are leveled that Sayward realizes her deprivation of its spiritual influences. As a child of the forest she had grown to maturity without benefit of religious training; when organized religion does come into the settlement, Sayward finds her spiritual feelings to be broader than any doc-trine.[32] Her consciousness of a Supreme Power behind the phe-nomena of the forest is arrived at intuitively, not doctrinally, and as she gains wisdom from her experiences with life she comes to what may be called a more transcendental conception of evil. Human causes and inevitable destiny account for what in the temporal sense are tragedies; but one can never "blame the Lord" for evil.[33] Sayward's great poise and natural relationship with the universe results in a spiritual serenity not unlike that sought by the Concord Idealists.

Richter's relationship to the primitivistic ideals of Emerson and Thoreau also helps to explain his great fascination for the Western frontier; for his fictional recovery of the frontier past is prompted chiefly by the symbolic power Americans have come

[31]   Richter, "Three Towns I Love", *Holiday*, XIV (December 1953), pp. 55, 56, 104. N.B. The appeal of the unstudied naturalness of the New Mexican towns is "inner, symbolic. It suggests a more simple, unregimented life, freedom from some of the demands of modern living" (p. 94).

[32]   *The Town*, p. 33.

[33]   *The Fields*, p. 66.

to associate with the West as a result of transcendental ideology and symbolism. The transcendentalists' affection for primitive environments and their celebration of nature and solitude coincided with the greatest westward expansion in our nation's long history of migration to the frontier. Consequently, it was almost inevitable, given the transcendentalist penchant for fronting physical facts as symbols of spirit, that the frontier should have taken on symbolic values for the American consciousness.[34] Both Emerson and Thoreau were conscious of shaping the West into a unique metaphoric vehicle that caught and compelled the American imagination. To Emerson, the higher reason was stimulated most when it could confront *frontiers* of thought. Thoreau declared that when he set out to walk, some instinct or impulse drew him inerringly westward.

Eastward I go only by force; but westward I go free ... I believe that the forest which I see in the western horizon stretches uninterruptedly toward the setting sun. ... Let me live where I will, on this side is the city, on that the wilderness, and ever I am leaving the city more and more, and withdrawing into the wilderness.[35]

Wilson Clough in *The Necessary Earth* has recently shown to what extent the frontier furnished American writers with a native metaphor in their search for a national expression; the experience of the early American upon frontiers of nature and solitude entered in a demonstrable way into the thinking and literature of this country; the frontier experience has been absorbed into the imagination of both writer and public and made to serve as a dynamic cultural trope.

The frontier in the mind of America is on its way to becoming the natural symbol for resolution, courage, the confrontation of hard realities from which there is no convenient escape, the courage of the

---

[34] Henry Nash Smith has demonstrated the evocative power of certain Western myths and symbols and has shown that even Frederick Jackson Turner's influential theory of the frontier's role in shaping American character and institutions was itself a projection of the mythical power of the West. See *Virgin Land: The American West as Symbol and Myth* (Cambridge, 1950).

[35] "Walking", *Walden and Other Writings of Henry David Thoreau*, pp. 607-608.

individual fighter who can rely on none other for his salvation. A native metaphor is born.[36]

Clough's useful and insightful study tacitly recognizes the central role played by Emerson and Thoreau in establishing the symbolic properties of the cluster of ideas associated with the frontier. Edwin Fussell also calls attention to the transcendental influence in causing the West symbolically to impinge upon the American mind, and, to a large degree, to form it.[37] Philosophically, writes Fussell, "the Western frontier became more and more entangled with Transcendental dialectic", and the complexity and ambiguity of the metaphor of the West has something to do with the transcendental mode of reconciling such opposites as nature-civilization, mind-matter, synthesis-analysis, self-society, and organism-mechanism.[38]

One of the more important things to note about the transcendental transformation of the physical frontier into a moral and spiritual metaphor is that it was accompanied by a sense of urgency in resisting tendencies in our national life. It was a way of attacking the increasingly central role the machine was coming to play in mid-nineteenth century America; the transcendentalist profoundly distrusted the machine because of its debilitating effects on man's physical and spiritual nature. It is a sure sign, said Emerson, that though society constantly changes from the barbarous to the civilized and scientific, this change is not necessarily amelioration. "For everything that is given something is taken. Society acquires new arts and loses old instincts." The savage has fewer things but more health and strength; "it may be a question whether machinery does not encumber; whether we have not lost by refinement some energy . . ., some vigor of wild virtue".[39]

Such notions, of course, were simply more recent expressions

[36] *The Necessary Earth: Nature and Solitude in American Literature* (Austin, 1964), p. 78.
[37] *Frontier: American Literature and the American West* (Princeton, 1965), p. viii.
[38] *Ibid.*, pp. 18-19.
[39] "Self-Reliance", *Works*, II, pp. 84, 85.

in an American context of the classic pastoral ideal, an ideal which still remains a significant force in American life. Although by nature optimists whose enthusiasm was rarely dampened, Emerson and Thoreau were among the first to sense a profound and ominous shift in the structure of American society. They stood on the edge of a change in our national condition that gave added significance to their celebration of the Americanized and transcendentalized version of the pastoral ideal, a middle ground between the highly developed agrarian civilization described and longed for in Virgil's *The Georgics* and the delicious primitive wilderness of Adamic innocence in the Edenic wilderness.

The period extending from about 1840 to 1860 is a turning point in our cultural history, and the Civil War itself was in many ways a symbolic conflict between an agrarian democracy on the one hand and a capitalistic and industrial democracy on the other. W. W. Rostow's study of the universal stages of industrial growth speaks of certain points which form the "great watershed in the life of modern societies" when the traditional resistance to development is overcome by the expansion and dominance of economic progress. According to Rostow, this watershed point began in America about 1844, a date which marks the middle period of the transcendental era.[40] The transcendentalists, more sensitive than most of their contemporaries, felt the earth tremors of this great subterranean movement of ideas and values, and their apprehension of the potentially destructive forces of the machine to both national life and private sensibility inaugurated an ill-defined note of social protest that continues to our day. Indeed, subsequent and recent studies of the impact technology has had and is having on the American character has born out the legitimacy of their concern.

One of the most fruitful ways of exploring the nature of the transcendental concern about the implications of a technological society is to observe this concern reflected symbolically in their literature. Leo Marx has done just this in *The Machine in the Garden*, which explores the significance of machine imagery in

[40] W. W. Rostow, *The Stages of Economic Growth, A Non-Communist Manifesto* (Cambridge, 1960), p. 7.

the works of representative American writers from the time of Irving, Hawthorne, Emerson, and Thoreau to the present.[41] In the traditional pastoral ideal, Marx points out, the writer could always retreat, if not in reality at least in fantasy, to an oasis of harmony and joy away from the artificiality of the city and into the naturalness of the country. In the 1840's, however, this literary mode is radically altered; a new pastoral mode emerges in which the serenity of a pastoral oasis is shattered by the disturbing presence of a locomotive, whose noise and grimy smoke invade and pollute the garden, destroying its tranquility and leaving in its wake an irritating fretfulness and vague anxiety. So often does this metaphoric design appear in the works of such men as Hawthorne, Emerson, and Thoreau that Marx sees here a literary paradigm of the chief crisis in modern civilization: the industrial invasion of the pastoral Eden in the American wilderness.

The recurring scene of the locomotive entering the garden thus becomes a modern version of an ancient literary device: the contrast between a world of rural peace and simplicity and a world of urban power and disturbing complexity.[42] Marx defines the anti-pastoral forces at work in our literature as the most significant tradition in American writing; industrialism imaged as machine technology "provides the counterforce in the American archetype of the pastoral design".[43]

Thoreau carried the transcendental protest against the technological corruption of the pastoral ideal to its logical conclusion, and, as Richter was later to do, he put into practice the ethics of austerity he had been preaching. The record of his economic retreat from the city to a simpler, more devoted life in the country is, of course, contained in *Walden*, a perfect wilderness haven marred only by the occasional appearances of a train whose tracks lay adjacent to Walden woods. The presence of the train is a constant reminder of the threat of commerce to the higher life,

---

[41] *The Machine in the Garden: Technology and the Pastoral Ideal in America* (New York, 1964).
[42] *Ibid.*, p. 19.
[43] *Ibid.*, p. 26.

however, and Thoreau's prose becomes hortatorical as he calls for the restoration of "simplicity, simplicity, simplicity"! The simple noun gives way to the imperative of "Simplify, simplify . . . The nation itself, with all its so-called internal improvements . . . is just such an unwieldy and overgrown establishment . . . ruined by luxury and heedless expense, by want of calculation and a worthy aim. . . ." [44]

This rhetoric might well have served Sayward in her vigorous arguments with Portius and Chancey. Portius as an ambitious lawyer is a chief advocate of economic and material progress. When a grain mill is set up in the wilderness, Portius is contemptuously amused at Sayward's stubborn refusal to patronize it.

"I was just going to say," he mentioned, "that when enterprizing men fetch labor-saving machinery into the wilderness, I think we should encourage and patronize them.

"I'm for keeping' up to the times when we kin afford it," Sayward said.[45]

It is not merely an impulse toward frugality that prompts Sayward's reply; her conservatism derives from an intuitive resistance against the acceleration of change-as-progress ushered in by the age of technology. "So long as the old works", she said, "I don't believe in throwing it out for the new." [46] Although she is not as eloquent as the transcendentalists, she is no less reluctant to see machines invade the garden. She is sensitive to a new consciousness of change accompanied by loss that makes even the simplest machine an ominous portent of worse to come.

Her hostile attitude toward the proposition that all technological "internal improvement" is necessary and beneficial is highlighted in her conflict with the canal company. It was agreed by the merchants and civil leaders that Americus stood in desperate need of one of the new navigable canals to keep alive local commerce and to compete with the other industrial cities in the state. Sayward is incensed when she learns that the canal route decided on would traverse her hard-earned land; but after a brief struggle

[44]   *Walden*, pp. 82-83 .
[45]   *The Fields*, p. 137.
[46]   *The Town*, p. 92.

she acquiesces, realizing that it is impossible to "fight the whole state and town to boot". Sick over the mutilation of her beloved land, her crops trampled down by the celebration crowd, Sayward sits stonily through the fourth of July commemoration speeches and toasts to "internal improvements" with the bitter taste of defeat in her mouth. Yet even in her bitterness she is amused at the expansionist devotion to progress reflected in the commemoration toasts. The first toast-master stands with raised glass and solemnly speaks.

The Fourth of July. The worthies of the Revolution on this day commenced the system of Internal improvement by breaking ground on the line of our Political Independence.

So that was it, Sayward told herself. Before they got through, they would have God Almighty making the first canal with his flood and Noah a building the first canal boat . . . Even Washington, she told herself, was not the father of his country anymore. No, he had to be the Father of Public Works and Internal Improvement.[47]

The final irony comes not too many years later when those who had supported the canal as the ultimate in commercial transportation turned their support to the incoming railroad. In time the canal, an ugly scar across Sayward's land, is hopelessly out of date, but not before it has permanently drained the beautiful creek that formerly graced Sayward's farm. Progress may be essential, but it profanes much of what it touches.

The railroad is even more distressing to Sayward than the canal, and the scene describing the arrival of the locomotive is a forceful statement of the machine in the garden, a bitter indictment of the anti-pastoral forces in technological advancement. Richter had already used the train as symbolic of technology's destruction of the past in his early short story, "Smoke Over the Prairie", in which Gant, the stubborn pioneer protagonist, loses his race with the locomotive and is crushed at the crossing. In the Ohio trilogy, Richter avoids such a melodramatic confrontation between the pastoral past and the industrial present, and concentrates rather on creating an undercurrent of foreboding

[47] *Ibid.*, p. 133.

and doom within an atmosphere of celebration and optimism. The day the train arrives has been set aside as a festive occasion; yet the engine's noisy presence brings a disturbing sense of destruction into the quiet tranquility of the village street, and Sayward sees the engine as a demonic agency of destruction.

Black and besotted, with a vicious iron point in front to cut you to pieces and a fierce stack belching smoke and fire, it looked like it came from where canal folks claimed, the pits of hell. On the side in sulphurous letters was the monster's name, SHAWANEE.[48]

Although members of the younger generation are filled with joy and excitement, the older pioneers stare at the engine "as if doomsday was at hand", and the physical presence of the locomotive brings Sayward a fresh awareness of immutable change and a sense of her own mortality.

Sayward's motives for resisting what the party of progress believes to be beneficial to mankind are seldom understood. To the townsmen she is a selfish anachronism, and even her youngest son's first published poem is a broad lampoon called "The Frog's Petition", which cruelly satirizes her for her refusal to permit the city to drain her Beaver Gats so that the industrial area could be extended. "When she wanted her land drained, she said, she would drain it herself." But her fierce independence is caricatured and ridiculed as her own youngest son turns against her the refrain which satirically calls for a "Return unto the status quo / of forty, fifty years ago." [49]

An ethics of austerity is one of renunciation. Thoreau and Emerson, as did Richter a hundred years later – and Sayward of the trilogy – perceived that although the decay of modernity may have many causes, one of the most important was, and is, the spirit of commerce, the growth of industrialism and the attendant appeal of the utilitarian ethic in private and public morality. To the transcendentalist, the most alarming effect of the growth of industrialism is the subordinating of all values to those of economics and technical progress. "The idea that if a thing is good

[48]   *Ibid.*, p. 380.
[49]   *Ibid.*, p. 314.

for a few people it must be better for a great many has taken over", writes Richter, "an idea dear to American progress and so fatal to beauty and charm." [50] Change, Richter reluctantly admits, is in large part irresistible, and chances are that "modern economics will probably win". In the meantime, man has a "choice between beauty and economics, charm and decay" by affirming a primitivistic ethic of austerity within the intellectual framework of transcendental thought. At its best, this affirmation of a choice is a feeble rear-guard action, a restatement of the transcendental revolt against materialism. Overtones of a tragic necessity in the inevitable dissolution of the human spirit in the age of technology, however, transform Richter's forward-looking restorative impulse into a lamentation of regret.

5. THE OHIO TRILOGY AS NOVEL OF THE SOIL

One of the most significant literary traditions to which the Ohio trilogy is related is that of the novel of the soil, a regionalist and pastoral tradition characterized by an affirmation of primitivist and transcendentalist values, and a consequent criticism of a false conception of the good life. Although the term "novel of the soil" was used in literary criticism during the period of the Southern agrarian reform to define a particular kind of protest in literary regionalism, it is a term that needs clarification.[51] The novel of the soil has been defined as "a special kind of regionalism in the novel in which the lives of people struggling for existence in remote rural sections are starkly portrayed" in the manner of realism or naturalism.[52] This definition unfortunately tends to restrict the type to such novels as Ellen Glasgow's *Barren Ground*,

---

[50] "Three Towns I Love", p. 58.
[51] N.B. It is hardly necessary to point out that the most significant concepts in regionalism were first articulated by the Southern agrarians, who redefined Jeffersonian principles and set forth a set of cultural and economic preferences to offset the growing system of large scale industrialism. See Donald Davidson, *The Attack on Leviathan* (Chapel Hill, 1938).
[52] William Flint Thrall and Addison Hibbard, *A Handbook to Literature* (New York, 1960), p. 325.

O. E. Rölvaag's *Giants in the Earth*, or Elizabeth Madox Roberts's *The Time of Man*, in which the struggle with the stubborn earth nearly overwhelms the reader with a sense of tragic futility and pessimism, even though he is led to see that this struggle elicits from the characters the integrity, self-respect, and strength needed to endure and triumph in the face of the bitter ordeals on the land.

But the temper of a novel of the soil such as the Ohio trilogy is more optimistic to the same extent that it is more primitivistic. It shows how life in a natural environment (in the case of the trilogy, the pioneer, rural, and village community of Moonshine Church) creates and indelibly marks the people living in it. The rural environment is symbolic of the natural order in the world, that is, the example of a universe in which an infinite number of independent forces concur so as to produce an order behind which can be detected the presence of an intelligent power.

This awakens in man the true stoic conception of *amor fati*: love of the order of the world. True stoicism, Simone Weil reminds us in her remarkable book, *The Need for Roots*, is based on the conception that the universe in which we find ourselves is above all perfect obedience to the will of the Creator. Thus,

The order of the world is to be loved because it is pure obedience to God. Whatever this universe accords us or inflicts on us, it does so exclusively out of obedience of this universe to God, places us in contact with the absolute good formed by the divine will; in virtue of this, everything without any exception, joys and sorrows alike, ought to be welcomed with the same inward attitude of love and thankfulness.[53]

Whenever a technological and commercial spirit invades the natural environment, the sense of a natural order is necessarily obscured or diminished. The environment is therefore more than a mere background; it becomes a key actor in the human drama. It participates in the action as a physical force making a distinct impression upon the mind and sensibilities of the characters, and

---

[53] Simone Weil, *The Need for Roots*, trans. Arthur Wells (Boston, 1952), p. 289.

as a total way of life – a set of values and manners and a frame of mind – which molds character and destiny.

One of the most important themes in a novel of the soil, therefore, is the vital relationship of man and nature. When man lives a life close to the earth, that is, facing nature directly and trusting her for a physical means of life (which means accepting her on her own terms and likely as not implies some form of constant, but satisfying, struggle), he has bred into him a spiritual contentment with work and life, and a kinship with nature that cannot be easily obtained in an urbanized environment.

The pioneer, the peasant, the farmer – i.e., anyone in personal contact with the elemental life – thus becomes the elemental figure, the symbol of man at his best, in direct and immediate intimacy with the creative power of reproduction and growth. When men are drawn into natural association one with another under these circumstances, there then occurs the organic growth of true community from the soil.

In addition, of course, the novel of the soil treats of other equally primitive and what may be called regionalist pastoral themes, most of which are overlapping: the superiority of the simple life, the spirituality of work and its value for happiness, the love of independence and self-reliance, the lack of deference to materialism and the profit motive, and the importance of roots as symbolized by attachment to the land, respect for tradition, and reverence for the past.

The concept of rootedness in the novel of the soil cannot be overstressed; Weil's belief in the importance of rootedness as a vital need of the human soul comes close to defining this concept:

To be rooted is perhaps the most important and least recognized need of the human soul. It is one of the hardest to define. A human being has roots by virtue of his real, active, and natural participation in the life of the community, which preserves in living shapes certain particular expectations for the future. Every human being needs to have multiple roots. It is necessary for him to draw well-nigh the whole of his moral, intellectual, and spiritual life by way of the environment of which he forms a natural part.[54]

[54] Weil, p. 43.

The values listed above, then, including the need for roots, are affirmed. But at the same time the novel of the soil implies a judgment of what is *not* of the soil. In short, it is a protest against those forces that would uproot man and deprive him of important primitive and traditional values. It is thus an implicit and explicit protest against the sterile pretensions of urban civilization.

Because of this protest, the novel of the soil takes on added social significance. It is almost a commonplace to recite the problems which the twentieth century has forced on the artist: man's dissociation and loss, the sterility of love and religion, the breakdown of tradition and the forces of convention and ties to family and community, the impact of the machine age and the crass materialism of modern life. Yet most contemporary fiction has been, and will probably continue to be, concerned with these same problems. Blanche Gelfant tells us that "The comprehensive theme of city fiction is personal dissociation: the prototype for the hero is the self-divided man. Dissociation is a pathological symptom which results from, and reflects, a larger social disorder." [55]

A recurring theme in the regional literature of economic and social protest – which includes the novel of the soil – has been rebellion against the economic motives of modern industrialism, which regionalist critics have felt to be the chief source of this larger social disorder reflected by the dissociation of modern man. Donald Davidson charges in *The Attack on Leviathan* that cosmopolitanism and industrialism – toward which American life has long been tending – have been marked by one signal defect: they "abstracted the economic function from its old place in the complex of human activities and made it the chief, and almost the only important, member of the hierarchy of social functions". [56]

It is true that this devotion to economic purpose has given man a higher standard of living; but, continues the regionalist argument, there is evidence that this has been accomplished at great

[55]   Blanche Housman Gelfant, *The American City Novel* (Norman, 1954), p. 21.
[56]   *The Attack on Leviathan*, p. 73.

cost to man's humanity and self-respect, ripping him from his roots and destroying his natural ties with tradition and the past, standardizing his mores by the sheer driving power of economic motive alone.[57]

As art, the novel of the soil can be a powerful expression of primitivistic and pastoral ideals, and as such, a compelling force in literary regionalism. By regionalism, of course, is meant – besides its implications for social criticism – something much more than local color in fiction. It implies not only that the artist must look at life from the vantage point he knows best, that is, through his own traditions, heritage, and experience, but also that he has a preference for certain aspects of this heritage and tradition which he fears is being challenged or endangered by some change in the human condition.[58]

Regionalist artists, Davidson has pointed out, were among the first to come to this realization:

... some of the dilemmas of an industrial civilization may be downed or avoided by reaffirming ties, local and native, which were once only shackles to be cast off. In its undeniable nostalgia this sectionalism contains a realistic answer to the question *"Whom shall my soul believe?"* Worn out with abstraction and novelty, plagued with divided counsels, some Americans have said "I will believe the old folks at home, who have kept alive through many treacherous outmodings some good secret of life ..." [59]

Regionalism in the novel of the soil, then, denotes the recreation in fiction of those social reactions characteristic of rural, village, and small town communities with a sustained suggestion that in

---

[57] Cf. Weil: "Money destroys human roots wherever it is able to penetrate, by turning desire for gain into the sole motive. It easily manages to outweigh all other motives because the effort it demands of the mind is so very much less" (p. 44).

[58] Richter's fondness for the simpler life of rural or small village communities was intensified by his own firsthand knowledge of what an industrial life is like. Much of his youth was spent in the coal-mining regions of Pennsylvania. For a time he worked as a clerk in the mammoth Westinghouse plant in Pittsburgh. Later he worked as a reporter on the Pittsburgh *Dispatch*, and his knowledge of the industrial life in the steel capital of America is not superficial.

[59] Davidson, p. 11.

these communities we may discover certain enduring values which are well-nigh becoming extinct elsewhere. But the emphasis is partly on the destructive elements of city life and is an indictment of the assumptions of modern progress for which the city has become the social expression and place of culture. In the twofold thematic structure of affirmation-protest, the regionalist codes of ethics and behavior are set off against those prevailing in the more cosmopolitan or urbanized centers. The rooted are set off against the rootless.

One way to highlight the Ohio trilogy's relationship to this regionalist tradition is briefly to show its thematic correspondence to a very fine novel of the soil, and one which may well serve as a prototype, Knut Hamsun's *Growth of the Soil*.[60] In almost Biblical simplicity and power, in the idiom of the region, both the trilogy and Hamsun's novel describe the development of a homestead out of the wilds and trace the growth of that alliance which develops between nature and man when he faces her directly, receiving spiritual and physical strength from his foothold upon the earth.

Growth of the Soil is divided into two books, the first providing the basis of values to be affirmed, the second describing the threat posed to these values by a commercial way of life. The meaning of the novel is implied in the contrasts between, on the one hand, those characters whose values and way of life are shaped by the land, and, on the other, those who represent the destructive influence of an urbanized environment. This meaning is made more explicit by the narrator's tempered comments, and by the critical evaluation of one of the characters, the perceptive but rootless Geissler.

The true tillers of the soil such as Isak and his son, Sivert, and Isak's wife, Inger (except for her partial dissociation following her sojourn in the city) embody the affirmative themes. Life in the wilds of Norway is constant activity, the work hard, and

---

[60] Knut Hamsun, *Growth of the Soil* (1917), trans. W. W. Worster (New York, 1921). Hereafter referred to as *Growth*. N.B. Hamsun's peasant novels are mentioned by Davidson in *The Attack on Levithan* (p. 71), as examples of a growing literature of protest against cosmopolitanism.

survival made possible only by developing a stoic conception of *amor fati*, and by practicing the simple virtues of frugality, simplicity, self-reliance, integrity, faithfulness, and honesty. These characters' relationship with nature awakens within them a spiritual sensitivity and provides adumbrations of something beyond. Sivert exemplifies the growth of this sensitivity by his felt kinship with the animals.

He knew the wether from the day when it had been a lamb, he under stood it and was one with it – a kinsman, a fellow creature. Once, a strange primitive impression flickered through his senses: it was a moment he never forgot. The wether was grazing quietly in the field; suddenly it threw up its head, stopped munching, simply stood there looking out. Sivert looked involuntarily in the same direction. No – nothing remarkable. But Sivert himself felt something strange within him; " 'Tis most as if he stood looking into the garden of Eden," he thought.[61]

In time the community of settlers increases as others are attracted to the wilds, but the keynote is independence, even within the sense of community kinship. Isak's felt responsibility to his family, his animals, and his land develops out of an attachment to a way of life and a set of values that grow with the soil.

In the Ohio trilogy, *The Trees* and *The Fields* constitute Richter's affirmation of the primitivistic values elicited by the frontier and agrarian environment. To recite the common problems and hardships which draw the settlers into a close-knit group is to recite the major episodes of the novels (e.g., the collective sense of need expressed in the building of Moonshine Church, the drought which sends the fathers and sons to Kentucky for food, the community's sympathetic involvement in Sulie's disappearance, Guerdon's snakebite, and Jude MacWhirter's death, the cooperative spirit expressed in the cabin-raisings and log-burnings, and so forth).

Our attention is always drawn to Sayward or some immediate member of her family, however, since the narrative is primarily concerned with the development of her consciousness. Sayward, as the representative pioneer, stands for the others in the growth

61   *Growth*, I, p. 167.

of her spiritual sensitivity. She becomes conscious of the cosmic destiny working in the affairs of men and nature, and she thus develops the stoic conception of obedience to the order in the world (e.g., her conception of Providence and her fear of interference in the destiny of others). Her knowledge of, and respect for, the transcendent power behind nature we have seen to be the result of her immediate contact with the forest and the earth, and the dominant note of the story, like that of Hamsun's, is quiet and patient strength, the will and the ability to endure, triumph in the face of adversity, and spiritual and cultural autonomy.

The second part of a novel of the soil is the protest which highlights the affirmative values by juxtaposing them against the debilitating effects of an urbanized and commercial way of life. Hamsun's protest is directed against the demoralization of character and dissociation of personality that take place in the city. First this is traced in Inger's change after her eight-year prison stay in Bergen (symbolically, she has been a prisoner of the city). Soon after her return Isak notices the change: "Inger – was she really grown so different in her heart through living among folks from the towns? The fact was that Inger had changed a good deal; she thought now less of their common good than of herself." [62] Inger has not only become self-centered, she is now physically weaker, lazier, given to gossip and idleness, unfaithful, and impressed with social rank as measured by wealth and the accumulation of material goods.

Inger has been corrupted by the urban community in Bergen, but slowly she is restored to her former scheme of values by the subtle influences of the land. "No one can live in the depths of the wilds and have time for such foolishness", the narrator comments editorially. "Happiness and nonsense are two different things." [63]

The second most detailed and graphic portrayal of character degeneration, this time irrevocable, is that of the oldest son, Eleseus. When Eleseus's small talent with letters is encouraged by a telegraph company engineer, Inger persuades Isak to let the boy go to town and study to be a clerk. But Eleseus's long sojourn in

[62]   *Ibid.*, p. 229.
[63]   *Ibid.*

the city during his formative years proves disastrous. He becomes a cheat, a spendthrift, shallow and lazy, and is described as a town dandy and fop with no depth, no grip, and no originality – in short, he is badly dissociated: "His town life had wrought a schism in himself, and made him finer than the others, made him weaker; he began indeed to feel that he must be homeless anywhere." [64] Eleseus is a failure and Hamsun tells us plainly the reason for this failure. The boy had started well enough but had been turned into "an artificial atmosphere, and warped, transformed".

Something unfortunate, ill-fated about this young man, as if something were rotting him from within. The engineer from the town, good man – better perhaps, if he had not discovered the lad in his youth and taken him up to make something out of him; the child has lost his roothold, and suffered thereby. All that he turns to now leads him back to something wanting in him, something dark against the light. . . .[65]

The contrast between the rooted and the rootless is sharply focused when commercial mining operations begin in the area, a contrast which is highlighted by the juxtaposition of diametrically opposed value systems, the one based on a self-sufficient agrarianism and the other on a delicately balanced economic system.[66]

To those who embrace commercial and cosmopolitan values, money is the object most in demand. Aronsen, a man who formerly owned a small village fishery, comes to the community with dreams of wealth. To realize these dreams he opens a store which caters to the needs of the miners, and not only their needs, but their whims (the miners show little discretion about what they purchase, being overcome quite readily by what glitters and dazzles). But Aronsen's reverence for the power of money is a

<hr />

[64] *Ibid.*, II, p. 19.
[65] *Ibid.*, p. 231.
[66] Cf. Davidson: An industrial system "must depend upon a scheme of correlations and balances vast in extension but delicate and complicated in their inner workings. Without pure devotion to economic purpose at every point in the gigantic scheme of manufacturing and distribution, the whole thing may break down, like an automobile stalled on the road by the failure of some part" (p. 73).

source of amusement to the local farmers. For example, his unsuccessful attempt to buy hay from one of the farmers who really
had none to spare is recounted mirthfully:

" 'Ho, d'you mean you don't want to make money?' said Aronsen.
Thinks money's everything in the world, seems like. Puts down a
hundred *Krone* note on the counter, and says 'Money!' 'Ay, Money's
well enough,' says I. 'Cash down' says he. Ay he's just a bit touched
that way, so to speak. ..." [67]

Aronsen's business flourishes for a time, but his affluence depends
upon the only commercial enterprise in the area, the copper
mine. When the mine folds and later reopens on the other side of
the mountain, he is forced to follow it and set up another store,
which later also fails when the second mining operation abruptly
closes down. The mine is forced to close when it cannot meet the
competition of lower prices from the copper mines in another part
of the world. Villagers, who are fairly content before the coming
of the mines, neglect their land for the more lucrative mining
jobs; but when the shutdown comes, they, like Aronsen, are left
with no way to maintain the high standard of living they have
come to expect as their right in the world, and they become dis-
gruntled and unhappy. The followers of the commercial enterprise are thus shown to be subject to the instability of world
markets, victims of forces beyond their power or comprehension.
    The novel's chief critic of the rootlessness inherent in the
commercial and urban way of life is one who ironically is caught
up in its tangled web – Geissler, the land speculator who is always
on the move, attending to his projects in Sweden and Norway
(and particularly his investments in the copperrich land on Isak's
farm). Geissler, although profiting materially from it, detests his
way of life. Modern man, he points out, having "learned all the
Jew and the Yankee can teach", is quick like lightning; but
lightning is destructive. The lust for wealth is like a disease,
crippling the soul; and when life crushes them, modern men com-
plain against it. Life should not be raged against, however: "Not

[67]   *Growth*, II, p. 118.

be stern and strict and just with life, but be merciful to it, and take its part. . . ." [68]

In Hamsun's most eulogistic passage, Geissler sets forth to Sivert his belief in the efficacy of a life on the soil:

Look at you folk at Sellanraa, now; looking up at blue peaks every day of your lives; no new-fangled inventions about that, but field and rocky peaks rooted deep in the past – but you've them for companionship. There you are, living in touch with heaven and earth, one with them, one with all these wide, deep-rooted things . . . Look, Nature's there for you and yours to have and enjoy. Man and Nature don't bombard each other, but go together; they don't compete, race one against the other, but go together . . . You've everything to live for, everything to believe in, being born and bringing forth, you are the needful on earth . . . What do you get out of it? An existence innocently and properly set towards all . . . Nothing can put you under orders and lord it over you.[69]

The tiller of the soil, affirms Hamsun, is a "ghost risen out of the past to point the future . . .", a man who has his powers above, his independence, his dreams, his loves, and his wealth of super-stitions.[70]

In the Ohio trilogy, the protest begins quite naturally in the third novel, *The Town*. Richter, as did Hamsun, realizes that the real enemy to traditional values is the inflated importance eco-nomic theory wins in our modern scheme of values. Thus the protest in *The Town* begins with Sayward's dissatisfaction with, and sense of alienation from, the "town breed", particularly be-cause their scheme of values is predicated by economic motive alone. During a meeting held at the Wheeler cabin to decide on a new name for the growing town, Sayward is struck by the contrast of its careful efficiency and brisk businesslike air with the meet-ings of the past. In the old days, because of the sense of commu-nity kinship, the thrust of the meetings – even those called for taxing purposes – was social; and when the meetings were over your "insides warmed and your hearts stretched" and "you felt like a brother and sister to all".

[68]   *Ibid.*, p. 246.
[69]   *Ibid.*, pp. 243-244.
[70]   *Ibid.*, p. 252.

Now these men tonight at Moonshine Church were different, town bodies, reckoning town things. Figures of money and time and such entered their talk. Hardly one spoke that he didn't mention so many dollars or hours and days it took to do something or so many boats tied up last week at one time and how many tons they carried. They were good enough folks and friendly to her and Portius . . . but they weren't the settler folks she and Portius used to know in the woods in the old days.[71]

In another conventional, yet delightfully contrived scene, the old ragged hunter, Worth Luckett, is the voice of protest. When complimented by Portius's Eastern sister, Cornelia, for opening up the country, he angrily retorts that he never would have, had he known what the Easterners would do with the land:

"And what do they want with it? Why, they want to make it just like the country they left back East. Already they've put in flour mills and wool mills and saw mills and fullin mills and all kinds of mills . . .!" He was hollering now. "Money, that's what they're crazy about. Money!" [72]

Of course the old hunter speaks as a woodsman who distrusts the settled pastoral life of the farmer as much as he does the commercial life of the townsman and therefore he cannot fully represent Richter's sympathies. Nevertheless he dramatizes Richter's sensitivity to the motive behind what the townsmen call the "progress of civilization" – i.e., the profit motive.

Portius, unlike Sayward, lacks any moral referents by which to judge the growth of the town. A native of Massachusetts, already a growing industrial state when he left it, he apparently has accepted the growth of towns and factories without questioning whether or not technological growth was invariably good. Sayward, on the other hand, has begun to see the social and personal implications of the machine age. Although she tries to live above the commercial spirit of the town, she is constantly galled by the necessity to give way little by little to the growth of the industrial city. The town swiftly becomes a crowded metropolis, filled with laborers who staff the increasing number of industries: the pack-

71 *The Town*, p. 52.
72 *Ibid.*, p. 238.

ing houses, looking glass works, cotton factory, comb factory, shipping houses, and others.

In time she finds herself ailing from a malaise which she finally traces to her deep dissatisfaction with the townsmen. It was "the pride and greed and great shakes of these town bodies that bothered her. Nothing was good enough for them anymore." [73] She chafed at the catapulting taxes which went for services she had not solicited. But her main source of annoyance was to see her beautiful old residential square, once spacious and tree-filled, transformed into an ugly market place by the merchants. (Her own mansion she stubbornly refuses to sell to be cut up into shops.) There are no limits to the insatiable demands of industrial expansion. "They even tried to buy the old cemetary and put up a bank and hardware store on the graves. Nothing could stop progress, they said, not even 'Mrs. Wheeler's mother's bones.' " [74] Nothing is too sacred for the townsmen to profane if by doing so they can realize a quick profit.

Chancey, like Eleseus in *Growth of the Soil*, represents the dissociated and rootless youth produced by an urban way of life. Chancey is over-protected and mollycoddled because of his weak physical condition, a circumstance which Richter shows to be a serious hindrance to his development. Reliant on others, resentful of work which he felt degrading both to mankind in general and to one in his social position in particular, Chancey grows into adulthood openly skeptical of and hostile to his mother's scheme of values. He is blind to his own self-pity and lack of depth and grip which have resulted from his deliberate and hostile rejection of the traditions, wisdom, experience, and teaching of the older generation; he is oblivious to the fact that he has cut himself off from values that are essential.

Simone Weil observes that for those people who are really uprooted, there are only two modes of behavior to choose from: "either to fall into spiritual lethargy resembling death . . ., or to hurl themselves into some form of activity necessarily designed

[73] *Ibid.*, p. 272.
[74] *Ibid.*, p. 273.

to uproot . . . those who are not yet uprooted, or only partly so".[75] Chancey gravitates toward the second mode. Not only does he reject the spiritual heritage from the past that his mother could have given him, but he also religiously tries to bury his heritage. In an impassioned speech to important conservative leaders of the infant state of Ohio, he tells them bitterly,

You gentlemen speak of the past. But the past is dead and gone. Soon you old men who belong to it will be gone, too. Only youth will be left. The old can never understand the problems of the youth. Only youth itself can. Youth is the native of its own times and carries with it the key to its own salvation.[76]

But all his attempts to "plough . . . these stick-in-the-muds loose from their earthy roots" fail, and he remains until his partial recovery at the end of the novel a pathetic example of the root-less, dissociated man who has experienced the breakdown of community and family ties; he reflects that ineffectuality of both love and religion which undeniably are symptoms of a larger disorder in our society.

Richter is criticizing the tendency of the present to hold the past in contempt. In our devotion to progress in the materialistic sense, he is suggesting, we have lost respect for the past as the record of providential purpose. An eternal chain of duty links the present generation with the past and the future, and we have no right irrevocably to alter the shape of things, or – in contempt of our ancestors and the rights of posterity – to ignore a spiritual heritage long in building. Deliberately ignoring the past will condemn us to repeat its mistakes. "Loss of the past, whether it be collectively or individually, is the supreme human tragedy", writes Simone Weil, "and we have thrown ours away just like a child picking off the petals of a rose." [77]

---

[75] *Weil*, p. 47.
[76] *The Town*, p. 387.
[77] Weil, p. 118. N.B. Weil further observes: "It would be useless to turn one's back on the past in order simply to concentrate on the future. It is a dangerous illusion to believe that such a thing is even possible. The opposition of future to past or past to future is absurd. The future brings us nothing, gives us nothing; it is we who in order to build it have to give it everything, our very life. But to be able to give, one has to possess; and

Richter's criticism of our neglect of the past, and hence of the spiritual treasures accumulated by those who have preceded us, has an undeniable validity, but to recall the past too often, if it is turned into a unique source of comfort in the face of present instability and misfortune, is no more than escape and can do a great deal of harm. Desire to preserve a vanishing way of life, when predicated as it is by Richter's deep strain of nostalgia and resentment at the relentless erosion of time leads to his idealizing the past and unfortunately, commitment to "the past for the sake of the past" can arrest genuine amelioration in the human condition and be as dangerous as the equally fallacious commitment to "progress for the sake of progress".

As in all questions of good judgment, a proper balance must be struck, and the importance of Richter's criticism is that his nostalgic reaction does call attention to the weakness in our modern predilection both to consider the past as dead and useless for the present, and to favor change for the sake of change. Certainly there is very little danger that our society is guilty of broadly idealizing the past to the neglect of the present, and Richter's reaction is a healthy reminder of our debt to our heritage.

As a writer, Richter's purpose is to communicate a personal discovery about his world, a discovery which he interprets in terms of his psycho-energic theories of creative evolution. But the implications of those theories, we have seen, have led him to affirm conventional and traditional primitivistic values, and have provided him with a particular historic image and point of view. As a social chronicle with a distinct thematic structure of affirmation and protest, the Ohio trilogy does place certain of today's social problems in an historical perspective, and it does explore their development over a period of time in an attempt to trace cause and effect. By contrasting the rural and the urban and by showing the progressive breakdown of traditional values that has accompanied the growth of urban values, the Ohio trilogy as an

---

we possess no other life, no other living sap, than the treasures stored up from the past and digested, assimilated and created afresh by us. Of all the human soul's needs, none is more vital than this one of the past" (p. 51).

historical novel of the soil successfully and movingly recreates the historical process of change by which the pioneer village became an industrial city. It also offers an interpretation and judgment of this rapid historical change – particularly of its by-product, the rootlessness of modern man.

6. THE HISTORICAL NOVEL AND THE ART OF FICTION

Richter's literary reputation rests in large part on his remarkable achievement in the genre of the historical novel. Critics and reviewers have long acclaimed his skill and craftsmanship in his fictional recovery of the past.[78] But the genre of the historical novel has long admitted of many levels of achievement; its perennial popularity has caused numbers of untalented and unskilled craftsmen to turn out scores of inferior novels, a state of affairs which has done much to bring the genre into ill repute.

It would seem advisable, therefore, to conclude this chapter by briefly defining the kind of historical fiction to which Richter's trilogy relates. For the Ohio trilogy is within a newer tradition of historical fiction which has, in the past three decades, captured the attention of the critics and won for itself a more respectable place in modern American literature. It is neither feasible nor necessary to trace in detail the emergence of the more significant historical novel; it will be enough to set forth the broad requirements of the genre, and to suggest briefly the essential characteristics which distinguish the inferior and commonplace historical novel so much with us from the real thing, and thus to gain an understanding of how Richter's craftsmanship and special talents combine to make of the Ohio trilogy a significant contribution to the genre.[79]

[78]   E.g., Carpenter, pp. 77-83; Kohler, pp. 363-368; Prescott, pp. 133-145; and Sutherland, pp. 413-422.

[79]   I am especially indebted to two studies of the historical novel for the discussion to follow: Ernest Leisy's *The American Historical Novel* (Norman, 1950), and R. M. Bertram's doctoral essay, "The Novel of America's Past: A Study of Five American Historical Novelists, 1925-1950" (unpublished Doctoral dissertation, The University of Michigan, Ann Arbor, 1954).

It is important to realize that the good historical novel is subject to the same demands made of all good fiction. But it is no less important to understand that it is subject to special requirements. The most general technical characteristic of the genre is the concept of past time in the sense of identifiable time, place and historical agent (such as a person, an event, or a clearly recognizable social, political, or economic phenomenon).

The action must be laid in the past anterior to the novelist's personal experience so that for knowledge of that past time – its authenticities and details, its cultural patterns and social climate – he must rely on research into the documents of the era. Although he is dealing with facts gleaned from these sources, it is understood that the novelist is free to take certain liberties with them in order to create that sustained illusion which is the essence of fictional truth. It is his responsibility as historian not to violate historical fact; but it is his responsibility as novelist to inform historical fact with a significance derived from his own observation of basic human truths.

It has become customary to divide the historical novel into three categories: the historical or costume romance (in the complete tradition of the romance), the period novel, which is more concerned with background details than with the whole of life, and the historical novel proper, which integrates character and setting and strikes an artistic balance in blending historical fact and fiction.[80]

If such a classification seems too arbitrary, a more reasonable division would simply be to differentiate between the earlier – and still extant – tradition of the historical romance, and the more recent tradition of the serious and realistic historical novel which

---

[80] Cf. Leisy, p. 18. Orville Prescott goes even farther in dividing the genre into five categories: *In My Opinion* (New York, 1952), p. 128. N.B. One of the significant defects of Leisy's classification of the historical novel, according to Kenneth Murdock, is Leisy's failure to distinguish "between tales in which the emphasis is on the depiction of the historical past and those in which it is on the development of a philosophical theory, the analysis of a mind or moral dilemma, or the presentation of characters and occurrences as symbols of values and issues not limited by time", Review of Leisy's *American Historical Novel, American Literature*, XXII (January 1951), p. 527.

self-consciously, although not always successfully, seeks to avoid the excesses of romance while subjecting itself to the more rigid requirements demanded by the art of fiction. Within this newer tradition, three distinct types may be defined: fictional biography, fictional accounts of great events with recognizable historical personages, and the realistic historical narrative peopled with fictional characters who, set apart from the noise and thunder of specific historical events, are preoccupied only with living their own lives from day to day, and whose significance is thus self-contained.

The majority of the historical novels, unfortunately, follow in the tradition of historical or costume romance.[81] In historical romance the emphasis is on action, on exciting narratives of adventure and love. Characters are usually accurately costumed, but for the most part they are wooden puppets unrealistically made to serve the action.

Historical romances are marked by the strong tendency to turn to improbable, melodramatic, and often cheaply sensational plots which may or may not be based on extensive research. As costume romance, of course, they have a certain appeal: i.e., for their pageantry, for their adventure, and for the escape they provide from the problems of a troubled present into an enchanted past where all conflicts are resolved. But seldom if ever are they triumphs of art and realism: the plots sprawl, the narratives lack compactness and cohesion, and the styles lack either grace or distinction.[82]

---

[81]   Earlier examples of the historical romance would include the adventure stories of William Gilmore Simms, Maurice Thompson's *Alice in Old Vincennes*, Charles Major's *When Knighthood Was in Flower*, and those romances of the Revolution and the Civil War by Winston Churchill. More recent novelists in this tradition include Ben Ames Williams, Kathleen Windsor, and Thomas Costain. Its tendencies, of course, can be seen in novelists of considerable achievement such as James Boyd and Kenneth Roberts.

[82]   Historical romances continue to be marked by these general faults. For a discussion of the structural deficiencies, prolixity, sensationalism, and brutality that still prevail in the modern historical romance, despite its "greater fidelity to psychological truth and more scientific documentation of material to guarantee historical accuracy", see Harlan Hatcher's "The

The shift away from historical romance to the more serious historical novel cannot, of course, be neatly pinned down. It began with those novelists who turned to the study of the past for other reasons than to exploit it for adventure and action, or to glorify and to sentimentalize it. Bertram has shown in his study of five novelists of America's past that more serious and competent craftsmen are turning their attention to the study of history for fictional materials on the assumption that the people and the problems of the past were much like those of the present, and with the conviction that the present generation should learn from their predecessors the importance of studying itself and meeting its obligations with courage and realism.

The shift to a more mature historical fiction is, from a literary point of view, extremely encouraging, especially as the novels become increasingly oriented toward realism. Historical writing, Bernard De Voto has pointed out, is following "the preference of the time for realistic writing, psychological inquiry, and social judgment in fiction".[83] Leisy comes essentially to the same conclusion in his study of the American historical novel.[84]

In treating historical materials according to the tenets of realism, novelists are first confronted with the problem of creating the sense of contemporaneity, that "indeterminateness, fluidity, and precariousness" characteristic of the flow of time in the present, while working with characters, details, experience and incidents that clearly belong to the past.[85] This is no small task.

New Vogue of Historical Fiction", *English Journal*, XXVI (December 1937), pp. 775-784.

[83] "Fiction and the Everlasting *IF*", *Harper's Magazine*, CLXXVII (June 1938), p. 42.

[84] Leisy, p. 216: The historical novel has "followed the tenets of realism in psychology and in social awareness".

[85] The historical novel, says Bartram, "reintroduces the dramatic 'if' among the accomplished facts of history, shows how narrowly success is distinguished in its making from failure, and recreates the errors, mischances, and coincidences that have had their part in the making of today. Historical fiction, joining a sound knowledge of the present and of the timeless truths of human character and motive to a careful assessment of past history, introduces indeterminateness, fluidity, and precariousness into the past and so transforms it momentarily into the present" (p. 9).

The realistic novelist strives to create the illusion of life-as-it-is-happening so that we seem to share the experience of the characters rather than simply to view them as actors who appear on stage to perform the historical roles assigned them. The historical novelist has become increasingly aware of his responsibility to recapture the spirit and flavor of an age as revealed in the everyday relations of the people; to this end he has come more and more to rely on the documents of social history.

The introduction of the realistic method, of psychological insight, and of themes of social judgment has not necessarily enabled historical novelists to escape the influence of historical romance, however. Novels recreating the past in terms of recognizable historical personages or recognizable historical events are too often impregnated with romance. Fictional biographies such as Howard Fast's *The Unvanquished* (1942), the story of Washington in the Revolution, *Citizen Tom Paine* (1943), and *The American* (1946), an imaginative biography of John Peter Altgeld, or Kenneth Robert's recreation of great men and great events in stories with fictional heroes and heroines such as *Arundel* (1930), *Rabble in Arms* (1933), and *Northwest Passage* (1937), are cases in point.

Although fictional biography has participated in the trend toward realism and the more serious attempts to weld subject and form into artistically satisfying wholes, the very nature of its subject matter poses serious problems for the novelist. John T. Flanagan, in his survey of the middle western historical novel, detects a significant shift away from the fictional treatment of heroes: "Particularly healthy is the tendency to get away from fictionalized biography of heroes and to democratize the novel by choosing the ordinary citizen as protagonist." [86]

But even so, the novel which makes use of purely fictitious characters drawn from the ranks of ordinary citizenry to tell the story of well-known historical events tends to partake of the romantic tradition. The great historical personages may fall into the background, but we are not permitted to forget that they are present, just off-stage, and shaping events which will embroil the

[86] "The Middle Western Historical Novel", *Journal of the Illinois State Historical Society*, XXXVII (March 1944), p. 46.

fictional hero. The story is usually told from the viewpoint of some private citizen caught up in a moment of public action, usually a national crisis destined to change the course of history. James Boyd's *Drums* (1925) and *Marching On* (1927), and Kenneth Robert's *Oliver Wiswell* (1940), illustrate this type of historical novel.

Long ago Paul Leicester Ford expressed the opinion that the historical novel's appeal lies in the conviction of truth which the mention of real persons, places, and events convey to the mind of the reader.[87] In a superficial way this may be true. But in point of fact, it is difficult to subdue the myths that have grown around historical characters and events, and any treatment of them cannot escape what Andrew Lytle calls their "preterit quality".[88] The dialogue invented and episodes imagined to fill out the "full" story of actual historical personages and events, and the motives inferred to explain the behavior of key participants tend to tax our willing suspension of disbelief and to put a strain on the illusion the author strives to create. It often gives us the uncomfortable feeling that this is, after all, conjecture, only *one* of the possible explanations, only *one* of the ways it might have been; in short, we are made too conscious of the fact that this is nothing more than the novelist's ingenious synthesis of historical fact and imagined probability. There is a constant tension between the fact-fiction synthesis and the feeling for the myths and legends surrounding the personages and events that we inevitably bring to our reading experience. The materials, when concerned with recognizable men and events, do not readily permit of the necessary detachment for imaginative truth.[89]

[87] "The American Historical Novel", *Atlantic Monthly*, LXXX (December 1897), pp. 721-728.
[88] Andrew Lytle, "Caroline Gordon and the Historical Image", *Sewanee River*, LVII (Autumn 1949), p. 560.
[89] Cf. John T. Flanagan, "A Half-Century of Middlewestern Fiction", p. 22: "In most of the novels which deal with [national celebrities] the fame of the man dwarfs the art of the writer. The novelist has difficulty in avoiding genuflections before the imminent greatness of his hero and is equally troubled by the need to humanize him. The usual result is stiff and unconvincing portraiture."

Many historical novelists try to overcome this obstacle by the most exhaustive research and documentary and factual accuracy possible, assuring authoritative raw materials and leaving as few of the actually recorded details to the imagination as possible. Kenneth Roberts and Walter D. Edmonds both exemplify this painfully keen literary conscience.

Roberts' methods of research for his sequence of American historical novels are well known. He read, studied, collated, annotated where possible, all available source materials, made copious notes and detailed summaries, drew or collated extant battle maps and battle plans, studied maps to trace with precision the exact routes traveled by armies, and even visited for firsthand observation the terrain dealt with in his novels. One of his typically documented novels is *Northwest Passage*, in which his use of accurate details, his knowledge of just what Roger's Rangers wore, what jokes they told, how they made their camps and cooked their meat – when they had it – make for an authentic and convincing realism. But the effect is unevenly sustained. "Roberts' best truth and best art", Bertram observes, "are in those taut scenes which describe a few nameless, ragged men going somewhere." [90]

Roberts is too preoccupied with fidelity to historic detail. The minutely detailed mapping out of Rogers' exact route, for example, borders on tedious antiquarianism. Despite Roberts' extensive documentation to insure realism, he often fails to achieve an artistic blending of fact and fiction. Nor does his realistic approach camouflage his intention to vindicate or condemn a person or a cause.

Edmonds perhaps more than Roberts is devoted to the minutiae of factual historical detail. His best known novel is *Drums Along the Mohawk* (1937), the action of which takes place within a seven-year span (the Revolutionary War) in a recognizable valley peopled both with imagined characters and actual personages whose recorded experiences make up part of the novel's action. Edmonds relies heavily on the "authenticity" which comes of

[90]   Bertram, p. 165.

using people who actually lived during that period of American history. (He is careful to list his fictitious characters in an Author's Note.)

As a chronicler of daily life, Edmonds reveals a canvas crowded with people busy doing just what the records tell him people *were* doing between 1776 and 1781 in the Mohawk valley. In his Author's Note, he even tells us that the snow storms, floods, and rains are historically accurate. Although the numerous scenes rendering the minutiae of daily life are usually colorful, Edmonds simply reports too many banal and dull details; he is overcome by the historicity of his materials, and achieves no perspective or foreshortening in his predilection to treat every object with the same emphasis.[91]

A new kind of historical novel has recently been emerging within the genre which reflects an attempt to avoid the weaknesses of fictional biography and fictional accounts of recognizable historical events. For want of a better term, this new type may simply be called the realistic historical narrative. The best of these narratives, such as A. B. Guthrie's gritty and lustily realistic *The Big Sky* (1947), and Conrad Richter's Ohio trilogy, are no less documentary than the novels of Roberts and Edmonds. But it is documentation of a different kind. Guthrie and Richter are both astute students of history. Richter particularly relies on historical materials; but he does not place himself under the obligation of being "historically accurate".[92] And yet no historical novelist has been held in higher esteem by the historians themselves.[93]

Richter's purpose in the trilogy is to shun the names, dates,

---

[91] *Ibid.*, p. 176.
[92] Harry R. Warfel, *American Novelists of Today* (New York, 1951), p. 354.
[93] E.g., Oscar Handlin, an eminent Harvard historian, reveals with what respect Richter is held as a chronicler of social history. "Social history puts a greater strain on literary expression and the sense of balance than any other kind . . . . [Historians] need to improve their human perception as well as their literary style if they except to be the teachers of social history that, for instance, . . . Conrad Richter is." "History as a Literary Art", *Harvard Guide to American History*, eds. Oscar Handlin *et al.* (Cambridge, 1955), p. 47.

and events that, because of their sensational or spectacular aspects, have found their way into the history books. The trilogy, he writes, is about those pioneers "whose names never figured in the history books but whose influence on their own times and country was incalculable". If the trilogy has had any other purpose than to tell some of their story, he continues,

it has been to try to impart to the reader the feeling of having lived for a little while in those earlier days and of having come in contact not with the sound and fury of dramatic historical events that is the fortune of the relative, and often uninteresting, few, but with the broader stuff of reality that was the lot of the greater majority of men and women who, if they did not experience the certain incidents related in these pages, lived through comparable events and emotions, for life is endlessly resourceful and inexhaustible.[94]

Richter does not stress the role of the individual as hero; in his narrative the common man gets the center of the stage, and the individual is subordinated to the family group.

A careful student of the idiom and speech patterns of the pioneers, Richter, like Guthrie in *The Big Sky*, tells his story in the language of the settlers.[95] His remarkable feeling for the authentic pioneer idiom and figures of speech does much to translate us almost bodily into the past to accomplish his purpose of making us feel we have "lived for a little while in those earlier days". The narrative description, the thoughts of the characters, and the realistic dialogue are of a kind; there is never the jarring shift back and forth between the literate narrator and the illiterate characters, no self-conscious solecisms of dialogue so characteristic of the typical pioneer tale. The speech patterns are natural, at times lyrical and possessed of a Biblical simplicity. Nothing reveals Richter's grasp of the peculiar qualities of time and place obtained through the documents better than his skill with the use of the pioneer's language.

Richter's careful research into documents, journals, letters,

[94]   *The Town*, p. ii.
[95]   Cf. Prescott: "But, in contrast to Mr. Richter who comes close to poetry in his use of archaic speech, Mr. Guthrie is harsh and gritty and violent." *In My Opinion*, p. 141.

diaries, newspapers, and social histories to insure the authenticity of material is well known. The acknowledgments of the trilogy reveal the great extent to which he has gone to inform himself of the cultural patterns and social climate of the past.

In a recent interview, Richter revealed that the chief work which "set him on the road" to the Ohio trilogy was "Howe's Historical Recollections" published in the 1840's.[96] A close reading of this rich and monumental work on early Ohio has indicated something of Richter's technique in freely availing himself of historical materials for his authentic fictional recovery of the past. In this one work alone Richter obtained nearly a hundred specific and identifiable details, anecdotes, and incidents which he incorporated into the narrative structure of the trilogy. A representative selection of these historical materials gathered from Howe has been included in an Appendix for further reference, and to give some idea of the "documentary authenticity" of Richter's material.[97]

It is significant to note, however, the kind of historical material available in Howe which Richter did *not* avail himself of. For example, Howe's *Collections* is filled with references to, and accounts of, the following: (1) violent and bloody Indian raids on isolated settlements;[98] (2) the bloody wars which erupted in Ohio in the late seventeen hundreds when Pontiac and Tecumseh united the Indian nations – with British backing – against further encroachments by the whites (including accounts of St. Clair's defeat and Wayne's victory over Tecumseh);[99] (3) incidents re-

[96] John K. Hutchens, "Pine Grove to Pulitzer and Back", p. 11. N.B. The title of this work is *Historical Collections of Ohio*; the interviewer apparently inadvertently added the prefix "Re-".
[97] In this study, the two-volume edition of Henry Howe's *Historical Collections of Ohio* (Cincinnati, 1907) is used.
[98] To be sure, Richter never lets us forget the Indian lurks just in the background, a frightening figure and potential menace. But Richter's intention is to avoid the sensational, and to reveal that undercurrent of tension and restrained emotion felt by the early pioneers, who well knew the constant possibility of Indian harassment.
[99] There is one offhand reference to Wayne's army. Louie Scurrah recounts his experiences when he kept Wayne's army supplied with game during a long seige by hostile Indians. The emphasis, however, is not on Scurrah's participation in the heroic event, but rather on his description of

lated to the War with England in 1812, the military implications of which touch much of Ohio's history (e.g., the fleet Commodore Perry built on Lake Erie and the naval battles fought off Ohio's shores); and (4) accounts of notables like the famous Indian fighter, Lew Wetzel, and the heroic Betty Zane.

The typical historical novel abounds in such events.[100] Indeed, such material could have supplied Richter with action of the most melodramatic possibilities; but he carefully avoids this kind of action so aptly suited for heroic deeds.[101] There is never that pervading sense of sensational history-in-the-making caught by those novelists who, in order to establish authenticity of time and place, feel impelled to touch on such historically significant material. Richter finds Howe's *Collections* a veritable gold mine, not for outstanding facts of history, but for the simpler details of a "broader reality", apart from the "sound and fury of dramatic" historical fact.

Richter defines a story as the record of human achievement; his first task in delineating that achievement in the historical trilogy was, of course, to collect volumes of homely and picturesque details, anecdotes, superstitions, and folklore which he could arrange, order, and synthesize to create a background of authenticities on which to weave his narrative.[102] These are the small authenticities without which life would not have been life

---

his ingenious "coal-pit fire", and how he shot and skinned deer while avoiding discovery by the savages (Scurrah's account is based on solid fact – see Appendix, B, 2).

[100]   John T. Flanagan in his survey, "The Middle Western Historical Novel", shows the popularity of these same materials which have long proved irresistible to historical novelists: e.g., James B. Naylor's *In the Days of St. Clair* (1902), *Under Mad Anthony's Banner* (1903 – Wayne's campaign), and *The Sign of the Prophet* (1901 – Tecumseh); Burton Stevenson's *The Heritage* (1902 – St. Clair and Wayne); Emerson Bennett's *The Pioneer's Daughter* (1851 – St. Clair); Thomas Boyd's *Shadow of Long Knives* (1928 – Wayne); Robert S. Harper's *Trumpet in the Wilderness* (1940 – Perry's Fleet); and Zane Grey's *Betty Zane* (1903 – Lew Wetzel and Betty Zane).

[101]   Cf. Kenneth J. Barnard, "Presentation of the West in Conrad Richter's Trilogy", *Northwest Ohio Quarterly*, XXIX (Autumn 1957), p. 232.

[102]   See Appendix, B, 1-13. Also, see John T. Flanagan, "Folklore in the Novels of Conrad Richter", *Midwest Folklore*, II (Spring, 1952), pp. 5-14.

on the Ohio frontier: the feeling of solitariness evoked by the forest; the way log cabins were raised and furnished; how trees were "ringed", felled, and "niggered off the land", and how the stumps dotted the town streets; the way corn was planted and how the Indians conducted their trading at the post; what the pioneers did to "over" the ague and fever and what they took for rattlesnake bites; what their superstitions were, what made them laugh and sing and cry, and how they welcomed the first circuit rider to bring religion to the settlement; what they did on Independence day and how they fought over the location of the county seat.

The details of setting are not simply described or allowed to accumulate for a total effect; rather they are dramatized as inner experience and by exposing them, opening them to us, Richter thus permits us to enter the lives of his pioneers with greater emotional immediacy. For example, rather than externally describing the dense and terrifying forest of the Ohio wilderness which nearly overwhelms the Lucketts at their arrival, Richter dramatizes as inner experience the confrontation of the scene and thus suggests almost poetically the impact on the family's imagination of the "monstrous butts". He accomplishes this inner dramatization by a sustained metaphor, equating the strange, dark, green subsurface world of uncivilized wilderness to the bottom of the sea.

For a moment Sayward reckoned that her father had fetched them unbeknownst to the Western ocean and what lay beneath was the late sun glittering on green-black water. Then she saw what they looked down on was a dark, illimitable expanse of wilderness. It was a sea of solid tree tops. . . . As far as the eye could reach, this lonely forest sea rolled on and on till its faint blue bellows broke against an incredible distant horizon.[103]

The feeling of looking out over a sea, experienced on the hill from where Sayward receives her vision, soon gives way to a sensation of being "down under the ocean of leaves", and Jary, her mother, views the dark forest as a huge well at the bottom of which the family is trapped.

[103]   *The Trees*, p. 8.

When Richter makes use of recorded detail, he often changes it only slightly. The following account recorded in Howe of a pioneer woman making tea and cakes in one kettle, for example, is lifted almost bodily and fleshed out by Richter to blend it into his narrative:

A year or two after we arrived, a visit was got up by the ladies in order to call on a neighboring family who lived a little out of the common way. The hostess was very much pleased to see them, and immediately commenced preparing the usual treat on such occasions – a cup of tea and its accompaniments. As she had but one fire-proof vessel in the house, an old broken bake kettle, it, of course, must take some time. In the first place some pork was tried up in the kettle to get lard – *secondly*, some cakes were made and fried in it – *thirdly*, some shortcakes were made in it – *fourthly*, it was used as a bucket to draw water – *fifthly*, the water was heated in it; and *sixthly* and lastly, the tea was put in and a very sociable dish of tea had.[104]

In Richter's hands, the anecdote serves to point up the essence of frontier privation, the matter-of-fact "make-do" spirit it engendered in the self-reliant pioneer women, and the significance of human companionship and social intercourse in the lonely Ohio forest. Sayward is visited by a new neighbor lady, Mrs. Covenhoven, and for the first time in her life she is called upon to entertain a guest and to serve refreshments.

"Well," she said, "I'll start a gittin' you some tea – if it's all the same to you."

"Oh, I don't want you to go to any trouble," Mrs. Covenhoven told her.

"It's no trouble," Sayward said. "My big kettle has soap in it. But I ain't a usin' the other."

"Oh, I kin do all I want with one."

Sayward took the small kettle and used it the first time to fry out bear's bacon for shortening she would need later on.

"Almost warm enough for a body to wash their hair," she said.

She used that kettle a second time to bake sour dough biscuit in, after she had poured the shortening in a gourd.

"You and your man have a mess of poke yit?" she made talk again. "It has plenty around."

When the biscuits were done, she used the kettle a third time to fry the shortcake in, first working the fresh shortening in the dough until it was ready.

"Pap got such a nice silver fox last winter," she said. "I wish you could a seed it."

Now she took the kettle a fourth time and used it as a bucket to draw and fetch water from the spring.

"I heered your man's a puttin' up a double cabin?"

"Not that one room isn't big enough for us," Mrs. Covenhoven explained modestly.

"No, one room's got plenty room for the six of us," Sayward agreed.

When the kettle started to simmer, she used it a fifth time, as a teapot, putting in a lick of dittany and sassafras root shavings. Then she poured out a pair of steaming wooden cups and set them with her two bread-stuffs on the trencher. ...

"Tea's done," she said gravely. "You kin draw up your stool." [105]

Richter borrows freely from much larger actual incidents and humorous anecdotes to provide the basis for significant episodes – sometimes the external action for whole chapters – in his trilogy.[106] For instance, Captain Peirce's account of the "great Hinckley Hunt" [107] provides Richter with the complete physical action for chapter six in *The Fields* ("His Own Man"). The chapter describes the organization of a great hunt to wipe out the wolves and bears which have been preying on the farmers' sheep and pigs. Numbering over five hundred men, armed with everything from muskets to butcherknives mounted on poles as lances, the army of hunters forces hundreds of wild animals into a natural conclave of brush and timber and there they kill great numbers of the entrapped beasts. After the hunt, the men celebrate by holding an unprecedented Bacchanalian feast of barbecued bear and straight whiskey.

Peirce's account and Richter's adaptation of it are almost identical down to the exact number of wolves, bear, and deer killed. But whereas Peirce's description of the hunt is characterized by a preterit quality and a dry matter-of-fact brevity, Richter has used his creative imagination to bring the scene to life: he

---

[105]   *The Trees*, pp. 106-108.
[106]   See Appendix, A, 1-12.
[107]   See Appendix, A, 7.

has filled the air with the shouts and laughter of excited men, the sound of dogs and hunting horns, the sharp crack of rifles and the smell of gunsmoke, the loud cries of terrified beasts in the last moments of the carnage; he has captured the tension and contagious excitement that charged the air with an electric current, and he lets us smell the burning logs and barbecuing bear meat, lets us hear the murmur of low voices as the evening settles down into serious story telling and the swapping of tales.

But more importantly, Richter introduces the element of conflict into the scene – not the external conflict of man and beast, but the tumultuous inner conflict of the young Wyitt here in his moment of truth. For the hunt is merely a background for Wyitt's time of decision "to be his own man", and to follow the "everhunter" instinct in his blood consciousness to his destiny somewhere in the forests of the West. Like his father before him, Wyitt cannot forsake his primitive level of evolutionary development; he has learned the meaning of the hunt and can no longer deny the "Monsey Indian blood" which would "out" despite his attempts to resist it. It is the achievement of the chapter that the action of the hunt moves quickly into the background, while in the foreground we are made aware of Wyitt's emotional upheaval. Once again, the details of the hunt are not described; they are dramatized as inner experience.

Richter also draws freely on humorous anecdotes told about remarkable people in Ohio's history in order to delineate his own imagined characters as infused with the spirit and essence of the age.[108] Richter's dissatisfaction with conventional interpretations of the early American character is due to the tendency of contemporary historians and writers to dress up people of today in the costumes of yesterday, forgetting, or unaware, that the early American had a peculiar quality of character strength and manhood elicited by the frontier environment. The problems of meeting life and death are the same; but the way the pioneers faced up to these problems reveals, Richter maintains, that they had a "crabbed" hardihood, self-reliance, and love for independence

---

[108]   See Appendix, C, 1-3.

quite conspicuous for their absence today.[109] He finds the temper of those early times imbedded partly in the keen sense of humor possessed, for example, by the many lawyers and judges described in Howe's *Collections*, the anecdotes of which furnish Richter with material for his delineation of Portius Wheeler.[110] His reliance on such authentic detail insures that the characters, in their own experiences, motives, actions, and understanding, are more authentically kept within the immediacy of their own moment of time.

It should be made clear that Richter finds himself under no obligation to maintain factual accuracy. Portius Wheeler of the trilogy helps draw up the bill that made Ohio into a State; but no document listing the representatives to the constitutional convention at Chillicothe in 1802 will give his name. Neither the county of Shawnee, nor its county seat, Americus, has ever been or will ever be on Ohio's maps; they have existed in a hundred counties and in a hundred county seats, but they have never existed in themselves. Resolve Wheeler, eldest son of Sayward, rises to become governor of the state, but the honor roll of Ohio's governors has never held his name; for he is a mythical governor, and as such Richter can attribute to him anecdotes told of many governors.[111]

Richter, in his attempt to create the illusion of reality, takes great liberties with factual detail but never with human truths; he concerns himself not with documenting a factual record, but with using the documents to create a believable record of human achievement. In this sense of documentation, few contemporary historical novelists are as thorough and representative as Richter.

The essential feature of Richter's use of detail is the quality of restraint achieved by his discriminating selection and his successful blending and integration of the details of setting with characters and action. Despite his heavy reliance on the documents for his material, Richter is never overcome by the historicity of that material. Bertram tells us that, when reading *Drums Along the*

---

[109] "That Early American Quality", pp. 26-30.
[110] See Appendix, C, 1.
[111] See Appendix, B, 13, for one.

Mohawk, we are forever bumping into Edmonds armed with his documents; Richter never overwhelms us with forced documentation. The details are not only sharp and realistic; they blend into the story of human life with its frustrations and its triumphs.

The key to this artistic triumph is his selectivity. The mass of human experience he finds recorded in Howe and in the other sources for his narrative is bare of tidy demarcations. Richter's skill lies in the discipline he imposes over this bulk of authentic but raw materials; this disciplining process he describes by the phrase "Experience, Selection and Order in Writing" (and by experience he also means that mental experience which includes research and knowledge).[112] The form he imposes on his subject matter, the cosmological pattern which gives the materials their peculiar unity and clarifies their meaning, is the result of his skill in the art of selection and order.

That intense effort to condense and interfuse in a single story stream all the thousand and one details of theme, ideas, background, color, character, incident and dialogue in the back of my mind – these things for me have to come out in their proper order and extent. Order to me is one of the most important elements in fiction and generally over-looked by the amateur and the verbose professional.[113]

The method of the trilogy is episodic; therefore it is doubly important for Richter to exercise rigid selectivity. He focuses on the revealing situation or crisis in the lives of his people, the illuminating episode which compresses and suggests so much of the meaning of life. Richter has learned the important literary truth that "the art of rendering life in fiction", as Edith Wharton once said, is to disengage "crucial moments from the welter of experience".[114]

By skillful and selective use of historical materials to get the most out of them for his realistic narrative, by creating a sense of contemporaneity void of antiquarianism, and by delineating believable characters from the ranks of common men and women – characters who reveal no knowledge transcending their own

---

[112] Correspondence to me, May 16, 1962.
[113] Quoted in Hutchens, p.11.
[114] Quoted in Prescott, p. 254.

time and place apart from their perception of enduring human truths obtained through experience – Richter has made a significant contribution to the genre of the historical novel. His grasp of the cultural pattern transcends the notebooks so that he illuminates this pattern with something like the emotional power of the poet.

But this is not the trilogy's only achievement. The narrative is framed by an historical and philosophical overview that adds an extra dimension to the story. The chief importance of using the past, writes Andrew Lytle, lies in its creating the "illusion of the contemporary within a context of historical perspective, so that while an action is taking place it is rendered in terms larger than those of its immediate appearance".[115]

Thus while we are watching the action take place, we are also aware that the actors reveal the essential meaning of their time. The value of the past for us, Richter believes, is that we can see from our present post of observation the pattern of a cosmic destiny operating in the affairs of men. This pattern, we have seen in chapters two and three, reveals the operation of natural laws in the universe which insure the eventual development of man through natural adversity and self-discipline.

The meaning of the trilogy as a historical novel rests on our perception of the beginning of a cultural loss which resulted when these natural laws were ignored or overlooked by man; and this loss is measured specifically by the disappearance of those values cherished by the hardy, self-reliant and stoic pioneers, and the substitution in their place of those more disturbing values deriving from the mercenary and comfort-seeking materialism of an industrial age.

We witness the story as a contemporary, but at the same time we are made aware of the philosophical undertones of the author's point of view. We see those forces which elicited that peculiar quality of inward strength in the pioneers; and we see how these characteristics give way before the worshippers of progress who, unaware of the "laws" of the universe, have created an environ-

115   "Forest of the South", *Critique*, I (Spring 1958), p. 4.

ment which robs them of their integrity of character, emasculates them, and threatens their emotional and physical development. That Richter enables the trilogy to carry the weight of this social judgment without subordinating the realistic narrative to thesis must be counted as a remarkable achievement in the genre of the historical novel.

CONCLUSION

Although Richter has earned a distinguished reputation as a novelist of American backgrounds, the actual relationship of his psychological and philosophical theories to the thematic, textural, and structural achievement of his fiction has generally been neglected, discounted, or misunderstood. In point of fact, however, his speculative and mystical theories of psycho-energics define a conception of man and cosmic order which significantly shapes all of his fiction, particularly his masterpiece, the Ohio trilogy. By determining to what extent his view of human behavior and destiny has informed his fiction, it has been possible to clarify the mystical and social implications of the Ohio trilogy, and more clearly to determine its contribution to American literature.

Gifted with keen powers of observation and a speculative turn of mind, Richter came to believe that the distinguishing features of the pattern of life were empirically demonstrable; furthermore, he convinced himself that this pattern of life revealed a teleological relationship between natural law, hardship and suffering, and the generic evolution of a spiritual temperament in human nature. His sustained attempt to reconcile the implications of a reductive science with the spiritual and mystical cravings of his mind by defining the primary mechanism of purposeful evolution relates Richter to the early tradition of evolutionary naturalism, with its tendencies to mix the waters and oils of naturalism and idealism and to rest its case on pseudo- and demi-scientific thought.

Building on the supposition that energy is the basis of all life phenomena (including mental and spiritual behavior), Richter sets forth two postulates: the distinguishing feature of life is limited energy, and the basic primal motive of the human organism is energy hunger. His pseudo-scientific theory of emergent evolution is based on the assumption that theurgic natural law insures a constant state of "inharmony" in the evolving organism by continually providing circumstances of pain, hardship, suffering, struggle, or privation to induce ever higher needs in the psychoenergic "realman". According to this conception, the physiological process of building up energy flows to meet the persistent energy hunger of the essential being of man is the *sine qua non* of inner evolution and the prelude to moral strength and spiritual growth.

Richter's primary concern has been to explain and justify pain and suffering in the human condition and to persuade his readers to cooperate with destiny by participating actively in their own physical and spiritual growth. Theoretically, this is accomplished by stoically embracing hardship and a regimen of self-discipline. In so doing, Richter theorizes, man may hopefully remove himself from some of the harsher stratagems of fate or at least be prepared to endure the inevitable natural adversity with a minimum of physical and emotional anguish.

In the last analysis, the primary value of Richter's philosophical works is for the light they shed on the textural and structural achievement of his fiction, especially the Ohio trilogy. His theories are a heterogeneous blend of keen observation, shrewd insight, pseudo-scientific and demi-scientific thought. Although he hits the nailhead part of the time and displays extraordinary gifts for the organization of ideas, he makes no new revelation about ultimate reality, and he tends to confuse an aspect of human behavior for the whole.

Nevertheless, his theories have provided him with a consistent conception of character, a structural principle of order, and a philosophical superstructure of meaning. Moreover, the larger adumbrations of his thought – i.e., a conception of man that recognizes the influence of heredity and experience on human

behavior, a conception of the cosmos which recognizes the primacy of providential purpose, and a conception of the role of suffering and tragedy in the growth of spiritual sensitivity and endurance – transcend the severe limitation of his basic assumption that
man is an evolving mechanism.

The moral ambivalence in Richter's cosmology is reflected in
a number of ambiguities inherent in his philosophical system. The
relationship between free will and determinism is never clearly
distinguished. More importantly, the easy optimism of an evolutionary theory, with its presupposition of movement from primitive simplicity toward an increasingly complex organization of
matter (inevitably reflected in human behavior and social structure), runs head-on into Richter's pervasive sense of loss and the
disintegration of things, of the "evil" of complexity, and hence
the desirability of primitive simplicity. To adapt an old Puritan
adage, "Believe like a Calvinist, but act and feel like an Ar-
minian," Richter believes like a Darwinian-Spencerian evolution-
ist, but feels like a modern physicist who is alarmed at the second
law of thermodynamics, a law which suggests that the expenditure
of energy in the universe tends toward a chaotic disintegration of
matter.

Much of the moral ambivalence in Richter's thought and fiction is related to the problem of evil, and the discrepancy between
his theoretical explanation of the efficacy of pain and suffering
and his emotional reaction against that necessity partly accounts
for the tragic vision in his fictional world. Actually, the notion
that struggle or pain is the instrument of a benevolent and divine
evolutionary process was long ago admitted by evolutionary
naturalists to be an unavoidable "harsh truth" inhering in an
ethical and teleological interpretation of Darwinian evolutionary
theory. Transcendentalizing scientific thought inevitably leads to
sticky problems of natural ethics.

It must be admitted, however, that Richter's thesis derives a
certain credibility and validity from its commerce with the classical biological theory of the struggle for survival. It is a generally
accepted empirical fact that, in a protective environment, all
living things appear to lose their versatility and adaptability. It

is not necessary to embrace an evolutionary as opposed to a creationist view of human origins to see that the pattern of struggle is apparently so deeply ingrained in the processes of life, that the removal of all obstacles serves only to atrophy the drive to survive.

The obstructions encountered in his environment, on the other hand, keep man alert, strong, and self-reliant; he is made tough and resourceful by adversity as he struggles against the innumerable emotional and physical obstacles perennially in the path of human experience. Such a self-evident truth, perhaps, is more compelling when expressed as mystical and poetical suggestion than as a scientific postulate. Richter's mystical adumbrations in his fiction of this truth are certainly more convincing and meaningful than his specific and detailed interpretation of it in his psychological and philosophical theories.

Richter's social interpretation of this principle, interestingly enough, is not unlike the conclusions John Steinbeck derives from a similar theory set forth in *The Sea of Cortez*. Steinbeck's amateurish yet insightful study of marine biology convinced him that with warm water and abundant food, marine animals retire into a sterile, sluggish, and vulnerable collective happiness. By analogy, Steinbeck reasoned that in a thoroughly collectivized state, mediocre efficiency may increase only at the cost of eliminating the swift, the clever, and the intelligent along with the incompetent; collective man inescapably abandons his versatility.[1]

It is the social implication of this biological principle that likewise alarms Richter. In setting forth a comprehensive view of man and the universe which presupposes the eventual triumph of progress, Richter is more immediately concerned about the possibility of inhibiting that progress; consequently, he finds himself caught in the dangerous crossfire of his own theories. In his attempt to account for the emergence of altruism as passion, he speculates that evolving man passes through an intermediate phase in which his evolved sympathy and desire to relieve the suffering of others is not balanced by a sufficient understanding

---

[1]   Frederick Bracha, "Steinbeck and the Biological View of Man", *Pacific Spectator*, II (Winter 1948), pp. 14-29.

of the role of hardship. The welfarist and collectivist intellect, even though predicated by altruistic motives, may thus inadvertently work against natural law by attempting to remove all circumstances of inharmony ("beneficial burdens") through deliberate manipulation of the social structure.

It is only through immediate experience with the living tissue of life that the sensitive altruist realizes the need to proceed cautiously in planning for human welfare if he is not to interfere in the cosmic destiny of his fellow beings. Contemporary society, in its commitment to economic materialism and collectivism, however, has become devoted to the cult of comfort, a cult which has caused the atrophy and emasculation of moral character and the dissociation of personality.

Richter's criticism of the cult of comfort, which emerges as themes of protest in *Early Americana, The Sea of Grass,* and the Ohio trilogy, is one of his major reasons for reacquainting us through historical fiction with our early American heritage. Richter's respect for pioneer values as a check to the moral bankruptcy which has attended the cult of comfort accounts for his lifelong preoccupation with the frontier experience as a source of literary materials. His study of the past provided him with an historic image: a change in the human condition attended by a cultural loss. He locates the beginning of this change in the historic transition from the rugged living conditions of the frontier community to the high living standards, but crass materialism, of the mid-nineteenth century industrial community.

The Ohio trilogy records this historic change in the human condition and points up the essence of the cultural loss by means of a thematic structure of affirmation and protest. *The Trees* and *The Fields* affirm pioneer values. The steady conflict with natural adversity on the wilderness frontier – apotheosized by the hard work of clearing a virgin forest to make way for homes, fields, and a reasonable security – causes the pioneers in the community of Moonshine Church constantly to summon and build up their energies for survival. In the process, Sayward, her family, and her neighbors develop a unique quality of mind and spirit, a quality of hardihood and ethical courage.

The Town, on the other hand, protests those social forces of economic materialism and collectivism which bring about the destruction of these values. The radical shift in attitude toward suffering and pain, which is reflected in the hypersensitivity, physical weakness, and moral confusion of Chancey Wheeler, the child of the industrial revolution, is in explicit contrast to the attitude shared by Sayward and her contemporaries. The pioneers, in their common sense philosophy, intuitively accepted the need for hardship and discipline in their lives. Tutored only by experience, they came to consider life's misfortunes and adversities to be providential, the wise dispensation and discipline of the gods. Furthermore, they came to that painful self-knowledge that the issues of life must be embraced personally. The great lesson experience teaches Sayward is that she cannot be strong for others without destroying their own strength.

The surface narrative of the Ohio trilogy is thus connected with a background meaning: the cosmic role of hardship and discipline as a means of grace. The theme of cosmic order and individual destiny gives unity to the three novels by providing a principle for selecting those details and episodes which enable Richter to coordinate structure and meaning. There is a consistent correlation between the artistic pattern of the Ohio trilogy and the philosophical structure of Richter's perception of the reality beneath the appearances.

The pervasive sense of cosmic order and the consistent conception of character and human behavior explain in large part the structural unity and coherence of the Ohio trilogy; however, the emotional power of the three novels owes much to another dimension of Richter's art – its tragic vision.

Although the enormous sense of loss reflected in the past-present polarity of the tales in *Early Americana* hint at a growing tragic awareness in Richter's art, it is not until *The Sea of Grass* and the Ohio trilogy that his tragic vision receives an impressive and symbolic expression, and that the relationship of this tragic sense to his psychological theories is made clear. In the action of both *The Sea of Grass* and the Ohio trilogy, Richter confronts the irreducible facts of suffering and death; and in his characteriza-

tion of Brock Chamberlain and Chancey Wheeler, he suggests
the immutable limitations imposed upon human personality by the
tyranny of blood consciousness and the irresistible flux of time.
Richter's later appeal to the Cronos myth to explain the hostility
between father and son in *The Waters of Kronos* illuminates his
earlier sense of loss at the tragic erosion of time, which has been
the subject of all of his fiction. The mechanistic determinism of
time-as-emasculator, the sense of mortality that grows heavier in
the Ohio trilogy, and the apparent helplessness of each succeeding
generation to be reconciled to the one that went before it contribute to an essentially tragic insight into the modern loss of identity
and sense of spiritual alienation characteristic of contemporary
man.

The present, in repudiating the past, suffers a tragic paraly-
sis of the spirit, and contemporary man thus stands alone, unaccommodated, condemned to search out the meaning of existence without any revelation save that of his own experience.

Richter's tragic vision empowers all of his art, but much of the
enduring appeal of the Ohio trilogy derives from its organic
relationship to the traditions of primitivism and transcendentalism;
its thematic structure of affirmation and protest, which helps to
order the realistic historical narrative, relates it to the regionalist
tradition of the novel of the soil, a tradition which embraces the
stoic values of primitivism, the tenacious confirmation of the
land, and the spiritual values which inhere in a transcendent
conception of the cosmos.

Although it is not all of the truth to say that Richter has devoted the major portion of his literary life to the meticulous re-
construction of an earlier world he might have loved and to the
analysis of a contemporary one he hated, there can be no question of his love affair with pioneer America and of his disaffec-
tion with contemporary civilization. His commitment to primitive
ideals is heightened by his personal sense of loss and nostalgia
which threatens at times to carry him to an uncritical preference
for the past. "His nostalgia, however, does not lead him to senti-
mentality", writes Granville Hicks, "and he is incapable of the
sensationalism that spoils so much of the fiction written about the

pioneers." [2] Moreover, Richter's philosophical convictions show that his preference for the past transcends mere sentiment and becomes a serious indictment of the modern preoccupation with economic materialism as the means to progress in the human condition.

It is not difficult to understand why Richter's temperament, so remarkably akin to that of the mid-nineteenth century transcendentalists, with their revolt against materialism, their distrust of the machine in the garden, and their symbolic interpretation of the frontier, prompted him to fasten his mind on the West, not only as a place in space and time, but as an image of the spiritual frontier all men must face in their encounter with cosmic order. His fictional recovery of the West in *Early Americana, The Sea of Grass*, and especially in the Ohio trilogy is not simply an attempt to recreate authentically the atmosphere of a unique experience in our national history; it is also an attempt to evoke the symbolic power of the West as metaphor and to make this power accessible to contemporary man.

In recreating the historical West in a prose style so rich in emotional immediacy and so happily lacking in that preterit quality which characterizes most frontier fiction, and in suggesting the intimate and mysterious continuity of past and present in the cultural consciousness of Americans, Richter has reacquainted us with a dynamic native metaphor, a metaphor which has played a significant role in shaping the American mind itself. That "early American quality" of mind – resolute, courageous, self-reliant, and willing to confront the hard realities of existence with determination and with confidence in future possibilities – is given apt metaphoric expression in the image of the Western frontier. Richter has long grasped the significance of what Archibald MacLeish has recently declared regarding the strength of America as a country of extremes, of many opposites made one: "The American dream has been a dream of the west, of the world farther on. . . . West is a country in the mind, and so eternal." [3]

[2] Granville Hicks, "Caught Between Two Ways of Life", *Saturday Review*, May 14, 1966, p. 27.
[3] Archibald MacLeish, "Sweet Land of Liberty", *Colliers* (July 8, 1955), pp. 54-55.

In predicting the literary future of the United States, Malcolm Cowley reflects on the implications of our disappearing natural landscapes. As the soil yields to factories, cities, suburbias, parking lots, super-highways, and automobile junkyards, fewer people will live in or even catch a glimpse of the open countryside. "All this will lead to the decline of certain familiar types of writing, especially nature poetry and novels of the soil." [4] The prediction is probably accurate; the novel of the soil, however, still has rich possibilities in the kind of *historical* fiction Richter writes.

Although an actual return to the soil is as unrealistic as a physical return to the past – and any social-political program based on this as a real possibility deserves the label of anachronism, a revitalizing return to the soil and to the past on the level of imagination is still a viable alternative in an increasingly urbanized and rootless world. In a poetic evocation of the Western wind, Edward Harris Heth argues that "it is not necessary to *be* there, to uproot ourselves who are already uprooted and return to the land . . ., but only *not* to put it out of mind, or cast the land from us as thoughtlessly as we discard a tin can. Remembered sights and sounds", he continues, "often carry in themselves more magical vitality than the sights and sounds themselves . . ." [5]

Richter's gift for projection and absorption into the early childhood of our still young culture, reacquainting us on the level of imagination with that state of mind which is our chief patrimony from the past, has found its finest expression in *The Trees*, *The Fields*, and *The Town*. As an historical novel of the soil, then, the Ohio trilogy affirms enduring primitivist and transcendentalist values: the growth of community from the soil; the superiority of a simple, unregimented life in a natural environment which evokes a spiritual sensitivity; the spirituality of work; the love of independence and self-reliance; the stoic conception of *amor fati*, or love of the order of the world; and the importance of roots as symbolized by attachment to the land, respect for

[4] Malcolm Cowley, "The Unsettled Literary Future of the U.S.", *Saturday Review*, June 9, 1962, p. 17.
[5] Edward Harris Heth, "Wait for the Western Wind", *Country Beautiful*, II (October 1962), p. 30.

tradition and community ties, and reverence for the past. In a novel of the soil, of course, the rooted, whose values are affirmed, are set off against the rootless, whose values are protested. Thus the Ohio trilogy protests those social forces of an industrial and urban civilization – particularly the inflated importance of economic motive – which threaten to uproot man.

This distinct thematic structure of affirmation and protest enables the Ohio trilogy, as a realistic historical narrative framed in a philosophical and mystical overview, to place today's social disorders in an historical perspective. By means of a skillful and selective use of documentary historical materials to create, not factual accuracy, but a restrained, realistic illusion of life in an ordered universe, Richter effectively recreates the historical process of change by which frontier America became industrial America.

The trilogy offers an interpretation and judgment of this rapid historical change – particularly of its by-product, the rootlessness of modern man – in terms of the cultural loss which has attended our disregard for the past as a record of providential purpose, and our headlong flight after novelty, change, and materialistic progress. Richter's use of the realistic historical narrative in the tradition of the novel of the soil to dramatize those forces which have shaped contemporary America, a dramatization empowered by Richter's tragic vision of the erosion of time and of the inevitability of suffering, makes of the Ohio trilogy a significant contribution to the genre of the historical novel, and to American literature.

APPENDIX

The following is a selective list showing the kind of factual details, anecdotes, and incidents Richter appropriates from Henry Howe's *Historical Collections of Ohio* for background authenticities, extended scenes of action, and delineation of character in the Ohio trilogy.

A. Incidents and humorous anecdotes providing the basis for significant episodes (sometimes whole chapters).

   1. A man travels miles through the wilderness to procure flour to make "real" bread for a sick and ailing wife (Howe, I, 551: cf. *Trees*, Ch. 5, "Bread", pp. 43-57 – Worth does this for Jary).

   2. Ague, fever, the swamp pestilence; frequency of attack; symptoms; deadliness; doctors forbid water to patients; how one patient crawled from his bed to a nearby stream to quench his thirst (Howe, I, 536-37; II, 725-27: cf. *Trees,* Ch. 11, "Corpse Candles", pp. 122-32).

   3. Small girl lost in the woods; separated from the cows; sensation of being lost in the forest; reaction of neighborhood; large search party organized, led by veteran hunter; clues found: play house, pieces of calico, footprints; search abandoned (Howe, I, 417-18, 490; II, 133, 850-51: cf. *Trees*, Ch. 14, "The Little Tyke", pp. 159-81 – Sulie's disappearance).

   4. Unusual frontier wedding; jovial but mischievous group

propose a match between a reluctant bachelor and a willing but timid maid; prospective groom primed with whiskey, restrained by force; long happy married life of the principals (Howe, I, 353: cf. *Trees*, Ch. 29, "It Came a Tuesday", pp. 263-86 – Jake Tench proposes match between the "solitary" – Portius Wheeler – and Ida Tull; Sayward steps in and marries Portius herself).

5. Special mode of clearing the virgin forest; "ringing the trees", and "niggering the butts", log-burnings and log-rollings (Howe, II, 207-208: cf. *Trees*, Ch. 20, "Black Land", pp. 287-302).

6. The "Great Hinckley Hunt"; clearing the woods of varmints (Howe, II, 203-206: *Fields*, Ch. 6, "His Own Man", pp. 69-83).

7. Account of the famine; settlers reduced to six kernels of corn apiece; young men go to Pennsylvania for corn; account of a plucky pioneer woman who kept her family alive by searching the mattresses for grain kernels, and by painfully stalking a lone turkey with only one shell for the gun (Howe, I, 266, 528: cf. *Fields*, Ch. 7, "The Fleshpots of Egypt", pp. 84-105 – famine in the settlement; men leave for Kentucky; Sayward searches bed ticks for grain; stalks and shoots turkey to keep family alive).

8. Two small boys alone in the woods; one bitten on the finger by a rattlesnake; chops off his own finger to save his life (Howe, I, 923: cf. *Fields*, Ch. 13, "The Nettle Patch", pp. 188-200 – Guerdon's snakebite; chops off his own finger).

9. Competition for the County Seat; use of political cartoon showing a man carrying off a court house in a wheelbarrow (Howe, I, 695; II, 424: cf. *Town*, Ch. 6, "County Seat", pp. 57-71 – conflict between Americus and Tateville).

10. Opening of the Ohio canal; celebration (Howe, II, 72: cf. *Town*, Ch. 11, "The Two Diggings", pp. 128-35 – Ohio canal goes through Americus).

11. Parents discover after thirty or forty years that their

daughter, who had been captured by the Indians, is still alive and married to an Indian in the western part of the territory; tragic reunion; daughter refuses to leave husband and family, or to return to white civilization (Howe, I, 297-98, 408; II, 451: cf. *Town*, Ch. 22, "Ant Sulie", pp. 255-70 – Sulie still alive, won't return).

12. Competition between neighboring towns reflected in famous sleigh-ride war; hundreds of sleighs behind a flag depicting a thumb-to-nose gesture invade town; invasion returned (Howe, II, 424f: cf. *Town*, Ch. 27, "Winter In", esp. pp. 329-35 – sleigh war between Americus and Tateville).

B. Smaller details and humorous anecdotes appropriated for background authenticities.

1. Making cakes and tea to entertain guest; how one kettle does the work of six (Howe, I, 566: cf. *Trees*, Ch. 9, "A Noggin of Tea", esp. pp. 105-108).

2. Indian fighter, Josiah Hunt, keeps Wayne's army supplied with game when Wayne's fort is under seige; description of "coal-pit fire", techniques for hunting and skinning deer in hostile Indian country (Howe, I, 699: cf. *Trees*, pp. 145-46).

3. Detailed description of building and furnishing a log schoolhouse (Howe, I, 534: cf. *Fields*, Ch. 11, "The Laurel Hut", esp. pp. 161-64 – building the "Academy").

4. Description of Fourierites, phalanxes; Cincinnati, the cultural and publishing center; gathering place for all causes (Howe, I, 420: cf. several references throughout *The Town*; Chancey attracted by phalanxes, goes to Cincinnati to edit radical paper).

5. Detailed description of pioneer day and Independence Day celebrations: cabin raising; speeches (Howe, I, 662, 885; II, 375, 729-30; cf. *Trees*, Ch. 16, "Public Day", pp. 198-215; *Town*, esp. pp. 287-91).

6. Description of eccentric Johnny Appleseed (John Chapman), his peculiar dress and manner, his Swedenborgian

religion (Howe, II, pp. 485f: cf. *Town*, pp. 368-70 –
Chancey comforted after Rosa's death by Johnny's
Swedenborgian sentiments).

7. Anecdote of the ignorant Mormonite who left his country
   because of the vision he had seen in the sky; the clouds
   had spelled F-A-M-I-N (Howe, II, 195: cf. *Fields*, p. 87,
   Luke Peter's vision).

8. At pioneer celebration, humorous song:
   (women) "Oh, for a man; Oh, for a man; oh! for
   a mansion in the skies."
   (men)   "Bring down sal; – bring down sal; – bring
   down salvation from above."
   (Howe, I, 885: cf. *Fields*, p. 117 –
   sung at first religious meeting).

9. Reading Virgil's *Aeneid*; at the point in the narrative
   where Aeneas tells Dido he must leave by the mandate of
   Jove, two agitated backwoodsmen in the audience leap to
   their feet and heap censure on a man who would concoct
   such a tale just to run out on a woman (Howe, I, 290: cf.
   Fields, pp. 168f – Jake and Billy hear Portius read).

10. Indian offered whiskey; after hesitating and quoting white
    preacher who had warned him drinking whiskey would
    send him to hell, the Indian concludes the preacher proba-
    bly "tell damn lie", and gratefully accepts the cup (Howe,
    I, 582: cf. *Town*, p. 61 – Portius and Little Turtle).

11. Important pioneer who operated a tavern and a ferry
    nearby was known for his fiercely democratic sense of
    sovereignty; he earned the nickname "King Charley", for
    kicking Louis Philippe, afterwards the famous king of
    France, out of his tavern when that worthy monarch
    complained of his accommodations during his travels as a
    refugee in America (Howe, I, 481: cf. *Town*, p. 85 –
    "King Sam" Sloper, operator of tavern and ferry, enjoyed
    the same reputation).

12. Description of Women's Temperance Crusades; anecdote
    of one young man who finds himself trapped in a saloon
    by a group of crusaders among whom are his sister,

sweetheart, mother, and mother-in-law-to-be; escapes out the back door (Howe, I, 428, 916: cf. *Town*, pp. 302f – Chancey trapped in Red Mule, escapes out the back).

13. A French Duke, traveling in America, wants to pay a visit of state to the Ohio governor, Jeremiah Morrow; he stops to ask a common laborer in a nearby field where the governor could be found and is flabbergasted to learn the laborer is himself the governor (Howe, II, 756: cf. *Town*, p. 428 – told of Resolve).

C. Humorous anecdotes appropriated to facilitate characterization.

   1. Portius Wheeler
      a. Accounts of hermits
         (1) An eccentric person named Jones, who dressed in deerskins and lived a solitary life in the wilderness; his background mysterious but probably banished from the East for his intemperance. He was a scholar who had brought with him many books and was fond of reading poetry aloud (Howe, I, 291).
         (2) Wadsworth was a graduate of Yale, but for some mysterious reason had come to the wilderness to be a recluse. He had rich relatives in Boston who occasionally pleaded in vain for his return (Howe, I, 490).
         (3) William Hewit had left his Virginia home where he had been a man of wealth to become a hermit in the wilderness. His background mysterious, but generally believed to have been a victim of misplaced love and faith (Howe, II, 430).
            (Portius Wheeler, trained for the bar, was known as the "solitary", and the "hermit". He had been mysteriously banished from the East where he had apparently been a member of a wealthy family.
            Reduced to wearing buckskins; scholarly and fond of poetry, he was often seen wandering up and down in front of his wretched log hut, reciting

Greek and Latin poets, and reading from Shakespeare. He was inordinately intemperate. After marrying Sayward he is rescued from his solitary ways, but when letters arrive from Boston bidding his return, he refuses, preferring to stay in the wilderness).

b. Humorous anecdotes about various frontier lawyers. The majority of biographical sketches in the *Collections* are about early day lawyers.

(1) Ben Tappen, chagrined that one of the presiding judges was late returning from court recess, piled the tardy judge's saddle bags (which contained lawbooks) on the bench in front of the judge's seat, and addressed them in absence of the judge (Howe, I, 972: cf. *Town*, p. 69).

(2) A man appearing before a pioneer judge in common pleas court, paid his fine for beating a man caught stealing his pigs. He was threatened with contempt for bragging in court how he beat the "damn hog thief", which action caused the defendant to yell at the judge: "If you'd steal a hog, damn you, I'd whip you too" (Howe, I, 696: cf. *Town*, p. 70).

(3) Nicholas Longworth lawyer and man of wealth, was famous for refusing to give money to organized charities. The "Lord's poor" are well cared for, he claimed. "But I will help the 'devil's poor', the miserable drunken dog that nobody else will do anything for but despise and kick" (Howe, I, 819: cf. *Town*, p. 391 – sentiment attributed to Portius; defines his temperament).

(4) A copy of the *Arabian Nights*, bound in black, was mistaken for a New Testament and used to swear in witnesses (Howe, I, 698: cf. *Town*, p. 399 – Portius, a skeptic, did this for his own private amusement).

(5) Numerous accounts of ostentatious brick mansions built by lawyers: cf. Portius's desire to have the biggest mansion in town.

(6) Numerous accounts of lawyers advocating the new canal policy and championing "progress" (e.g., Howe, I, 650: cf. *Town*, pp. 128f).

2. Jake Tench

  a. Accounts of ruffians and rowdy backwoodsmen.

    (1) The rowdy group who plan wedding between non-courting bachelor and old maid (see A, 4).

    (2) Description of the "Fighting Funks", the most notorious of whom was Jake. They loved whiskey and brawls. One of the Funks once skinned a pig whole to get a wineskin to carry home his whiskey in (Howe, I, 603: cf. *Trees*, p. 297).

    (3) Jamie Shaw was a religious enthusiast fond of rolling on the floor at the height of his religious ecstasy. Once a rowdy urchin dropped a bullet in his mouth when Jamie was in a supine position and he nearly choked to death (Howe, II, 269: cf. *Fields*, p. 29 – Jake does this to Scovel Harris).

    (4) John Driskel, a rowdy and belligerent man, bit off a man's ear in a fight; the victim, watching his chance, leaped on Driskel and bit off the man's nose in exchange (Howe, II, 839: cf. *Town*, pp. 217-218 – Jake loses an ear but gains a nose).

3. Chancey Wheeler

  a. Anecdote of Jeremiah Reynolds; Jeremiah and his step-brother were known as "Job's Oxen", and at a log-rolling, Jeremiah was unable to hold up his end of a log. In fun a by-stander said "One of Job's oxen was a calf" (Howe, I, 431: cf. *Town*, "The Off-ox", p. 289).

  b. Anecdote about Rev. Armstrong. At a log-rolling Armstrong found his end of the log too heavy. When his partner said "More handspike?" (meaning to lighten

Armstrong's load), the Rev. misunderstood and quickly
said "No more stick for me; I have already as much as
I can carry", much to the amusement of those about
(Howe, I, 697: cf. *Town*, p. 289 – part of the same
incident involving a. above).

   c. Account of William Gallagher's poem, "Fifty Years
Ago; a Song of the Western Pioneer" which ends with
the refrain, "In the days when we were pioneers, /
Fifty Years ago"), and of his poem "The Spotted
Fawn", about a beautiful Indian princess who with her
lover was slain on her wedding day by cruel white
hunters. Howe includes a parody of this ballad which
paralleled the fate of the Indian maiden with that of a
young frog stoned to death by boys (Howe, I, 721-14:
cf. *Town*, pp. 313-14 – Chancey writes a broad lampoon attacking his mother for her refusal to permit the
city to drain her Beaver Gats. Entitled "The Frog's
Petition", it is inspired by the satire on Gallagher's "The
Spotted Frog" and his poem "Fifty Years Ago". Every
verse calls for a reasonable – from a frog's point of
view – return to a way of life more suited to a frog's
needs. Each verse ends with the refrain, "Return unto
the status quo / Of forty, fifty years ago").

D. Details which tend to define Richter's point of view toward
his materials.
   1. Howe's attitude toward pioneers; e.g., the following account of John Welch: "His history illustrates the pluck of
that early race which started in life when Ohio was a
wilderness. Beginning with battling with trees, and con-
quering them so as to give the ground a fair chance for
the sunbeams, they went forth into the battle of life among
their fellow men regarding them somewhat as 'trees
walking'. Success was of course assured." (Howe, I, 278).
   2. Attitude toward trees and forest.
      a. Trees described as "angry", "threatening" the settlers
       · (Howe, I, 317).

   b. Accounts of famed trees left standing as a reminder of
   the old days, finally to be overcome by a storm (Howe,
   I, 545).
   c. Accounts of terrible and frightening grandeur of the
   forest, and the indescribable feeling of "solitariness"
   experienced by the first settlers (Howe, I, 193f).
3. Social equality of pioneers.
   a. Consciously democratic; no aristocratic distinctions
   (Howe, I, 555).
   b. Spirit of sharing and brotherhood; hostility toward
   mercenaries and speculators (Howe, II, 245).
4. Contrast between past and present; nostalgia of pioneers.
   a. Settler complains that modern materialism and affluence
   have destroyed the sense of gratitude and joy at living,
   at being supplied with life's necessities (Howe, I, 217).
   b. Old timer looking back bemoans loss of that "primitive
   simplicity!" and regrets the animosities brought on by
   increased wealth (Howe, I, 566).
   c. Settlers regret afterwards that they hadn't left a few
   more trees standing (Howe, II, 855).
   d. Howe's repeated observation that the individualistic
   olden days made it possible for every village to have
   its colorful characters whose individuality provided
   "moral entertainment" (Howe, II, 269, 448).

BIBLIOGRAPHY

Barnard, Kenneth J., "Presentation of the West in Conrad Richter's Trilogy", *Northwest Ohio Quarterly*, XXIX (Autumn 1957), pp. 224-234.

Bertram, R. M., "The Novel of America's Past: A Study of Five Historical Novelists, 1925-50", Unpublished Doctoral Dissertation, University of Michigan, Ann Arbor, 1954.

"Birth of the Mind", *Literary Digest*, XCIV (July 9, 1927), p. 24.

Boas, George, *Essays on Primitivism and Related Ideas in the Middle Ages* (Baltimore, The Johns Hopkins Press, 1948).

Borgese, G. A., "Primitivism", *Dictionary of World Literature*, Revised edition, ed. Joseph T. Shipley (Paterson, New Jersey, Littlefield, Adams and Company, 1960), p. 318.

Bracha, Frederick, "Steinbeck and the Biological View of Man", *Pacific Spectator*, II (Winter 1948), pp. 14-29.

Bromfield, Louis, "Another Volume in Mr. Richter's Fine Frontier Saga", *New York Herald Tribune Book Review*, April 23, 1950, p. 5.

——, "A Fine Novel of Pioneers in Ohio", *New York Herald Tribune Weekly Book Review*, March 31, 1946, p. 3.

Carpenter, Frederic I., "Conrad Richter's Pioneers: Reality and Myth", *College English*, XII (November 1950), pp. 77-83.

Cathcart, E. P., "Energy of Expenditure", *Scientific Monthly*, XXI (November 1925), pp. 508-510.

Clough, Wilson, *The Necessary Earth: Nature and Solitude in American Literature* (Austin, University of Texas Press, 1964).

Cowley, Malcolm, "The Unsettled Literary Future of the U.S.", *Saturday Review*, June 9, 1962, pp. 15-17.

Davidson, Donald, *The Attack on Leviathan* (Chapel Hill, The University of North Carolina Press, 1938).

Dempsey, David, "In the Footsteps of the Nazarene", *Saturday Review*, April 28, 1962, p. 19.

De Voto, Bernard, "Fiction and the Everlasting *IF*", *Harper's Magazine*, CLXXVII (June 1938), pp. 42-49.

Dudden, Arthur P., "Nostalgia and the American", *Journal of the History of Ideas*, XXII (October-December 1961), pp. 515-530.

Edmonds, Walter D., "A Novelist Takes Stock", *Atlantic Monthly*, CLXXII (July 1941), pp. 73-77.

"Electrical Theory of Memory", *Scientific American*, CXXVI (April 1922), p. 249 f.

Emerson, Ralph Waldo, *The Complete Works of Ralph Waldo Emerson*, 12 vols. (New York, Houghton Mifflin and Company, 1903-04).

Finger, Charles J., "The Old Southwest", *Saturday Review of Literature*, August 8, 1936, p. 7.

Fiske, John, *The Miscellaneous Writings of John Fiske*, 12 vols. (New York, Houghton Mifflin and Company, 1902).

Flanagan, John T., "Conrad Richter: Romancer of the Southwest", *Southwest Review*, XLIII (Summer 1958), pp. 189-196.

——, "Folklore in the Novels of Conrad Richter", *Midwest Folklore*, II (Spring 1952), pp. 5-14.

——, "A Half-Century of Middlewestern Fiction", *Critique*, II (Winter 1959), pp. 16-34.

——, "The Middle Western Historical Novel", *Journal of the Illinois State Historical Society*, XXXVII (March 1944), pp. 7-47.

Ford, Paul Leicester, "The American Historical Novel", *Atlantic Monthly*, LXXX (December 1897), pp. 721-728.

Frye, Hall, *Romance and Tragedy*, 2nd ed. (Lincoln, University of Nebraska Press, 1961).

Fussell, Edwin, *Frontier: American Literature and the American West* (Princeton, Princeton University Press, 1965).

Gaston, Jr., Edwin W., *Conrad Richter* (New Haven, Twayne Publishers Inc., 1965).

Gates, G., *Mechanism and Meaning* (New York, The Grafton Press, 1928).

Gelfant, Blanche Housman, *The American City Novel* (Norman, The University of Oklahoma Press, 1954).

Greenwald, Dorothy, "Forest of Ohio", *Boston Evening Transcript*, March 2, 1940, p. 1.

Haldane, J. S., *Mechanics, Life and Personality* (New York, E. P. Dutton and Co., Inc., 1928).

Hamsun, Knut, *Growth of the Soil*, Translated by W. W. Worster (New York, Grosset and Dunlap, Publishers, 1921).

Handlin, Oscar, "History as a Literary Art", *Harvard Guide to American History*, ed. Oscar Handlin *et al.* (Cambridge, The Belknap Press of Harvard University Press, 1955), pp. 44-49.

Hatcher, Harlan, "The New Vogue of Historical Fiction", *English Journal*, XXVI (December 1937), pp. 775-784.

Heth, Edward Harris, "Wait for the Western Wind", *Country Beautiful*, II (October 1962), pp. 26-31.

Hicks, Granville, "Caught Between Two Ways of Life", *Saturday Review*, May 14, 1966, p. 27.

Howe, Henry, *Historical Collections of Ohio*, 2 vols. (Cincinnati, Published by the State of Ohio, 1907).

Hucky, G., "Human Body as an Electrical System", *Scientific American*, LXXXII (July 1, 1916), pp. 2-3.

Hutchens, John K., "Pine Grove to Pulitzer and Back", *New York Herald*

Tribune Book Review, April 22, 1962, p. 3.

Hyman, L. H., "Suggestions Regarding the Causes of Bioelectric Phenomena", *Science*, XLVII (November 22, 1918), pp. 518-524.

Jackson, J. A. and Salisbury, H. M., *Outwitting Our Nerves* (New York, Century Company, 1928).

Kessler, Jascha, "Ashes of the Phoenix: A Study of Primitivism and Myth-Making in D. H. Lawrence's *The Plumed Serpent*", Unpublished Doctoral Dissertation, The University of Michigan, Ann Arbor, 1957.

Kohler, Dayton, "Conrad Richter: Early Americana", *English Journal*, XXXV (September 1946), pp. 363-369.

Krikorian, Y. H., ed., *Naturalism and the Human Spirit* (New York, Columbia University Press, 1944).

Krutch, Joseph Wood, "In the World of a Hermit", *New York Times Book Review*, June 5, 1955, p. 18.

La Hood, Marvin, "A Study of the Major Themes in the Work of Conrad Richter and His Place in the Tradition of the American Frontier Novel", Unpublished Doctoral Dissertation, University of Notre Dame, 1962.

Langer, Suzanne K., *Philosophy in a New Key*, 2nd ed. (Cambridge, Harvard University Press, 1951).

Lawrence, D. H., *Studies in Classic American Literature* (New York, Albert and Charles Boni, Inc., 1930).

Leisy, Ernest, *The American Historical Novel* (Norman, The University of Oklahoma Press, 1950).

Lodge, Sir Oliver, *Beyond Physics* (New York, Greenberg, Publisher, Inc., 1931).

——, *Electrons* (New York, The Macmillan Company, 1907).

——, *Life and Matter* (New York, G. P. Putnam's Sons, 1907).

——, *Making of Man* (New York, People's Library, 1924).

Lovejoy, Arthur O. *et al.*, *A Documentary History of Primitivism and Related Ideas* (Baltimore, The Johns Hopkins Press, 1935).

Lytle, Andrew, "Caroline Gordon and the Historical Image", *Sewanee Review*, LVII (Autumn 1949), pp. 560-586.

——, "The Forest of the South", *Critique*, I (Spring 1958), pp. 3-9.

MacLeish, Archibald, "Sweet Land of Liberty", *Colliers* (July 8, 1955), pp. 54-55.

Marx, Leo, *The Machine in the Garden: Technology and the Pastoral Ideal in America* (New York, Oxford University Press, 1964).

Myers, Henry, *Tragedy: A View of Life* (Ithaca, Cornell University Press, 1956).

"The Mythology of Classical Greece", *Larousse Encyclopedia of Mythology*, pp. 89-96.

Penfield, Wilder, "The Physiological Basis of the Mind", *Man and Civilization: Control of the Mind*, ed. Seymour M. Farber and Roger H. L. Wilson, pp. 3-17 (New York, McGraw Hill, 1961).

Prescott, Orville, *In My Opinion* (New York, The Bobbs-Merrill Company, Inc., 1952).

Quinn, A. H., *Edgar Allen Poe: A Critical Biography* (New York, D. Appleton-Century Co., Inc., 1941).

Richter, Conrad, *Always Young and Fair* (New York, Alfred A. Knopf, 1947).

——, *A Country of Strangers* (New York, Alfred A. Knopf, 1966).

——, "Doctor Hanray's Second Chance", *Saturday Evening Post*, CCII (June 10, 1950), pp. 22-23.

——, *Early Americana and Other Stories* (New York, Alfred A. Knopf, 1936).

——, *The Fields* (New York, Alfred A. Knopf, 1946).

——, *Human Vibration* (Harrisburg, Pennsylvania, Handy Book Corporation, 1925).

——, "The Iron Lady", *Saturday Evening Post*, CCXXX (July 13, 1957), pp. 20-21.

——, *The Lady* (New York, Alfred A. Knopf, 1957).

——, *The Light in the Forest* (New York, Alfred A. Knopf, 1953).

——, *The Mountain on the Desert* (New York, Alfred A. Knopf, 1955).

——, "New Mexico Was Our Fate", *New Mexico Magazine*, XXXV (March 1957), pp. 20-21.

——, *Principles in Bio-Physics* (Harrisburg, Pennsylvania, Good Books Corporation, 1927).

——, "The Rawhide Knot", *Saturday Evening Post*, CCX (January 1, 1938), pp. 18-19.

——, *The Sea of Grass* (New York, Alfred A. Knopf, 1937).

——, *A Simple Honorable Man* (New York, Alfred A. Knopf, 1962).

——, "Sinister Journey", *Saturday Evening Post*, CCVI (September 26, 1953), pp. 36-37.

——, *Tacey Cromwell* (New York, Alfred A. Knopf, 1942).

——, "That Early American Quality", *Atlantic Monthly*, CLXXXVI (September 1950), pp. 26-30.

——, "Three Towns I Love", *Holiday*, XIV (December 1953), pp. 54-59.

——, *The Town* (New York, Alfred A. Knopf, 1950).

——, *The Trees* (New York, Alfred A. Knopf, 1940).

——, "Valley from the Past", *Country Beautiful*, II (April 1963), pp. 8-14.

——, *The Waters of Kronos* (New York, Alfred A. Knopf, 1960).

Rosenberger, Coleman, "Mr. Richter's Magic Touch", *New York Herald Tribune Book Review*, April 17, 1960, p. 1.

Seitz, D. C., "Life Maintained by Electricity Within the Body", *Outlook*, CXLIII (August 18, 1926), pp. 540-542.

Sewall, Richard, *The Vision of Tragedy* (New Haven, Yale University Press, 1959).

Smith, Henry Nash, *Virgin Land: The American West as Symbol and Myth* (Cambridge, Harvard University Press, 1950).

Sutherland, Bruce, "Conrad Richter's Americana", *New Mexico Quarterly Review*, XV (Winter 1945), pp. 413-422.

"This Once Ideal Village", *Saturday Evening Post*, CCXIX (October 12, 1946), p. 4.

Thomson, J. A., *Concerning Evolution* (New Haven, Yale University Press, 1925).

——, *Darwinism and Human Life* (New York, Henry Holt and Company, 1917).

——, *Everyday Biology* (New York, George H. Doran Company, 1924).

——, *The Outline of Science* (New York, G. P. Putnam's Sons, 1924).

Thoreau, Henry David, *Walden and Other Writings of Henry David Thoreau*, ed. Brooks Atkinson (New York, The Modern Library, 1950).

Thrall, William Flint and Addison Hibbard, *A Handbook to Literature*, Revised Edition (New York, The Odyssey Press, 1960).

Tinker, Chauncey, *Nature's Simple Plan* (Princeton, Princeton University Press, 1922).

United States Catalog, Books in Print, 1928, January 1, 1928, p. 2412.

Wagenknecht, Edward, *Cavalcade of the American Novel* (New York, Henry Holt and Company, 1952).

Walton, E. L., "Pioneer Tales from the West", *New York Herald Tribune Books*, August 2, 1936, p. 6.

Warfel, Harry R., *American Novelists of Today* (New York, American Book Company, 1951).

Weil, Simone, *The Need for Roots*, Translated by Arthur Wells (Boston, The Beacon Press, 1952).

Wellek, Rene and Austin Warren, *Theory of Literature* (New York, Harcourt, Brace and Company, Inc., 1949).

White, Stewart Edward, *Credo* (New York, Doubleday, Page, and Company, 1925).

Young, David Lee, "The Art of Conrad Richter", Unpublished Doctoral Dissertation, The Ohio State University, 1964.

INDEX

STUDIES IN ENGLISH LITERATURE

30. GEORGE R. LEVINE: *Henry Fielding and the Dry Mock: A Study of the Techniques of Irony in His Early Works.* 1967. 160 pp.
Gld. 20.—

31. ERIC LAGUARDIA: *Nature Redeemed: The Imitation of Order in Three Renaissance Poems.* 1966. 180 pp.   Gld. 21.50

32. RONALD EDGAR BARNES: *The Dramatic Comedy of William Somerset Maugham.* 1968. 180 pp.   Gld. 21.—

33. F. PARVIN SHARPLESS: *The Literary Criticism of John Stuart Mill.* 1968. 250 pp.   Gld. 28.—

34. ROBERT DONALD SPECTOR: *English Literary Periodicals and the Climate of Opinion during the Seven Year's War.* 1966. 408 pp.
Gld. 43.—

35. BETTY J. LITTLETON: *"Clyomon and Clamydes": A Critical Edition.* 1968. 199 pp.   Gld. 26.—

37. JOHN H. DORENKAMP: *"Beggar's Bush": A Critical Edition.* 1968. 200 pp.   Gld. 25.—

38. JAMES H. CONOVER: *Thomas Dekker: An Analysis of Dramatic Structure.* 1969. 250 pp.   Gld. 34.—

39. D. C. YELTON: *Mimesis and Metaphor: An Inquiry into the Genesis and Scope of Conrad's Symbolic Imagery.* 1968. 366 pp.
Gld. 32.—

40. COBURN GUM: *The Aristophanic Comedies of Ben Jonson: A Comparative Study of Jonson and Aristophanes.* 1969. 207 pp.
Gld. 30.—

41. SHEROD M. COOPER: *The Sonnets of Astrophel and Stella: A Stylistic Study.* 1968. 184 pp.   Gld. 26.—

42. MARION TAYLOR: *A New Look at the Old Sources of Hamlet.* 1968. 79 pp.   Gld. 15.—

43. CHARLES S. HENSLEY: *The Later Career of George Wither.* 1969. 156 pp.   Gld. 24.—

44. JOHN POLLARD GUINN: *Shelley's Political Thought.* 1969. 134 pp.
Gld. 18.—

45. GERALD E. ENSCOE: *Eros and the Romantics: Sexual Love as a Theme in Coleridge, Shelley and Keats.* 1968.   Gld. 20.—

46. CHARLES J. LEES: *The Poetry of Walter Haddon.* 1967. 314 pp.
Gld. 36.—

48. KENNETH B. NEWELL: *Structure in Four Novels by H. G. Wells.* 1968. 120 pp.   Gld. 18.—

49. STANTON DE VOREN HOFFMAN: *Comedy and Form in the Fiction of Joseph Conrad.* 1969. 138 pp.   Gld. 21.—

52. WILLIAM R. BRASHEAR: *The Living Will: A Study of Tennyson and Nineteenth-Century Subjectivism.* 1969. 178 pp.   Gld. 30.—

54. ROBERT F. LEE: *Conrad's Colonialism.* 1969. 148 pp.   Gld. 26.—

All volumes clothbound.

MOUTON — PUBLISHERS — THE HAGUE